COMMUNITY SOCIAL WORK PRACTICE IN AN URBAN CONTEXT

The Potential of a Capacity-Enhancement Perspective

Melvin Delgado

New York   Oxford
OXFORD UNIVERSITY PRESS
2000

Oxford University Press

Oxford   New York
Athens   Auckland   Bangkok   Bogotá   Buenos Aires   Calcutta
Cape Town   Chennai   Dar es Salaam   Delhi   Florence   Hong Kong   Istanbul
Karachi   Kuala Lumpur   Madrid   Melbourne   Mexico City   Mumbai
Nairobi   Paris   São Paulo   Singapore   Taipei   Tokyo   Toronto   Warsaw

and associated companies in
Berlin   Ibadan

Published by Oxford University Press, Inc.,
198 Madison Avenue, New York, New York, 10016
http://www.oup-usa.org

Library of Congress Cataloging-in-Publication Data

Delgado, Melvin.
    Community social work practice in an urban context : the potential
of a capacity enhancement perspective / Melvin Delgado.
        p.   cm.
    Includes bibliographical references.
    ISBN 0–19–512546–0 (cloth : alk. paper). — ISBN 0–19–512547–9
(pbk. : alk. paper)
    1. Social Service.   2. Sociology. Urban.   I. Title.
HV40.D4394 1999
361.3′2—dc21   98–49973
                                                                  CIP

ISBN 0-19-5125460-0 (cloth)
Printing (last digit): 1

Printed in the United States of America
on acid-free paper

COMMUNITY SOCIAL WORK
PRACTICE IN AN URBAN CONTEXT

To Denise, Laura, and Barbara

Contents

List of Figures

Acknowledgments

A book of this nature could not have been possible without the assistance of numerous individuals and organizations. First, I must start with my university. I thank Dean Wilma Peebles-Wilkins, of the School of Social Work, Boston University, for her support throughout the entire process. Her encouragement and financial assistance made this book possible. Suzana Hogan, Sequence Administrative Assistance, facilitated the publication process. Several graduate assistants (Keva Barton, Gabriella Quintana, Kate Sheridan, and Myrna Chan MacRae) worked on this book, and they must be thanked for their diligent work in obtaining literature, developing case illustrations, locating photographs, and obtaining copyright permissions.

With regard to external sources, I thank the following individuals because of the critical role they played in providing literature and case material or allowing their photographs to be used in this book: Nancy Abbate (Chicago), Joann Barber (Community Builders), Doris Bloch (Los Angeles Regional Foodbank), Kyle Cundy (Community Builders Association), Tom Arie-Donch (Sacramento), Carrie Friedman (Gallery 37), Jane Golden (City of Philadelphia's Mural Arts Program), Sam Kornhauser (Schoolworks), Marilyn Linsdrom (Neighborhood Safe Art Spot), Victor Ochoa (San Diego), the Pennsylvania Horticultural Society, Jon Pounds (Chicago Public Art Group), James Prigoff (Sacramento), Elizabeth Stookey Sunde (the Public Domain Foundation), and Bruce Whitting (Coxsackie, New York).

I also wish to thank David Wenocur (University of Maryland School of Social Work) for his review of the initial prospectus and kind encouragement throughout the research and writing process and the anonymous reviewers of my final draft and their helpful suggestions for revisions. Finally, a thank-you to Layla Voll and Phillip Laughlin at Oxford University Press for their efforts in getting this book to press.

COMMUNITY SOCIAL WORK
PRACTICE IN AN URBAN CONTEXT

I

SETTING THE CONTEXT

Section 1 establishes a foundation for viewing community capacity enhancement as a legitimate form of practice for community social work. Chapter 1 (Introduction) introduces the goals of the book, examines the concept of community capacity enhancement, and places this approach within an urban context. In addition to describing the research methods used and the limitations of the book, Chapter 2 (Setting the Context for Urban Community Social Work Practice) examines the nature and definition of cities and several key concepts that play critical roles in increasing our understanding of a model of community capacity enhancement.

Chapter 3 (A Foundation for Community Capacity-Enhancement Practice) describes how community capacity enhancement has been conceptualized and grounds this model in the professional literature. Chapter 4 (Framework for Community Capacity-Enhancement Practice) presents a practice framework that lends itself to capacity-enhancement work within an urban context. Finally, Chapter 5, (Guiding Principles for Community Capacity-Enhancement Practice) lays out a set of six principles that should guide any form of community capacity-enhancement initiatives.

1

Introduction

This chaper gives the reader a context from which to understand the importance of urban-centered practice for the social work profession in the twenty-first century. It traces how the author became interested in a community-assets perspective and why the development of urban-specific interventions are so critical to community social work practice. In addition, it outlines the goals for the book, defines some of the key terms that are used, and describes the research methods used in selecting and analyzing case studies.

A Context for Urban Practice

The practice of macro social work—defined here as the purposeful design of interventions that target organizations and communities—has received renewed attention in the professional literature (Jeffries, 1996; Mondros & Wilson, 1994; Rothman, 1996; Weil, 1996). A number of new textbooks and a journal specifically devoted to community practice (*Journal of Community Practice*) have been published in the past few years (Brueggemann, 1996; Delgado, 1998c; Hardcastle, Wenocur, & Powers, 1997; Medoff & Sklar, 1994; Netting, Kettner, & McMurty, 1993; Rivera & Erlich, 1998a).

These scholarly publications have injected the field of social work with new techniques, critiques, and paradigms and have stimulated important dialogues on macro practice. These developments, including widespread recognition that the social work profession cannot consist solely of interventions focused on individuals and small groups, have generated excitement about macro practice and captured the imagination of practitioners and academics alike. Although these recent publications have made significant contributions to the profession, their focus, with some exceptions, has been on generic macro practice, and they have only indirectly targeted urban areas, low-income communities of color, and other undervalued groups.

Knowledge of urban environment is critical for enhancing social workers' understanding of low-income communities of color (Leadbeater & Way, 1996); this is not to say that low-income groups of color do not reside in suburban or rural communities across the United States. Undervalued groups reside in all areas of the United States and are by no means restricted to urban areas. Those who live in rural areas or suburbia also face considerable challenges in obtaining social and economic justice.

Surburban and rural areas share all the problems found in cities and struggle to address issues of substance abuse, family violence, HIV/AIDS, delinquency, crime, gangs, and under- and unemployment. However, an urban context presents a series of challenges that the profession must acknowledge and respond to accordingly. The sheer magnitude of social problems found in urban areas is compounded by residential segregation, increased vigilance by the police and criminal justice system, and limited formal resources to address issues (Bursik & Grasmick, 1993; Butterfield, 1992, 1994; Jackson, 1989; Leary, 1994; Purdy, 1995; Terry, 1994a, 1994b; Wilkerson, 1994). For example, in the United States, household crime rates are the highest in central-city sections of metropolitan areas, and so are arrest and incarceration rates (Walker, Spohn, & DeLone, 1996). These rates, in turn, fall disproportionately on communities of color. Because of this situation, urban communities have a heightened sense of suspicion and an increased sense of "helplessness."

This state of crisis is, arguable, not felt by suburban or rural areas, although they, too, share many of the same struggles as De Vita (1996, p. 11) noted: "Although both whites and minorities have left the cities for the suburbs, the exodus of whites has been much more rapid. The result is an increasing concentration of minority residents in central cities. Left behind, especially in the older cities of the Frostbelt, were large numbers of minorities—many of them poor, unskilled, and unable to follow the employment opportunities that were shifting to the suburbs, exurbs, and Sunbelt. This concentration of poor and disadvantaged minorities in distressed urban neighborhoods has been cited as an important factor in the growth of an isolated 'urban underclass.'" When people of color, particularly African Americans and Latinos, move to the suburbs, they continue to face residential segregation (DeVita, 1996).

A renewed emphasis on community-based practice presents a series of opportunities and challenges for social work practice. The community as an arena for practice provides practitioners with sufficient flexibility to initiate various types of interventions that are informed and determined by a community's assets and needs. Thus, practitioners do not have to be "problem driven" in the conventional sense of the term as it is often used in issue-based organizing.

The use of the community to build, in turn, is an often-overlooked strategy for achieving multiple community-focused goals. "What is community built? Community built is a dynamic new process of creation based on old community traditions: a collaboration between professionals and community volunteers resulting in a structure that transforms the public space; be it a mural, playground, park, museum, public garden, neighborhood center, historic restoration, housing or other project accomplished through community initiative and collective energy" (Community Built Conference, 1997, p. 1).

Community capacity enhancement, as is noted in Chapter 3, offers social workers the best of all worlds for practice—an opportunity to tap community assets in addressing community concerns and needs. In commenting on the importance of community capacity enhancement, Poole (1997, p. 169) stated: "We have now entered the era of community renewal in the United States. Although there is reason to fear a return to the 'lost world of community,' it is urgent that we find ways to strengthen those characteristics of communities that enable them to care for their members, especially those who are most vulnerable to dramatic shifts in national policy." Thus, enhancement should never be confused with letting a community address its needs and problems without outside assistance; enhancement-centered intervention, in turn, must be conceptualized as a collaborative partnership between the practitioner and the community.

Historically, this society has underestimated the importance of urban areas in the well-being of the country and, in so doing, has undervalued the importance and experiences of those who have sought social and political refuge in cities (Abrahamson, 1996; Halpern, 1995; Weisbrod & Worthy, 1997). Keating, Krumholz, and Starr (1996) noted that neighborhood initiatives are both a strategy and a metaphor for how America deals with its most significant urban problems, unfortunately with dismal results. Furthermore, some (see, for example, Hynes, 1995) argue that economically, U.S. inner cities have much more in common with the cities of Third World countries and should be viewed from that perspective in making the case for attention and intervention.

In 1995, approximately 37 percent of the world's population lived in cities; in 1995, that proportion increased to 45 percent, and it should reach 50 percent in 2000 and 65 percent (8 billion people) in 2025 (Dow, 1997; Badshah, 1996; Kirdar, 1997b; Streeten, 1997). Moreover, about 75 percent of the populations of industrialized countries and of Latin America reside in cities (Emmerij, 1997).

From a slightly different perspective it is estimated that as late as 1800, only 3 percent of the world's population lived in cities with 100,000 or more residents (Lofland, 1998). The number of metropolises in the world with populations over 1 million has tripled over the past thirty-five years, with estimates that there will be 611 by 2010 and 40 added every five years thereafter; if this rate of increase materializes, there will be 639 metropolises of this size by 2025 (Lofland, 1998). In the United States during the 1980s, the population of urban areas increased by over 20 million, from 167.1 million to 187.1 million (12 percent). By 1990, approximately 75.2 percent of the U.S. population lived in urban areas, up from 73.7 percent in 1980, with California having the highest percentage of its total population (92.6 percent) living in urban areas (Andrews & Fonseca, 1995; Wright, 1997). Furthermore, the percentage of people in urban areas is projected to continue to increase in the future ("America in the '90s," 1991; Rusk, 1995). Communities of color, particularly those that are low income, a population group that social work is invested in serving, are even more urbanized than the general population. This fact increases the importance of urban areas for social work practice (Barringer, 1997; Delgado, 1998b, in press; Fellin, 1995; Pear, 1992; Roberts, 1994).

This concentration, in combination with a host of social problems, makes urban areas a high priority for targeting interventions. As (Emmerij, 1997, p. 105) stated: "The urban question has many dimensions, including poverty, housing, unemployment and underemployment, slums, crime, drugs, and street children. But the urban question amounts to more than the sum total of its different problem areas. It is difficult to express what this 'value added' is, but it certainly has a lot to do with the quality of life, or the lack of it, in the urban setting. The quality of life affects both the poor and rich, as the urban situation deteriorates."

The importance of social work practice in urban areas has historical, current, and future significance. The profession's origins are deeply rooted in urban areas across the United States, and the founders of the profession developed and advanced practice with urban areas as a focus. Jane Addams and her colleagues played a significant role in the creation of the settlement house movement in the late nineteenth century. One of the primary goals of the movement was environmental reform, which was accomplished through the creation of groups that stressed action at the community level (Lubove, 1983), such as community gardening and other activities, that can be labeled community capacity enhancement today (Balgopal & Vassil, 1983). Currently, the profession plays an active role in attempting to address a myriad of social problems that are heavily concentrated in cities (Ewalt, 1997). In addition, the future of the profession will rest on how well social work can address urban issues, particularly as the populations it has historically served and the country become more urbanized. Nevertheless, the profession has been challenged to develop interventions that have a specific urban focus and effectively address the needs of population groups that are of color, undocumented, low income, and considered marginal by policy makers and key stakeholders.

Social work has not succeeded in this regard for a variety of reasons, two of which are the lack of vision and its inability to develop appropriate paradigms for engaging and serving these communities (Iglehart & Becerra, 1995; Specht & Courtney, 1994). Thus, there is a desperate need for the profession to reexamine urban-based community practice with undervalued communities. Delgado (1998c) addressed this need in *Social Work Practice in Nontraditional Urban Settings*. This book examined the role and importance of informal settings that social workers often overlook in their search for culturally meaningful service delivery strategies and focused on urban areas and communities of color. However, *Community Social Work Practice in an Urban Context* takes a different, yet complementary, perspective on urban practice by stressing an ecological and community-specific approach to intervention.

The need to develop urban-focused social work practice also requires the creation of models that build on community assets. These models must be sensitive to changing community conditions and the composition of residents and require the development of culturally competent practice methods. A model, according to Jeffries (1996, pp. 101–102), "is a simplification of reality that is encapsulating in its essential characteristics. To have analytical value a model should specify key variables to be considered in assessing a situation in order to develop and evaluate possible action plans. Thus a model should enable prediction of likely outcomes if a particular plan of action is pursued." Furthermore, a model serves to advance knowledge and generate competing explanations for events; hence, the field of urban-focused community practice, as the case in point in this book, benefits from this systematic attention.

An analysis of urban areas will reveal "unconventional" "assets" that provide a window through which a community shares its priorities, concerns, and hopes with the outside world (McKnight, 1997; McKnight & Kretzmann, 1990). Lewis Mumford (quoted in Kirdar, (1997a, p. 105)) viewed the city as a marvelous place to live in: "The city is the most precious collective invention of civilization . . . second to language itself in the manifestation of culture." Community asset-focused markers and projects lead to a better understanding of a community's capacities and are interventions that actively build upon and involve residents in addressing their concerns.

The presence of four types of what the author calls "community asset markers" serve this function extremely well: (1) murals, (2) gardens, (3) community-initiated playgrounds, and (4) sculptures. These markers provide a perspective on urban communities that, with rare exceptions, is often overlooked or undervalued by social workers and other human service providers. Yet, when these markers examined within the context in which they are found or initiated, they have profound implications for social work practice. Hynes (1995, p. 156) noted the importance of viewing gardens through a different lens: "At first glance, community gardens may seem an unlikely and unremarkable means of urban renewal. An anachronism? A naive throwback to preindustrial times? . . . In fact, the urban community garden, with its potential for feeding households, and generating local cottage industry, with its power to restore a measure of community life, and with its capacity to recycle organic wastes, is thriving throughout the world."

An urban ecological model of community social work practice, like any model based on ecological factors, stresses the delineation of multiple key factors that are interrelated and affect how individuals and communities interact with each other. Each part of this ecology exerts influences on the other parts. This model also stresses that the identification of indigenous resources and the involvement of the community in all aspects of intervention, empowerment, and capacity enhancement are central to any meaningful intervention or initiative. The social work literature includes numerous publications on strengths, empowerment, and participation. However, the concept of capacity enhancement, a key element of this book, is still in desperate need of conceptualization and operationalization (Poole, 1997).

Author's Interest in the Topic

The author became actively interested in murals, gardens, playgrounds, and sculptures when he conducted research on urban-based nontraditional settings. Initially, the presence of murals near nontraditional settings made them a subject of interest because they portrayed the community to an "outsider." However, field-based research uncovered numerous occasions in which murals served as backdrops for gardens and sculptures were centrally located within the gardens. This integration highlighted their presence in a community. Nevertheless, the author initially focused only on murals and gardens and thought of sculptures merely as "decorative." However, Nancy Abbate, a colleague (personal communication, November 13, 1996) in Chicago pointed out that community-built sculptures are much more than decorative—that they, too, fulfill other expressive and instrumental goals of a community. This point leads to the topic of community-initiated playgrounds.

A graduate student (Myrna Chan MacRae) introduced the author to the topic of playgrounds. In conducting a review of the literature on murals, gardens, and sculptures, she uncovered several newspaper articles describing and attesting to the importance of playgrounds in uniting communities, urban as well as suburban. These four projects—murals, gardens, sculptures, and playgrounds—can exist in isolation or invarious combinations with each other.

The primary lesson the author wants to share with readers is that social work practice is, in many ways, a journey with a series of unexpected stops and detours. The topic of this book was never "planned" in the conventional use of the word in macro practice. It just happened. However, it happened because of the author's commitment to communities and willingness and desire to visit communities throughout the United States. This propensity gave him the opportunity to "stumble" across this important dimension of community that has profound implications for social work practice.

The writing of this book represented an opportunity for the author to bring together various topics of interest into a form that makes it accessible to students as well as practitioners. Although he has published articles on many of the topics addressed in this book, the limitations of article writing (most notably limited space), did not allow him to explore murals, particularly the relationship among murals, gardens, playgrounds, and sculptures, fully. Thus, he was inspired to devote a considerable amount of time, energy, and other resources to this endeavor, with the aim of conveying to the profession a different way of looking at communities—a perspective predicated on community assets.

Goals of the Book

This book has three primary goals: (1) to ground social workers within a community-practice, urban context, from which to gain a better understanding of urban-based communities of color; (2) to examine, from an ecological perspective, the role of murals, gardens, playgrounds, and sculptures (as examples of community assets, when present) and capacity-enhancement strategies (when nonexistent as projects); and (3) to provide a practice framework, case examples, and detailed strategies for assessing, mapping, engaging, and evaluating communities in the development of murals, gardens, playgrounds, and sculptures. As a result, this book provides both descriptions and prescriptions to inform community practice based on an assets perspective.

Capacity Enhancement versus Development

The author has deliberately used the term *enhancement*, rather than the conventional term *development*, in this book. The difference between capacity enhancement and development may seem artificial to the reader, since both terms seem to have the same meaning. And, according to the *Oxford English Dictionary* (1972) there is no discernable difference between the two. *Enhancement* is to "lift, raise up, set up . . . or increase in price value, importance attractiveness" (p. 869), whereas development refers to the process used to achieve and end "result or product; a . . . form of some earlier and more rudimentary organism, structure or system" (p. 708).

Kretzmann and McKnight (1996a, p. 1), two influential and outspoken proponents of the use of community assets, defined asset-based community development as "the range of approaches that work from the principle that a community can be built only by focusing on the strengths and capacities of the citizens and associations that call that community 'home.'" The reader, like the author, can feel comfortable with the manner in which Kretzmann and McKnight used the term *development*. However, the concept of development is rarely used this way.

Despite the seemingly minimal difference in the definitions of these two terms, the author prefers the term *enhancement* because it fundamentally implies that there is a resource-asset in place and that all one needs to do is foster its growth. To use the metaphor of a seed, after a seed is planted, all it needs is water and sunshine. With *development*, the assumption is that there is no resource and, as a consequence, the practitioner must create it through some form of active intervention. To use the same metaphor, at first there is no seed; it must be created. Then the seed can be planted and nourished for it to grow. The conventional manner in which *development* is used is generally, with some important exceptions, deficit driven. The use of *enhancement*, in contrast, forces the individual to think only from an assets perspective.

Research Methods

Any effort to gain a better understanding of how community capacity-enhancement initiatives work must, by necessity, use a variety of approaches (quantitative and qualitative) and techniques that capture the richness, intricacies, and complexities of community-based interventions (Andranovich & Riposa, 1993; Marin & Marin, 1991; Patton, 1987; Stanfield & Dennis, 1993). Multiple lenses provide viewers, in this case researchers and practitioners, with an appreciation of how major community stakeholders, including residents, experience and view a particular phenomenon.

The work of Kingry-Westergaard and Kelly (1990) has stressed the need to use multiple methods to study ecological phenomena because of the complexities of relationships and systems. These methods are best utilized in collaboration between the researcher and the participants. As Jason (1997, p. 103) stated: "The ecological endeavor is a discovery process in which researchers and participants share the different constructions of their contexts, learn about events and processes that help define their understanding of their contexts, and work together to define the research activity."

A focus on community assets, however, presents an additional set of challenges because of the paucity of studies that have specifically targeted the strengths of low-income urban-based communities. Unfortunately, quantitative data are usually collected by governmental entities with a focus on problems (the deficit paradigm) and hence are of limited use in developing or understanding community capacity enhancement. This limitation, which is by no means minor, severely constricts the usefulness of existing data. Qualitative methods, particularly those that incorporate ethnographic techniques, offer the most promise for understanding community capacity-enhancement practice.

Ethnographic research takes into account both tangible and intangible factors and acknowledges that local people have the most in-depth knowledge of local circumstances (Facio, 1993; Martinez-Brawley, 1990; Williams, 1993). In addition, ethnography acknowledges and embraces the diversity of groups and communities. In so doing, it stresses the importance of the researcher developing collaborative relationships with community residents, local stakeholders, and other interested parties (Burawoy, 1991a, 1991b; Sells, Smith, & Newfield, 1997; Spradley, 1979). This collaborative approach to research necessitates that the researcher approach the subject matter being studied from a perspective of respect, a willingness to be open minded about local interpretations of acts and behaviors, and an understanding that it takes a certain amount of time (in some instances, less time and in others, more time) before a group or community comes to trust and feel confident in the researcher's ability to reflect their reality. Thus, ethnographic research offers the greatest potential for use in communities that are marginal and thus distrustful of outsiders, particularly academics who wish to "study" them.

Case studies, which may be defined as the strategic use of materials and information that illustrate key conceptual constructs with practice implications, are an excellent tool for bringing together multiple approaches and methods and weaving the results into a coherent "story" (Stake, 1995; Yin, 1994). Case studies must address five key elements to be useful for practitioners. They must give (1) sufficient detail to allow the reader to grasp the context in which the intervention occurred, (2) provide sufficient details on the intervention itself (theoretical underpinnings and operationalization), (3) highlight critical aspects that needed to be surmounted to achieve success, (4) illustrate techniques and approaches to help practitioners transfer newly acquired knowledge to their particular situations, and (5) summarize the lessons learned to facilitate the exchange of knowledge between the writer and the practitioners.

Due to limited financial resources, this book used existing data whenever possible and useful. Every effort was made to locate and use research and case studies to increase the generalizability of the model and thereby reduce costs. Follow-up with key informants identified in the chapters and the solicitation of materials were also used to enhance the stories. Last, the book relies on primary research utilizing ethnomethodological techniques that was specifically conducted for this book.

Photographs

The author was fortunate to get permission from the publisher to include photographs that were supplied through the generosity of many artists and provide an important visual perspective that is often missing from social work books. Of the eighteen photographs that are included, eight are of murals.

The author thought that although the other capacity-enhancement projects covered in this book lent themselves to visual representation, murals did so to a much greater extent. Furthermore, no amount of description of the images in murals could do justice to their actual manifestation. The author hopes that these visual images will help the reader to appreciate more fully the powerful messages that community capacity-enhancement projects transmit to their communities.

Words of Caution

Caution is needed whenever any paradigm is embraced that actively seeks to involve a community in designing and implementing changes that reflect their hopes and needs. Paradigms that are based upon self-help, natural sup-ports, and the like are appealing to all interested parties because they affirm an individual's ability and need to address areas of concern actively. How-ever, a number of authors have questioned whether an emphasis on locally driven initiatives may lead the government to stop providing resources and assistance (Delgado, in press).

A focus on community capacity enhancement, which ultimately results in residents playing active and significant roles in developing murals, gar-dens, playgrounds, and sculptures, must not be used as an excuse for providers and funders to disengage from communities in which these projects are conducted. Any shift in focus that results in local initiatives must not place a disproportionate onus on a community.

This book focuses on exploring the types of assets that can be found in communities (economic, social, cultural, and political resources) and how they can be used in the creation of a partnership with social workers and other helping professionals. This partnership, however, must be based on mutual respect and trust, with an understanding that the community is the best judge of what it needs and what is good for it. This orientation neces-sitates a radical rethinking of what social workers think about the people they serve (Delgado, 1998c, in press).

Expected Criticism of the Book

Although this book stresses four types of urban community capacity-enhancement projects, this does not mean that these types are the only ones that are possible or advisable. Such a statement would be foolhardy and mis-leading. Furthermore, the book would appeal only to those social workers who are interested in murals, gardens, playgrounds, and sculptures. Rather, these projects are meant to serve as examples. The attractiveness of com-munity capacity enhancement is its limitless potential for work with under-valued communities.

These four types of projects are highlighted to illustrate their use in as-sessments and interventions. The author hopes that these projects awaken in the reader a spark that will lead to the creation of other types of com-munity-enhancement projects that are based upon the cultural backgrounds of the community residents they seek to engage—the true meaning of cul-tural competence! Local circumstances must dictate the nature of these projects, and residents' backgrounds must be taken into account.

This book is not about turning social workers into part-time muralists, gardeners, builders, and sculptors, although these occupations are appealing and fulfill important roles in society. At the least, they present opportuni-ties for channeling creative energies. However, it is not possible to conceive of using murals, gardens, playgrounds, and sculptures without having some knowledge of the kind of planning that they entail. Most social workers probably do not have these types of skills or knowledge of these areas. Consequently, it is essential to develop an appreciation of what these types of projects and activities require of participants.

There is a tremendous need in the field to develop community asset-based interventions that take into account local-based hopes, concerns, needs, circumstances, and abilities. Social work has moved slowly, but steadily, toward using, if not embracing, a strengths perspective in practice. However, the literature has focused inordinately on strength-based work with individuals and has often neglected communities. Because of this propensity, the field is in desperate need of examples of the use of strength-based principles in work with communities, especially communities that are urban based, of color, and low income. There are many undervalued groups in urban areas that do not have these characteristics. Thus, the book is limited by its focus on one sector, although it is a significant and growing community that has great importance to the profession.

The author is fully prepared for a wide range of criticisms of this book. Many critics will say that the issues confronting low-income communities of color are no different from those confronting other low-income groups or not sufficiently different to warrant an entire book devoted to them. Other critics will say that the issues that low-income communities of color face are not restricted to urban areas and can be found in suburbia and rural areas as well. Still others will say that any social work text that focuses on urban practice is misguided because most social workers do not practice in cities. Last, critics may also say that a "scholarly" book must be based on "scholarly" sources, and that this book relies too much on unconventional sources—namely, newspaper articles; locally written documents, such as newsletters; and the like.

The author contends that the issues confronting low-income communities of color are dramatically different when placed in an urban, rather than a suburban or rural, context. To say otherwise is to say that interventions do not have to take context into account—that what works in a rural setting must also work in an urban setting. To deny context, however, is to deny the history and experiences of urban low-income communities of color in the United States.

Cities often represented a refuge for many undervalued groups because of the perceived opportunities for advancement and their hopes of finding social acceptance. The author argues that cities are a unique context in which social problems are manifested in a way that takes the environment into account. He wrote this book for a specific audience—social workers and other helping professionals, who have an interest and commitment to working in urban areas using an assets approach to undervalued communities. This is not to say that undervalued groups are not struggling to address a host of social problems in suburban and rural areas. Nevertheless, they have assets that must be identified and enhanced at every opportunity.

Finally, the author makes no apologies for using popular media sources in this book. In fact, the paucity of professional publications on the projects addressed here was the rationale for writing such a book. It would be a sad day for the field if it was said that major developments occurring in communities must be reported in the scholarly literature before it is legitimate to include them in a social work curriculum. The social work academic community was slow to respond to the AIDS epidemic because of this bias. In short, the author believes that social work is at least six years behind what is reported in the popular literature. This book represents an attempt to cut that time by a few years regarding urban-based communities.

Limitations of the Book

The process of writing a book about a new practice paradigm and just four types of urban-based community enhancement projects is not without its share of limitations, which the author must openly acknowledge. Any new paradigm will be subject to increased scrutiny concerning its ideology, applicability, and effectiveness. A paradigm based on community assets is still in its infancy and, as a result, requires much more thought, research, and critique before it is widely embraced. The author would have preferred to have drawn upon extensive research studies and in-depth cases to buttress the worthiness of a community capacity-enhancement paradigm. However, it was not possible to do so because of the dearth of such materials. It is hoped that this situation will change in the future.

The four types of projects outlined in this book were selected because of the author's experience with them and contacts in the field and because they were representative of the types of projects that are possible in urban open spaces. These projects all require the use of physical space, some more than others, and are accomplishments (physical development) that can be viewed, studied, and debated within and outside a community.

These projects essentially rely on volunteers giving their time, money, and expertise on behalf of a community. This is not to say that this is the only or, for that matter, the most frequent, form of volunteerism in a community. However, volunteerism related to murals, gardens, playgrounds, and sculptures results in a physical "artifact" that is visible to the entire community. Yes, volunteers can play important roles in soup kitchens and visiting the frail and isolated for example, which are important tasks in a community's life. However, this form of involvement does not necessarily enhance the volunteers' capacity to help or result in an artifact that stands as a testament of a community's will not only to survive, but to thrive.

There are countless other types of community capacity-enhancement projects that social workers and other providers can initiate. This book is limited by the selection of just four types. Although it could have taken a broader perspective and addressed many other types of projects, such an approach, although appealing from a generalizability point of view, would have sacrificed depth for breadth. Consequently, one of the strengths of this book is also its major weakness—namely, that it is highly focused, or, as some critics would say, too narrow.

The author struggled to identify the best case illustrations of community capacity enhancement. When he located a case, it became a challenge to gather as much data as possible through interviews and reviews of available material, including newspaper articles, pictures, and other accounts. Owing to time and financial limitations, the author could not gather as much information as he would have liked, and he was sometimes more successful in developing cases than at other times. Thus, the depth and detail available in the case illustrations can be considered uneven.

Every effort was made to provide sufficient details concerning the skills and knowledge areas that are necessary to initiate community capacity-enhancement projects. However, the author struggled with how much detail to provide without missing the central point. As a result, he assumed that the reader has a basic knowledge of urban issues and challenges related to practice in cities and is comfortable working in urban areas. For readers who have a limited knowlege of urban issues and practice-related challenges and do not feel comfortable practicing in this context, the book may be of limited use.

The review of the literature also proved challenging. The paucity of scholarly materials on community capacity enhancement, particularly those written by social workers, made the process of reviewing the literature arduous and unsatisfying. The author found a limited, but growing, body of literature on individual strengths but few publications on community assets. This situation may reflect an evolutionary pattern in which the field starts with individuals and eventually expands to communities.

Probably the most disturbing part of reviewing the literature was the paucity of strengths-based literature focused on communities of color, urban based or otherwise. Although the author had the same experience when writing *Social Work Practice in Nontraditional Urban Settings* (Delgado, 1998c), it was no less disturbing several years had passed since he wrote that book. In essence, much work needs to be done in this arena before the profession can realize its potential for serving urban-based communities of color. Thus, this book is limited in the extent to which it can systematically build on the work of other social work academics and move the concept of community capacity enhancement to a new level.

Finally, although the author worked diligently to ground this book in the professional literature, particularly acknowledging how social work used community-based activities during several early periods in its history, this book is not a history book. Consequently, the author has drawn on the historical literature to highlight key themes. The section on Urban-Focused Practice in Chapter 2 presents an overview, rather than an in-depth examination, of key historical periods in the profession. The author thought that far better qualified scholars have written on these periods and that the reader would be best served by reading those books. In addition, an in-depth discussion of these periods would have drawn away from the central goals of the book. Thus, the author acknowledges that the community-enhancement projects recommended here are not new. However, the profession has not embraced these projects to any great extent in present-day practice and must do so to be strategically placed in the twenty-first century.

Conclusion

The importance of cities for the nation and for social work will continue to increase well into the next century, particularly as newcomers enter the United States in record numbers. However, major structural changes in the economy (the demise of manufacturing jobs and the increase in service-related jobs), combined with dramatic changes in the racial and ethnic com-positions of cities, presents a series of challenges for the country and the profession.

The increased "coloring" of urban areas, along with the corresponding increase in diversity within communities of color, requires social work, along with other helping professions, to develop new paradigms for analyzing the assets and needs of these communities. Interventions must be developed that have multiple goals, one of which must be to unite disparate groups in search of common goals. The creation of a community is much more than physi-cal developments or buildings; it entails the development of "community spirit," or "connectedness," to ensure that all residents, regardless of their cultural or linguistic backgrounds, feel they are part of a community with a future that is worth working toward.

Warren (1998) used the term *symbiosis* to describe the interconnected-ness of cities with suburbs and rural areas and highlighted the need for the nation not to lose sight of cities. He explained that "the unmet and press-ing needs of our cities, and our mandate to conserve the earth's resources—apparently divergent areas of concerns—are in fact opposite sides of the same coin. When people abandon cities to settle in suburbs or countryside, they may well be finding solutions for their own households, and for their own generation. However, without effective land use planning, today's small town refuge in the Rockies will become tomorrow's Los Angeles, complete with traffic, smog, and destruction of habitat. To flee the problem is not to solve it." (p. 3). Cities cannot be easily ignored or marginalized by the society. They have importance in themselves and in their relationship with the rest of the nation.

2

Setting the Context for Urban Community Social Work Practice

This chapter presents a context for understanding urban-based macro practice. This understanding requires the reader to know what is meant by *urban*, "to have an awareness of an urban political-economic context and the importance of community, and to understand the role of "open space" and how macro practice is urban specific.

An urban context requires the creation of interventions that are based on urban realities. However, perceptions of urban areas play influential roles in dictating how practice is visualized (Breitbart, 1998; Marcuse, 1997; Moe & Wilkie, 1997; Watts & Jagers, 1998). Vergara (1995, p. 2) summed up America's views toward inner cities as follows: "Ghettos, as intrinsic to the identity of the United States as New England villages, vast national parks, and leafy suburbs, nevertheless remain unique in their social and physical isolation from the nation's mainstream. Discarded and dangerous places, they are rarely visited by outsiders, becoming familiar to the larger population only through television and movies." These sentiments serve as formidable barriers to the development of urban initiatives based on urban realities, rather than stereotypes, and increase the importance of social workers devising ways of gathering data and other information in which to base their experiences and perceptions.

One focus of this book is how events in the profession's history have shaped how communities of color have been viewed and practice has been conceptualized. Communities of color have expanded numerically over the past two decades and have accounted for a disproportionate percentage of the population increase in the United States (Murdock, 1995). Of the total net increase in the nation's population from 1980 to 1990, 66 percent was due to the growth of communities of color. The proportion of white non-Latinos declined by 3 percent from 1980 to 1990 as the proportion of all other groups increased. Culturally competent practitioners must have a keen understanding of the profile of the consumers they serve, including their projections for the immediate future. Rapidly changing demographics, in addition, present considerable challenges to policy makers, planners, managers, and other practitioners in their efforts to develop and deliver culturally competent services (Murdock, 1995).

Definition of *Urban*

The terms *urban, city,* and *metropolitan,* are often used interchangeably in the professional literature. These terms, however, do not have universal meaning. The term *city* is defined and operationalized differently by economists, demographers, social scientists, and political scientists (Kirdar, 1997a). the expansion of the term *urban* to include *metropolis, urbanized region, functional urban area,* and *megalopolis,* complicates the definition of the term (Flanagan, 1993; Rusk, 1995). According to the *Oxford English Dictionary* (1972, p. 3570), the term *urban* is defined as follows: "Pertaining to or characteristic of, occurring or taking place in, a city or town. . . . Constituting, forming, or including city, town, or bourogh, or part of such."

This definition is broad and highlights why it is possible for practitioners to view the term *urban* from dramatically different perspectives: (1) a geographic entity with distinct boundaries, (2) a place consisting of residents who share certain characteristics, and (3) an entity that houses a disproportionate number of social problems. The third perspective may help to explain why the term is usually associated with such negative descriptors as "plight," "slum," "blight," "crime," "ghetto," "epidemic," "decay," "problems," and "violence," to list but a few (Campbell, 1996; Lee, 1994a, 1994b, 1994c).

A city, according to the U.S. Bureau of the Census, is defined as a geographic entity with a population of 2,500 or more residents; metropolitan statistical areas, in turn, are defined as counties or equaivalents if they contain an officially defined city of 50,000 or more or have an urbanized area of 50,000 or more residents and a total metropolitan population of over 100,000 (Andrews & Fonseca, 1995). According to the 1990 U.S. census, approximately 48 percent of all metropolitan areas had populations of 2.5 million or greater, and 20 percent had populations of 1 million to 2.499 million, 12 percent had populations of 500,000 to 999,999, 11 percent had populations of 250,000 to 499,999, 8 percent had populations of 100,000 to 249,999, and 1 percent had fewer than 100,000 residents (U.S. Bureau of the Census, 1995).

The term *urban* can also refer to what is called "edge cities." Edge cities are geographic entities that fulfill important economic functions (they are where jobs are found) and are located close to major cities. Travel between the edge cities and major cities is facilitated by highways and transportation systems. Edge cities, although they have considerably smaller populations, are often considered extensions of the major cities.

When the term *urban* is used within a social science or social work practice context, it rarely encompasses community assets. It usually refers to a geographic entity (the inner city) consisting of subareas with high concentrations of undervalued groups with social problems. These subareas usually elicit negative public reactions and are targets of "special" initiatives. In essence, when the nation refers to the "urban problem," it invariably means people of color who have low incomes and live in segregated sections of cities. The interplay of these dimensions provides a context from which to undertake urban-focused assessments and interventions.

Urban Political-Economic Context

The 1980s and 1990s witnessed a dramatic shift in employment patterns among urban workers across the United States. As Moore and Pinderhughes (1993, p. xxv) noted: "By the late 1980s there was a consensus that the geographic shift in the location of job growth was a manifestation of a second and more important aspect of economic restructuring—the shift from a manufacturing to a service economy, and the increasing globalization of the economy. This was a major transformation, and it became obvious that traditional manufacturing was not going to revive."

Economic restructuring, according to Wilson (1987) refers to "deindustrialization," the termination or relocation of jobs and the increased polarization of jobs (the decline of middle-level jobs). Although economic restructuring affects all residents, it has had a greater impact on communities of color (Morales & Bonilla, 1993; Slessarev, 1997). Jobs that historically paid relatively high wages and included benefit packages were replaced by service jobs with low wages and often limited or no benefits. These service jobs are highly sensitive to economic shifts, making employees vulnerable to layoffs. In addition, most service-related jobs are nonunionized, further weakening the stability of wage earners and those who are dependent on them (Mills & Lubuele, 1997).

Consequently, it is imperative that social workers view the forces that have an impact on major urban areas of the United States within a broader context—one that is more global than national or local in nature (Dow, 1997; Dugger, 1998; Feagin, 1998b; Kirdar, 1997b; Simai, 1997; Sontag, 1998; Sontag & Dugger, 1998; Gallup, 1979). Taaffe and Fisher (1997, p. 49) summed up this interconnectedness quite well: "Little that happens in local communities these days is not affected by the dramatic changes occurring in the global economy. The new global economy is characterized by an increased velocity and competitiveness of transnational capital in a world undergoing profound technological changes."

These global forces can best be categorized into four types: (1) major economic changes from a manufacturing to a service system; (2) the influx of newcomers, documented and undocumented, who are radically changing the composition of cities; (3) the continued growth in the number of megacities (populations over 1 million); and (4) technological innovations requiring higher levels of formal education and highly specialized skills.

Dispersal and immigration patterns during the 1980s and 1990s for newcomers, documented or undocumented, were the result of global economic changes and political instability, particularly in Asia, the Caribbean, and Latin America According to Rivera and Erlich (1998b, p. 244), "Despite the slow expansion in the suburbs, smaller towns, and rural areas, it is no accident that the changing and emerging communities described by the authors are largely an urban phenomenon. The inner cities within inner cities continue to offer shelter to new arrivals mainly because of housing costs, employment possibilities, and ethnic support structures. . . . Those people who have managed to escape the inner cities since the 1960s have been replaced by a wide variety of immigrant and migrant populations."

The new influx of unskilled labor into cities exacerbated the difficult labor market, forcing newcomers into service jobs (some of whom were paid "under the table") and further depressing pay scales (Feagin & Smith, 1998). Economic uncertainty within the Southern hemisphers is projected to either persist or intensify well into the next century (Morales & Bonilla, 1993).

The magnitude of the social problems confronting major cities, particularly those often referred to as central cities, must be placed within a context that highlights the seriousness of the challenge (Downs, 1997; McCord, 1997; Mose, 1997; National Research Council, 1994; Slessarev, 1997; Venkatesh, 1997). For example, the number of people receiving public assistance in Chicago is greater than the combined populations of the following 13 states: Alaska, Delaware, Idaho, Kansas, Montana, Nebraska, Nevada, New Hampshire, South Dakota, North Dakota, Utah, Vermont, and Wyoming (De Parle, 1997). To put it another way, the number of families on public assistance who are living in Chicago's Cabrini-Green housing development is greater than the entire population of Wyoming (De Parle, 1997).

The technological, economic, demographic, and political forces that operate in the United States are formidable and by no means restricted to this country. Nevertheless, their impact is far greater on urban areas and undervalued communities, such as those that are low income and of color, than on others. These forces, in turn, have had profound influences on the lives of individuals and families. The stressors and consequences associated with urban living cannot be separated from global forces (Barringer, 1997).

Quest for Community

The importance of belonging to and having a sense of community in urban areas is ever present in contemporary society. According to Cohen and

Phillips (1997, p. 471), a sense of community is an important foundation for enhancing a community-development process: "Feeling a part of a community fosters a sense of ownership. . . . and serves as a deterrent to alienation. This sense of belonging acts as a strong defense against environmental and social factors that prey on many residents and social work services, provided in a variety of modalities, can enhance the community-building process."

Although almost anyone would agree that a sense of community is important, the concept of community is ambiguous. Like *urban, community* is a term than is subject to a variety of definitions interpretations of its essential elements and focus as Germain (1991, p. 38) put it, "Community is an ambiguous concept. . . . For community social workers, the community is the client unit served. For other social workers, the community is the environment in which individuals and families live who are being served. It is in the community that many of the society's social, economic, and political processes and events impinge on residents. And despite the transience of populations and the dispersion of residents' interests and affiliations to areas outside the community, the community influences the development and function of its residents in many ways."

The surge in the number of books providing advice on how best to achieve a sense of community attests to the importance of the issue in all sectors of the United States (Blakely & Snyder, 1997; Brown, 1995; Chavis, 1997; Garr, 1995; Jason, 1997; Oldenburg, 1991; McKnight, 1995; Moe & Wilkie, 1997; Schwartz, 1997; Williamson, 1997; Wuthnow, 1991, 1995). These books touch on four key themes: (1) residents' lack of connectedness and disengagement from participating in community-centered life and activities, (2) the stressors associated with major economic restructuring (the undervaluing of certain groups on the basis of their positions in the economic structure), (3) the increasing ethnic and racial diversity of communities (thereby limiting exchanges because of linguistic and cultural differences), and (4) increased competition for what are perceived to be limited resources to meet the social needs of residents.

Cottrell (1976) identified seven critical ingredients that must be present for communities to be able to function effectively, grow, and respond to changes. That is, communities must (1) have a commitment for residents to act effectively, (2) possess a vision that encompasses all sectors and stresses interconnectedness; (3) give each sector the opportunity to voice its perspectives and hopes, (4) create constructive channels through which conflict can be successfully addressed, (5) develop systems and machanisms for facilitating interactions and exchanges, (6) be able to manage relations with the external community, and (7) maintain open channels of communication among all segments. These factors are closely interrelated. Consequently, a community's failure to achieve any of these goals will severely impede its ability to function effectively. The failure to attain multiple goals, in turn, would have disastrous consequences for a community.

Keating (1996, p. 1) examined the changes in urban America from a historical perspective and noted: "With the decline of central cities in the late twentieth century, most of their neighborhoods have suffered too. They have often lost population, jobs, and a sense of community as public services have been reduced and community institutions (churches, schools, and civic organizations) have declined, disappeared, or moved to the suburbs. Nevertheless, urban neighborhoods retain an important place in civic life." Yemma (1997, p. A18) made a similar observation in examining South Central Los Angeles: "As in South Central Los Angeles, urban neighborhoods everywhere are becoming browner. Middle-class blacks, meanwhile, are moving to the suburbs, helping to integrate those once all-white enclaves but also leaving neighborhoods like South Central Los Angeles to increasingly poor and old blacks, and young Latino immigrants." As a result, the continued abandonment of neighborhoods in major urban areas will present significant social and economic challenges to the country, further increasing the lacuna between the suburbs and urban areas (De Vita, 1996).

There is little dispute that the concept of community is vital to everyone's well-being. Walter (1997) argued that the essence of community building rests on the inclination to conceptualize community as an inclusive, dynamic system that includes all people. Successful community practice is possible only if all the dimensions of community are actively engaged.

Thus, the dismal state of community increases the importance of activities that bring disparate groups together in pursuit of communal goals (Albrecht, 1994; Chase, 1990; Mose, 1997; Selznick, 1996; Vitek, 1996). Social work, too, has pursued approaches, although usually unsuccessfully, to reach out and serve undervalued groups and communities through projects that seek to create a sense of community (Delgado, in press; Forte, 1997; Specht & Courtney, 1994).

Open Space

A number of studies have shown the importance of the interconnectedness among family, community, and land use (Arie-Donch, 1998; Buss, 1995; Feagin, 1998a; Jason, 1997; Lofland, 1998; Longo, 1997; Gallagher, 1993; Schneekluth & Shibley, 1993; Streeten, 1997). The concept of open spaces (sometimes referred to as "urban oases" or what Lofland, 1998, called "memorialized locales") in urban communities has not received sufficient attention from social workers and other helping professionals (Warren, 1998). Lofland (1988) placed the concept of memorialized locales within the broader construct of the "public realm." Memorialized locales are defined as "small pieces of the public realm that, because of events that happened and/or because of some object (e.g., a statue) [mural, garden, playground, or sculpture] take on, for some set of persons, the aura of 'sacred places.'. . . . Of course, not all sacred places are in the public realm. . . . But when they are—precisely because of their 'publicness'—they can become lightening rods for feelings of 'community' and for expression of conflict."

Historically, open spaces have generally beeen relegated to parks. Arie-Donch (1990, p. 1), traced the impact of governmental disinvestment in urban parks and noted the implications for communities:

> During the 1970s, many parks and recreation departments began to treat the small neighborhood park as more of a liability than an asset. With rising maintenance costs and decreasing budgets, park directors were looking to cut costs and generate revenues for their departments. The district and regional parks became priorities, with funding becoming severely limited for development of neighborhood parks. These mega parks have a higher user cost effectiveness than small neighborhood parks, and are able to generate additional revenues for parks departments through user fees. However, what has often been overlooked in the analysis of neighborhood parks is their important cultural and aesthetic contributions to a community's development.

The importance of available open space in urban areas is often overlooked in urban and social planning endeavors. "Because it is sometimes dismissed as a frill, access to natural areas is a poor contender for limited public funds. But, by large majorities, people who live in cities regard access to open space as among the most important factors in their well-being and the vitality of their neighborhoods" (Trust for Public Land, 1994, p. 14). Recent initiatives by state and city governments to open up land that was previously not available for development because of toxic contamination have provided local communities with opportunities to use these plots for a variety of projects, including large-scale gardening (Renkin, 1998).

Cities, particularly those that are older and considered highly industrialized, have started programs to raze abandoned and commercial buildings (Johnson, 1998). Cities, such as Buffalo, New York (10,000 homes); Camden, New Jersey (3,000 homes); Philadelphia (26,000 homes of which 19,000 are beyond repair); Providence, Rhode Island (800 homes); and St. Louis, Missouri (6,000 homes) are examples of these types of programs (Johnson, 1998). Residents have the opportunity to convert the open spaces that result from the demolitions to a variety of uses, such as gardens and parks.

However, the creation of open space through the demolition of buildings is not universally applauded, as evidenced in Bridgeport and New Haven, Connecticut, and other cities across the United States. Critics have argued that tearing down buildings lessens the housing available for poor and working-class families. In New Haven, demolitions of buildings have resulted in the creation of over 100 gardens. In New York City, open spaces resulted in gardens and a greater sense of community. Nevertheless, city agencies have attempted to "reclaim" open spaces that were turned into gardens, in an effort to build additional housing (Finkel, 1998; Martin, 1998). Consequently, the availability of open spaces must be placed within the local context to determine whether it is "good" or "bad" for a community.

Breitbart (1998) contended that urban public places have slowly disappeared or been subject to greater control by authorities, which have severely limited who is considered acceptable to use them; urban youths, particularly those who are of color and have low incomes, have been singled out as being undesirable and dangerous. Efforts to control their free movement have resulted in increased police vigilance and activities. Thus, public open spaces, such as parks, are essentially off-limits to these individuals, and no alternatives are provided for them.

Maser (1997, p. 167) stresses the importance of open spaces, which are often available in fixed amounts in cities, as settings for engendering a sense of community: "Open space for communal use is not only central to the notion of community but also is increasingly becoming a premium of a community's continued livability and the stability of the value of its real estate. Of course, continued economic growth, at the expense of open space, will line the pockets of a few people in the present, but it will ultimately pick the pockets of everyone in the future."

In addition to facilitating residents' development of a sense of community, open spaces provide urban communities with the opportunity to determine what the primary purpose of these spaces should be, such as for recreation, the generation of food, or reflection (Kessler, 1997; Leinberger & Berens, 1997; Martin, 1997; Rosen, 1997; Rosenfeld, 1997; Warren, 1998).

In short, open spaces are much more than trees, grass, and flowers; these spaces can best be conceptualized as islands of safety and neighborliness (urban forms of plazas) that provide an opportunity for a community to come together (Falender, 1998; Rosenfeld, 1997; Warren, 1998). The continued development of cities in the United States has often been conceptualized along narrow lines, namely, the construction of buildings. However, as is the case in Boston, development can be broadened to include the creation of open spaces. As Falender (1998, p. E1) noted, "But for the new Boston to stay faithful to the old—a livable, walkable city on the water's edge—people must champion the growth of open spaces as aggressively as they do the ascent of office towers."

These spaces, in turn, allow a community to control the nature of activities within its borders and give residents the opportunity to come together and undertake a variety of projects that benefit the community (Warren, 1998), including gardens, playgrounds, sculptures, and murals. One program in Phoenix, Arizona, created an open space for recreational purposes, such as rollerblading, biking, basketball, and congregation, by getting the city to close off a street every Saturday, thus allowing the community residents to come together (Smith, 1996).

Open spaces and potential open spaces can be found throughout urban neighborhoods. Unused industrial and commerical buildings can be torn down or converted into other uses by a community (Warren, 1998). Thus, open spaces can be made available if residents have imagination and are willing to organize to achieve their goals. In essence, the availability of open spaces provides a community with an outlet for creativity and the development of socially constructive projects—projects that address local needs and systematically build upon a community's capacity to help itself.

Urban-Focused Practice

There is a growing acknowledgment that urban areas have long suffered from neglect of various kinds and that the nation must forge innovative solutions to the problems that are "endemic" to urban living, particularly for those who are undervalued, have suffered from dislocation (geographic and economic), and discrimination (Ewalt, 1997). However, as was stated in Chapter 1, but bears repeating, urban areas do not have a monopoly on social problems. Nevertheless, ecological factors increase the severity of the problems and influence how interventions are conceptualized and implemented; these interventions are often fragmented, disempowering, and superficial (Bullard & Johnson, 1997).

The goal of strengthening communities and social reform can be traced back to the nineteenth century, to the beginning of the social work profession and Chicago's Hull House (Brieland, 1990; Landers, 1998; Lubove, 1983; Margolin, 1997; Trolander, 1988). The provision of social support and the decrease of social isolation for newcomers to this country can accomplished more effectively and efficiently through the active involvement of the community. Brieland (1990, p. 138) raised a series of questions about what has happened to the profession since the days of Jane Addams: "The model of committed people fulfilling themselves by living amid the poor is outdated, but how can social workers demonstrate their essential commitment in the next century? How do service providers ensure that they identify with their clients and thus reduce the barriers that separate them from mainstream society? How and where do social workers expend their efforts for advocacy, even social reform?"

There are many answers to Brieland's questions, all with profound implications for the profession. The embrace of community capacity enhancement by community-oriented social workers is a twenty-first century version of the goals of the settlement house movement. By strategically and systematically focusing on assets, the profession can take an important step toward recapturing its zeal for meaningful change.

Historically, efforts to address urban-specific issues and needs have suffered from the lack of comprehensive planning and relied almost exclusively on a deficit perspective to inform policy and interventions (Chaskin, & Chipenda-Dansokho, 1997; Halpern, 1995; Morrison et al., 1997; Naparstek & Dooley, 1997). This bias has resulted in numerous failed attempts to deal with urban-based issues and has alienated communities in the process. Furthermore, the adoption of a deficit perspective has diverted much time and energy from the development of an asset perspective; in essence, the process of "retooling" that is necessary has suffered from misguided foci.

Urban-focused initiatives must be based on an in-depth understanding of urban realities (population density and trends, diversity of composition, interrelationship of social problems, and the impact of economic restructuring on communities) and be comprehensive, targeting formal and informal resources (McKay, Stoewe, McCadam, & Gonzalez, 1998). Major urban areas across the United States are increasingly becoming communities of color, with high concentrations of population groups that have been labeled the "underclass" (Jennings, 1994; Moore & Pinderhughes, 1993).

As a result, initiatives must take into account local languages and cultures and must actively seek to create opportunities for residents to participate in their communities (Erkut, Fields, Sing, & Marx, 1996). Maser's (1997, p. 102) description of the importance of participation in community development is applicable to capacity enhancement: "Because local community development is a democratic process that works only when it is accessible to and implemented by the majority of the population, it is necessary to involve as many members of a community as possible in the process of improving democracy through participation. The more diverse the participants are in the democratic process of community development, the more accurately the community will be represented, the greater will be the sense of equality in rights and duties, and the truer the outcome."

Conclusion

There is little question that urban areas in the United States are experiencing major changes and, in some cases, upheavals. These changes, which have been slow in coming, should continue well into the next century and have dramatic implications for the country and the helping professions. Urban-based communities of color have and will continue to pose great challenges for social work. The importance of cultural competence in all aspects of service delivery requires practitioners to be keenly aware of how communities are changing. It is no longer feasible to think of communities of color as monolithic in structure and composition; these communities are dynamic and ever changing in composition and demographic characteristics.

Social work, too, seems to be at a crossroads in how best to embrace and address urban issues. That it is not to say that suburban and rural areas do not share these issues because they do. However, the magnitude of the issues in urban areas, combined with the denisty of the population, limited formal resources, and history of ill-advised policies, necessitates the development of interventions based on this reality (Halpern, 1995; McKay et al., 1998; Walberg, Reyes, Weissberg, & Kuster, 1997).

3

A Foundation for Community Capacity-Enhancement Practice

It is a tremendous challenge for practitioners to translate practice theory into effective practice. As Poole (1997, p. 167) stated: "It is one thing to develop a theory of intervention but quite another to understand the problem within the context of a particular community and to match the intervention with local norms and practices. Failure to do so spells early defeats for . . . projects and weakens the capacity of communities to solve their own problems." Thus, a major challenge for the profession is to translate a vision of what urban-based comunity capacity-enhancement practice should be into a reality for practitioners and to do so in a manner that is sufficiently flexible to allow for modifications to reflect local realities. That is no simple feat.

This chapter provides a brief review of several theoretical schools of thought that have direct applicability to community capacity-enhancement practice in an urban environment. The reader will be exposed to what is meant by community capacity enhancement and to three perspectives that have been influential in providing a foundation for this approach to community practice.

The profession's embrace of an ecological perspective offers great appeal for examining urban-based issues and interventions (Schriver, 1997). No single theory could possibly explain urban-based social problems, since there are prodigious social, economic, political, and technological forces active in this arena. An ecological perspective is a sufficiently broad conceptual framework to encompass multiple theories, concepts, and practices (Poole, 1997). Therefore, it offers great promise for analyzing urban murals, gardens, playgrounds, and sculptures.

The model of urban community practice espoused in this book uses as-sets as a central focus and builds on the professional literature, with an emphasis on oppressed groups of color. Community practice in an urban environment must be viewed within the context of other models of macro practice, and its essential qualities are examined here in light of Weil's (1996) and Weil and Gamble's (1995) five characteristics. The use of these characteristics facilitates the identification of commonalities with other macro-practice models and highlights the unique features of the community practice orientation used in this book.

Community Capacity Enhancement

The incorporation of an assets perspective into community-focused initiatives can be referred to as community capacity enhancement. The strategy of community capacity enhancement is perhaps the best approach from which to operationalize a strengths perspective in the development of culturally competent initiatives (Williams, 1994). This strategy is predicated on five assumptions involving a community: (1) The community has the will and the resources to help itself; (2) it knows what is best for itself; (3) ownership of the strategy rests within, rather than outside, the community: (4) partnerships involving organizations and communities are the preferred route for initiatives; and (5) the use of strengths in one area will translate into strengths in other areas—in short, community capacity enhancement will have a ripple affect.

Community capacity-enhancement projects must not only systematically enhance residents' skills and knowledge, but result in significant physical changes in the environment. This latter goal takes on greater urgency when the community being targeted is struggling to meet a host of social and environmental problems, such as deteriorating buildings and the lack of safe and open spaces. The incorporation of physical environmental changes in the community also reinforces the importance of combining capacity-enhancement goals related to individuals and creating environmental changes.

Community capacity enhancement, as is discussed later in this chapter, must never be confused with policies that have systematically withdrawn resources from communities under the pretense that they can and should help themselves. According to Gorham and Kingley (1997, p. 366), "The residents of neighborhoods must feel that they cannot sit by idly and wait for local government to solve all of their problems. They also have a legitimate claim on help from their city's treasury, but they are likely to achieve their objectives more effectively if they view such assistance only as one among a number of required inputs. They need to organize, assess, mobilize, and build upon their own internal assets and to proactively seek to control their own destinies." Community capacity enhancement, as a result, requires the creation of a partnership between a community and external sources—the government, foundations, corporations, and so forth. This partnership, in turn, builds on a community's assets in the process of addressing current severe social problems.

The social work profession's embrace of comunity capacity-enhancement approaches has necessitated a search for innovative intervention strategies. In an excellent summary of the community capacity-enhancement literature, Poole (1997), stressed the need for social workers to include a repertoire of skills in community practice but acknowledged that the profession must make adjustments in how it translates theoretical knowledge and undertakes applied research. Urban-based communities, particularly those composed of newcomers to this country, have many potential indigenous resources that social workers often do not recognize.

Efforts to mobilize indigenous comunity resources to address community needs and problems can be called community capacity-enhancement strategies or initiatives. McLeroy, Steckler, Kegar, Burdine, and Wizotsky (1996), leading exponents of community capacity development, highlighted key community characteristics that play a critical role in identifying social and health problems and mobilizing residents to address them. Community capacity-enhancement strategies seek to strengthen these characteristics in the development of solutions to community problems (Finn & Checkoway, 1998).

Community capacity enhancement can be viewed from a multifaceted perspective: (1) as a goal, (2) a strategy, (3) a set of guiding principles, (4) a method, and (5) a process. These approaches are practiced differently, depending on individual social workers, their organization, goals, and the community they are working with to achieve change. Macro projects to develop murals, gardens, playgrounds, and sculptures are representative of community capacity-enhancement initiatives.

Poole (1997) traced the recent national interest in using community capacity-building strategies to achieve social and public health goals to four trends: (1) recent innovations in public health and primary health projects; (2) the need for coordinated community-based networks of managed care; (3) the advent of the "New Federalism," which gives states and communities greater control over block grants; and (4) public suspicion of governmental institutions.

There are at least eight important dimensions of community capacity-enhancement initiatives (1) participation and leadership (Mitlin & Thompson, 1995), (2) access to and the efficient use of formal and informal resources (Delgado, 1998c; Kretzmann & McKnight, 1993), (3) social and interorganizational networks (Medoff & Sklar, 1994; Poole, 1997), (4) the creation of a "sense of community" (Chavis & Wandersman, 1990), (5) a community history of collective action, (6) community power (McLeroy et al., 1994), (7) shared core values (Holmstrom, 1996a, 1996b; Jason, 1997), and (8) the capacity to engage in critical reflection (Garr, 1995).

The Foundation for Community Capacity Enhancement

A community capacity-enhancement paradigm does not just spring up overnight in the professional literature. This perspective owes a great deal of credit to various approaches, most notably the strengths-assets, empowerment, and community participation approaches. Numerous scholars and practitioners have written on these subjects and laid the prerequisite foundation for community capacity enhancement.

The term *strengths* has many synonyms—assets, coping, competence, effectiveness, protective factors, resilience, and wellness—to mention but a few of the most common in the professional literature. Most definitions of cultural competence directly or indirectly incorporate key elements of what can be considered strengths. Although Saleebey (1992a, p. 7) did specifically not providing a definition, he noted that the strengths perspectives "is powered by a . . . faith; you can build little of lasting value on pathology and problem, but you may build an enduring edifice out of strength and possibility inherent in each individual. . . . No matter how a harsh environment tests the mettle of inhabitants, it can also be understood as a lush topography of resources and possibilities."

Despite the recently emerged considerable body of literature on the concepts and use of the strengths perspective, the concept is not new to social work. Ross and Lappin (1967) stated the importance of developing an awareness of the community from a multifaceted perspective involving both needs and indigenous resources. Billingsley (1968) noted both the strengths of and areas that needed improvment among African American families in the late 1960s, but stressed that the former were more influential than the society recognized. In the early 1970s, Hill (1972) also stressed the importance of understanding how survival and coping have helped African American families through arduous times. Collins and Pancoast (1976) and Froland, Pancoast, Chapman, and Kimboko (1981) were among the early pioneers in advocating the use of a strengths perspective through natural support systems.

Although these and other authors have used variations of the strengths perspective, the construct was labeled as such only in the early 1990s, although its roots are extensive. Furthermore, the concept has only recently been more widely applied to communities of color (Delgado, 1997a; Delgado & Barton, 1998; Delgado & Humm-Delgado, 1982; Logan, 1996a, 1996b, 1996c; Medoff & Sklar, 1994; Smith, 1996). As the concept of strengths has worked its way into the literature on communities of color, it has been transformed to take into account the impact of culture and context, with an emphasis on community, and, hence, changes have been made in the strengths paradigm, so it is more applicable to communities of color.

A strengths perspective is an important breakthrough in social work practice and an influential contribution to the development of a community capacity-enhancement approach, but it is limited by its emphasis on individuals (Chapin, 1995). An emphasis on individuals, although a critical element of community, does not lend itself to identifying and tapping the broader community and nonhuman factors. A community assets perspective, in turn, not only identifies and taps individuals, but takes into account groups, open space, physical structures, and natural factors.

This broader viewpoint allows practitioners to consider factors related to space, such as its availability and location; the transformation of poorly used space into socially productive areas; and physical factors like nontraditional settings, building walls, and natural assets. Thus, a community assets perspective, like an ecological approach, facilitates an understanding of how communities are challenged to change and to consider human and nonhuman assets in the creation of capacity-enhancement initiatives. In essence, this approach is an excellent paradigm for practice and complements the key concepts covered in this book.

The practice of empowerment is firmly rooted in social work (Gutierrez, 1990; Gutierrez, Parsons, & Cox, 1998; Lee, 1994). Solomon (1976, p. 19) defined empowerment as "a process whereby the social worker engages in a set of activities with the client . . . that aim to reduce the powerlessness that has been created by negative valuations based on membership in a stigmatized group." The manner in which this concept is operationalized, however, depends upon the context, which takes into account the physical surroundings and the characteristics of individuals who are the focus of empowerment. Holmes (1992) noted that empowerment and strengths are closely intertwined concepts. Nevertheless, the concept of empowerment must be operationalized according to the context in which it is practiced; thus, its principles would be applied differently in a rural than in an urban community.

The involvement of consumers and communities in determining their own future is an essential aspect of the role that social workers can play in bringing about change. There are a variety of ways to encourage and include communities in designing and implementing activities and services to meet their needs. For example, participatory elements can be incorporated into assessment technolgies (Mitlin & Thompson, 1995). The concept of community participation, however, takes on added significance in urban-based practice. This participation must be based upon the careful assessment of a community's history of participation, skills, needs, and goals. Murals, playgrounds, gardens, and sculptures are excellent projects for achieving community participation; in fact, success is not possible without such participation.

Essential Characteristics of a Community Capacity-Enhancement Model

Weil (1996) and Weil and Gamble (1995) developed a framework for examining the characteristics of macro-practice models as a means of facilitating comparisons between them: (1) desired outcomes: is the primary focus to enhance community capacities, create social change, or develop social services; (2) primary system targeted for change: indigenous stakeholders or informal service providers internal to the community, organizations serving the community, or external institutions or authorities; (3) primary constituency: neighborhood residents, political entities, or formal organizations based or serving the community; (4) scope of concern: quality of life, socioeconomic support, social justice in the community, or building political power; and (5) social work roles: a combination or any or all the following roles, such as educator, organizer, facilitator, researcher, advocate, mediator, manager, generator of funds, planner, or spokesperson.

The application of this framework to the community capacity-enhancement model addressed in this book highlights key characteristics of the model that practitioners must be well aware of to achieve maximum results. Although Weil's (1996) and Weil and Gamble's (1995) framework does not include a category that is exclusively devoted to community capacity enhancement, these types of projects can be placed in their community social and economic development category. Their framework's five dimensions lend themselves well to categorizing community capacity-enhancement projects like murals, gardens, playgrounds, and sculptures.

Their desired outcome category stresses development from a grassroots perspective and the preparation of citizens for the key tasks they must address in carrying out this form of intervention. Community capacity enhancement also stresses participation from the ground up and enhancement of residents' skills. The category system targeted for change highlights a number of formal and informal institutions; likewise, community capacity enhancement stresses the importance of targeting formal and informal resources, with the latter focused on generating income and donations.

The primary constituency category focuses on marginalized or undervalued groups in the community, as does community capacity enhancement. The category scope of concern emphasizes the generation of income, social support, and the enhancement of skills—goals that are similar to those found in community capacity enhancement. Finally, the category social work roles highlights a multiplicity of roles, such as negotiator, promoter, teacher, planner, and manager, that are comparable to those required by community capacity enhancement.

Conclusion

There is no question that practice is greatly influenced by context. However, a context that is urban based presents an additional set of challenges to the profession because of the dynamic forces that operate in the society and, for that matter, in the world. The major political and economic forces that are changing the extent to which cities can be self-sustaining appear to be beyond the control of any set of individuals or country.

The demographic changes within U.S. cities, in turn, have resulted in an incrased rate of "coloring" of the population and concentration of poverty, bringing groups together that have little in common in regard to their cultural backgrounds, languages, and experiences with a highly urbanized and industrialized society. Nevertheless, their residence in neighborhoods provides an important context for sharing and working together in pursuit of similar communal goals if the "right" projects are initiated by social workers and others in positions of authority.

Community capacity enhancement, as conceptualized and operationalized in this book, must be grounded in the operative reality of the community it seeks to address and be as free as humanly possible from oppressive and deficit-driven definitions of success. Therefore, evaluation approaches, methods, and instruments must be congruent with community norms, gather data on what all parties consider important questions, and minimize any disruptive impact on the functioning of a community.

4

Framework for Capacity-Enhancement Practice

Practice frameworks fulfill a number of important functions for practitioners, in addition to guiding them in the development, implementation, and evaluation of interventions. Macro practice, like its clinical practice counterpart, must develop interventions that have systematically been well thought out, to increase the likelihood that they will achieve the desired results.

The framework used in this book for conceptualizing community capacity-enhancement practice consists of five phases that place equal emphasis on assessment, mapping, engagement, planning (includes implementation), and evaluation. The framework is highly dynamic and should not be viewed as linear in nature.

This chapter provides the reader with an in-depth understanding of what these different phases consist of and how they interrelate and grounds them within an ecological perspective toward practice. The five-phase framework is also presented in Chapter 8, where numerous examples are provided to illustrate how the framework is closely tied to community capacity-enhancement practice.

Urban Ecological Perspective

An ecological perspective lends itself to the development of an in-depth understanding of human behavior within its social and cultural contexts (Jason, 1997; McLeroy, Steckler, Goodwin, & Burdine, 1992; Poole, 1997; Warren, 1998). The study of and practice with urban-based low-income communities of color require such an approach. Since Lewin's (1951) initial contribution to the understanding of the interdependence between people and their environments, an ecological approach has found wide appeal among helping professionals, most notably in psychology (Jason, 1997; Rappaport, 1977; Reppucci, 1987; Seidman, 1991), and in social work (Balgopal & Vassil, 1983; Callahan, 1997; Germain, 1979, 1991; Greene & Watkins, 1998; Hartman, 1979; Jack, 1997; Kemp, Whittaker, & Tracy, 1997; Longres, 1995).

There are numerous definitions of an ecological perspective. However, Germain's (1991, pp. 15–16) best captures how this approach is used in this book: "Ecology is the science that studies the relations between organisms and their environment. . . . [I use it] as a metaphor. It facilitates our taking a holistic view of people and environments as a unit in which neither can be fully understood except in the context of its relationship to the other. That relationship is characterized by continuous reciprocal exchanges, or transactions, in which people and environments influence, shape, and sometimes change each other." Thus, an ecological perspective provides a broad-enough framework through which numerous theories can be brought to bear in pursuit of a better understanding of behavior.

The application of an ecological perspective to urban-based, low-income communities of color requires researchers and practitioners to have a higher sensitivity to the complexities inherent in studying and working with these communities. An ecological perspective toward community and all the elements of which it consists, such as the residents, population density, housing structure (buildings that may be high rise and have minimal open space), formal and informal organizations, and natural resources, provide community social workers with a framework from which to examine and intervene in the larger environment. In essence, communities cannot be isolated from the cities in which they are located, the country, the hemisphere, or the world.

The concept of ecology is widely used in the field. However, when applied specifically to cities, it takes on a different significance from that usually associated with individuals. Once an ecological perspective toward cities is expanded to include nonhuman factors, it provides a viewpoint rarely used with urban areas. As a result, cities can be viewed as natural ecosystems (Trefil, 1994). An urban ecological perspective gives practitioners a better understanding of change, the existence of niches, adaptation, and so on. However, it still considers people the central factors in urban communities (Trefil, 1994).

Thus, the concept of urban ecology provides a rich context for analyzing the role of murals, gardens, playgrounds, and sculptures in the lives of undervalued communities. This conceptualization, in addition, lends itself well to the inclusion of the other concepts that are used in this book and ties social work practice into an urban context.

Limitations

An ecological perspective, like any other theoretical point of view, is not without its limitations and critics (Falck, 1988; Gottdiener, 1994). Fraser and

Galinsky (1997) argued that an ecological perspective, like a systems approach, lacks the specificaity needed for use in practice. Gottdiener (1994, p. 40), an urban sociologist, took issue with the urban ecological concept because of its narrow focus: "The limitations of contemporary urban ecology are already in evidence. It possesses a biological reductionist view of human relations which ignores the influences of class, status, and political power. Thus, it disregards the healthy appreciation of the early ecologists for the competitive struggle— as reflected in space by gangs, crime, and so on—in favor of a cooperative view of all human interaction. Second, it is schematically conservative because of its focus on adaptation and functional integration." Another major criticism of an ecological perspective is its emphasis on adaptation to an ever-changing environment (Robbins, Chatterjee, & Canda, 1998; Schriver, 1997), lending itself to use by neoconservatives.

Framework for Practice

A framework is a tool that practitioners can use to help them conceptualize how best to approach the development of an intervention. A framework's usefulness is increased if it is conceptualized as a dynamic process for bringing about change in a community or organization, as the case may be. Most frameworks generally consist of four distinct phases: (1) assessment, (2) engagement, (3) planning, and (4) evaluation. However, the macro-practice framework used in this book consists of five phases. The engagement tasks are sufficiently important to be integrated throughout the framework, but they also warrant a separate phase; a mapping phase has also been added because of its importance for analysis and interactions. It is important to remember that the phases are closely interactive with each other and that in focusing on one phase, practitioners must not forget the implications of actions for the other phases.

In essence, a practitioner does not have the luxury of focusing exclusively on assessment, for example, without keeping in mind how to undertake a map, actively seeking support (engagement), noting what kind of service will be widely received, taking into account implementation considerations, and thinking about evaluation factors. An effective practitioner can consider one phase a foreground and the others backgrounds, but never lose sight of the importance of the other phases.

Each phase of a community practice framework has both analytical and interactional dimensions. An analytical dimension integrates key theoretical content; an interactional dimension refers to sociopolitical considerations at the practice level, strategies, and techniques (Googins, Capoccia, & Kaufman, 1983). McLaughlin's (1994, p. 66) description of the importance of "local knowledge" illustrates this point: "Effective leaders use local knowledge and credibility to craft programs and resources that provide the connective tissue between estranged, cynical inner-city youth and the broader social institutions essential to their productive futures and positive conceptions of self. This connective tissue is spun from personal knowledge of youngsters and their setting and from knowledge of social, political, and economic resources in the larger community. These effective leaders . . . enlarge the opportunities available to youth and [provide] the introductions and confidence necessary to access."

Successful community practice cannot be achieved without combining theory and politics. A practice perspective requies social workers to use their analytical abilities to determine the most applicable theories to be applied on the basis of local circumstances and to be able to modify theory to increase its applicability to different community groups. In essence, the author fully expects practitioners to be sufficiently flexible in how they interpret theory and to apply it to a "real" live situation. A framework with a dynamic foundation allows practitioners to incorporate the vicissitudes of practice in a manner that still provides them with guidelines for intervention.

Murals, gardens, playgrounds, and sculptures are sufficiently different from each other to appeal to different communities and subgroups. Although these four types of projects can involve the use of a steering committee, no committee should decide to undertake all four types of enhancement projects simultaneously. These projects can be labor intensive, require different types of expertise and materials, and can tax even the most energetic and committed community. Thus, the phasing in of the projects is highly recommended. This decision, however, must be based upon a careful recommended. This decision, however, must be based upon a careful assessment of the community, including the resources that are available for such interventions.

Assessment

The assessment phase is probably the most important phase in any form of intervention. It is during this phase that the practitioner and community come together to share their thoughts, hopes, and concerns and to set commonly agreed-upon goals for intervention. If properly accomplished, this phase sets the foundation for all the other phases in any form of intervention, asset or needs based. Consequently, the time, energy, and funds invested in undertaking an assessment will pay countless dividends in the future of any intervention.

Assessment can be defined as "a systematic set of procedures undertaken for the purposes of setting priorities and making decisions about program or organizational improvement and allocation of resources" (Witkin & Altschuld, 1995, p. 4). As a result, it plays a critical role in both asset and needs paradigms, but takes on added significance with asset paradigms because of the paucity of data on community strengths. This form of assessment can rarely rely upon existing normative and expressed data because of their reliance on "problems."

An assessment associated with a community capacity-enhancement project, such as those covered in this book stresses the identification of indigenous individual, organizational, or environmental resources; it also seeks to generate ideas about how these resources can be tapped in the development of an intervention and in enlisting community support for all phases of a project.

Asset-based assessment, like its needs counterpart, uses a variety of approaches and techniques that must be based on local circumstances and takes into account the characteristics of the population of a community. Thus, no "standard" procedures and techniques are equally applicable in all communities. There are, however, key principles that will guide practitioners in making culturally competent decisions about the best, most efficient, and least disruptive ways of undertaking as assessment.

The following four principles can guide practitioners throughout the decision-making process of an assessment: (1) The assessment methods and tools must reflect local norms and experiences to minimize bias by the practitioner; (2) local residents must play an active and meaningful role throughout all phases of the assessment, including being hired and trained as interviewers and for other appropriate roles; (3) after the assessment, practitioners must systematically seek community input into the design of a program and logistical decisions; and (4) assessment must systematically build upon previous community capacity assessments, rather than reinvent the wheel, so to speak.

Factors to consider. Although numerous factors must be considered in planning and implementing an asset assessment, ten factors stand out as being the most challenging for a practitioner who is undertaking a community capacity-enhancement project, such as the ones covered in this book.

Time required and season. Although most individuals, organizations, and communities prefer to focus an assessment on their strengths and assets, this paradigm is new and not easily understood. Consequently, an assessment based upon an asset paradigm may be time consuming to undertake and complete. In addition, since most resource directories that are commonly found in government offices and nonprofit agencies list "formal" resources, they will be of limited usefulness in asset assessments. Thus, any asset assessment that is planned must entail interviewers going into the community and actually talking with a variety of individuals, some, if not most of whom have never been approached for their opinions. Such a community venture takes a lot of time and is best done when the weather is conducive to be out-of-doors.

Delgado's (1995, p. 72) experience conducting an asset assessment in a Latino community during the winter proved challenging: "It is strongly recommended that assessment not be undertaken during the winter months or major holidays—in the Holyoke case, Christmas. Winter weather is not conducive to door-to-door surveys, severely hampering scheduling. . . . Cold weather . . . also limited the amount of time interviewers could be in the field. In turning to busy holiday periods, several establishments did not want to be bothered during the most profitable time of the year." Cold weather, snow, and busy holidays necessitate numerous return visits for interviews and not only make the assessment more costly, but can have a dampening impact on the interviewers.

Funds. The expense of undertaking asset assessments does not have to be prohibitive. However, if an assessment seeks to enhance residents' capacities in the process, every effort must be made to hire residents to conduct it. Since residents must be paid during the training period, as well as during the actual interview phase, the cost may be much higher than is typically expected (Delgado, 1998a). However, if the assessment phase is conceptualized as capacity enhancement, then the cost is low relative to the benefits to be derived. Furthermore, hiring community residents is a mechanism for keeping money in the community, rather than paying outsiders and having the money leave the community (Kretzmann & McKnight, 1996a).

Space. It is highly recommended that practitioners locate space within the community to serve as a headquarters for the study. A community location offers tremendous advantages for conducting as asset assessment (Delgado, 1998a). First, being based in a community minimizes the distance between the staff and residents. Second, residents have a place they can go to to seek additional information about the assessment or even to register a complaint.

Third, having a community base increases the contact that the staff has with the community, facilitates street contacts, and increases staff's knowledge of the community (Goldstein, Spunt, Miller, & Bellucci, 1990). Fourth, having a community headquarters reduces the amount of time the staff spends traveling to and from the assessment sites. Consequently, the benefits of having a community-based site are multiple for both the community and the staff.

Opportunities for community participation. Participatory approaches play a critical role in the development of assessment strategies involving community capacity-enhancement initiatives. According to Mitlin and Thompson (1995, p. 237), "the development of participatory approaches in urban areas has been encouraged by two factors. Their initial development was closely associated with the need to rapidly gather accurate information about the people involved in or affected by a project. . . . Second, information collection has been shown to be one means by which local residents realize and fully appreciate the value of their own knowledge and gain increasing confidence in their capacity to be important agents in development." The information that is gathered must be "owned" by the community if it is to have meaning and inform interventions.

Upkeep and follow-up. Community capacity-enhancement assessments are based in the community, not in an office. Consequently, practitioners must be able to set up the operations of an assessment within a community context, thus facilitating the implementation and support process. Unlike conventional needs assessments that can be more easily lodged in the agency, capacity-enhancement assessments require staff actively to "work" the streets in an effort to locate existing projects, such as murals, and potential spaces for projects.

The street focus of community capacity-enhancement assessments can be facilitated if practitioners establish a working base in the community. As is discussed in much greater detail in Chapter 8, a community base facilitates the process and helps practitioners gain access to the community and the community gain access to the practitioner. In addition, field staff require close supervision and support in gathering important data.

This support may require supervisors to go out with the field staff, particularly during the initial phase of the assessment, to help them refine their observational and recording skills. It must be remembered that no amount of training can prepare field staff for all the circumstances they will encounter in the community. Thus, early and close support will prove labor intensive, but will ultimately result in better data and much-needed community support of the undertaking.

Needs and goals. Assessments involving the four community capacity-enhancement projects covered in this book must also determine the nature of the goals of these projects. Are the goals of gardening, for example, to grow food that can be sold to generate income, to supplement tight budgets, or to be primarily recreational? This determination, in turn, has important implicications for future projects. Murals, for example, may have be painted because of the community's need to convey important messages to internal or external constituencies. The nature of these messages can inform the practitioner of the issues that a community considers to be important. The case of Chicano Park in San Diego (see Chapters 7 and 8) is an excellent example of how messages are conveyed to the community and the outside world.

The creation of a playground may be a means of creating safe alternatives to street play. When a community systematically includes benches or sculptures that seek to foster communication and exchange, a playground takes on added meaning for a community with goals that go beyond entertainment for children. Consequently, the determination of a community's goals in creating projects informs the practitioner and sets the stage for future projects as well.

Research on existing murals, gardens, sculptures, and playgrounds. Unlike most asset assessments that focus specifically on evaluating the capacities of persons, assessments involving murals, gardens, sculptures, and playgrounds require a different set of skills and abilities. The location of these types of asset markers is usually straightforward. However, assessing the circumstances that led to their creation and the circumstances surrounding their continued presence requires the use of innovative, if not unorthodox, approaches.

Katz's (1998, p. 135) comments on the importance of public space in the lives of urban youths highlights how this dimension of community must be captured in any successful assessment: "With public space deteriorated and perceived as unsafe from a variety of perspectives both social and physical, young people have fewer opportunities for autonomous outdoor play or 'hanging out.' This lack has implications for many aspects of their healthy development, the building of culture, and the construction of identity." Thus, an assessment must identify the public places where young or old residents congregate or if there are no such places, the reasons for their absence.

Involvement of the external community. The very nature of funding requires practitioners to play close attention to external forces, even though they are primarily interested in internal, community-based forces. Practitioners who are employed by organizations must be accountable to both funders and the community. As a result, every effort must be made to ensure continued support for community capacity-enhancement projects, such as murals, gardens, playgrounds, and sculptures.

The involvement of the external community, however, should not be conceptualized as being only the practitioner's responsibility. In fact, the involvement of residents during this aspect not only increases the likelihood that external sources will respect the process, but it will help the residents further enhance their political skills. The use of an advisory committee of residents can be an excellent mechanism for involving the community in this facet of assessment.

Degree of negotiation (internal and external). It is highly recommended that practitioners develop one advisory committee consisting of internal and external members or two committees, one with internal members and the other with external members. Asset-based assessments for murals, gardens, playgrounds, and sculptures involve prolonged walking around a community, interviewing residents in the street, taking pictures, and the like. These activities generate curiosity among residents and stakeholders alike.

Any mechanism that can help the practitioner gain access to the community must be seriously considered. Advisory committees can play an influential role not only in obtaining community cooperation and support for the assessment, but in providing important leverage for obtaining external support once the study has been completed and recommendations for programs are made.

There are a number of considerations involved in deciding whether to have one or two committees. If the practitioner believes that combining the groups may prove too challenging for the endeavor because of past differences between members or organizations, he or she should establish two committees—one representing professionals, formal organizations, and key stakeholders, and the other representing residents (Delgado, 1996a). If two committees are established, it is essential to make sure that each committee is informed of what the other recommended and their respective concerns and roles. Such communication minimizes each group's concerns about the other and increases the likelihood that the assessment will receive maximum support.

History of previous projects. Asset assessments, like their needs counterpart, must never be undertaken without first understanding a community's history with these types of activities. Communities that have had negative experiences with assessments will, in all likelihood, be resistant to involvement, even if the current assessment is asset based. Undervalued communities generally have found that researchers enter them, solicit personal information, and issue reports and recommendations that are stigmatizing, but that little or no positive change results from the intrusion (Andranovich & Riposa, 1993; Marin & Marin, 1991).

In addition, practitioners need to review as many previous studies as possible so they do not duplicate prior questions and can systematically build on what is already known about the community. Unfortunately, any studies that were done were probably deficit based and hence of little help to practitioners who are using an asset paradigm. Furthermore, if an asset study study was conducted, it is unlikely that it examined murals, gardens, playgrounds, and sculptures. Therefore, a new study is usually necessary.

Assessment approaches. Assessment approaches that are focused on community capacity enhancement, like needs assessments, have both "hard" and "impressionistic" aspects. The former usually entail reviews of data gathered by institutions; the latter often involve the mapping of the feelings and perceptions of residents and key stakeholders sanctioned by the community.

Systematic community studies. No one method or approach to community asset assessment can do justice to the richness and complexity of communities (Hancock & Minkler, 1997; Marti-Costa & Serrano-Garcia, 1983). Consequently, it is essential to conceptualize the assessment process as a multimethod one, with a clear, if not exclusive, tendency to use methods that rely on interactive and personal contacts.

The systematic use of tools in studying communities offers tremendous advantages to social service agencies and other organizations, although it can be time consuming and costly, depending upon the tools' level of sophistication. The professional literature has identified a number of approaches to the systematic study of communities, the most popular ones being a review of the professional literature, asset assessment, and examination of the media.

A reviewing the professional literature is often recommended as part of any assessment, needs- or asset driven. The process is not labor intensive or costly and may yield articles on a particular topic that is pertinent to the community being assessed. The authors of these articles may be in a position to share unpublished material, such as questionnaires, guidelines, and manuals, that can save the practitioner countless hours re-creating them from scratch. Furthermore, the literature and authors may provide valuable advice to the practitioner about potential challenges and recommend strategies to minimize barriers—in essence, a consultation.

Client-driven assessment. Residents who specifically mention the need for recreational space for their children, concerns about the physical appearance of their neighborhood, or the need for activities that eliminate isolation and bring members of the community together, to list but three areas, are an important source of data. Another source are residents who speak fondly of a local garden or playground that plays an important role in the community's life.

Unfortunately, most social service-oriented organizations have not identified the need for community capacity enhancement as a "category" for gathering data. These agencies are usually funded through some form of categorical grants, and these funds are targeted to addressing some form of problem. Rarely are these problems sufficiently broad to encompass such issues as isolation, lack of alternatives, and beautification of the community. Nevertheless, a community capacity-enhancement assessment may require community social workers to contact key social services and other types of organizations to elicit their opinions. The use of a key-informant method, for example, may be the most cost-efficient approach to tap client-driven data.

Stakeholder-generated data. Practitioners must actively seek the opinions, reactions, and impressions of community residents and stakeholders to achieve a more well-rounded assessment of a community (Mercier, 1997). These individuals are in a propitious position to comment on the community historically and currently; in addition, they can play an influential role in other aspects of a project, particularly in development and evaluation.

It is important for practitioners to conceptualize stakeholders from a broader perspective than is usually operationalized, namely, as key leaders, elected or otherwise. Many individuals may not fit neatly into such categories but still wield a great deal of influence or have information that would be useful in assessing or planning murals, gardens, playgrounds, or sculptures. Consequently, every effort must be made to reach a cross-section of a community's stakeholders.

Context-related data. Practitioners must conceptualize community capacity-enhancement assessment as consisting of two phases: (1) identification and basic information gathering and (2) in-depth data gathering. In the first phase, a team of field interviewers usual covers a predetermined area, according to how the community defines itself, and notes the location of any mural, garden, playground, and sculpture, for example. Then the field researcher records the location of these sites and their proximity to key community landmarks or institutions; takes photographs with sufficient details so they can be analyzed, and notes any features that are unusual or worth noting.

These notes may include the condition of the project, its relationship to nearby projects that are similar or different, aspects of the location that are difficult to record, and so forth. They will play an important role in contextualizing the project and assisting with the analysis, particularly if the project is different from others in the community.

The field researcher also attempts to gather preliminary information, such as on which groups sponsored the project and the relationship of themes to the profile of current residents. This information is used to developing an interview schedule that will allow for the more in-depth gathering of information.

In the second phase, data are analyzed, and the next steps for gathering additional information are planned and coordinated. For example, if there is a group of mural artists living in the community who are often asked to paint murals on the walls of stores, an effort would be made to locate the coordinator of this group, if any, to discuss these artists' work. This coordinator can be asked to suggest artists to be interviewed and perhaps to facilitate this process. For another example, a community-built playground may have a dedication attached it that has information on the individuals or groups that built it; attempts can be made to contact these persons or groups.

This phase also involves locating local media outlets, particularly newspapers and community newsletters sponsored by local organizations, to obtain articles written on the project and the names of people who played influential roles in its construction. Reporters may also be interviewed, since their perspectives as "outsiders" may provide valuable information that is overlooked by insiders who take certain aspects of the project for granted. Police data, the number of arrests and complaints traced to vacant lots, may be another important source of information.

The use of detailed photographs is an important dimension of the assessment because it facilitates an analysis of the project without requiring the staff to go to the sites over and over again to make observations and notes and gives all members of the assessment team the same information. It should be pointed out, however, that there is no substitute for visiting a project even though it is time consuming to do so.

The analysis of photographs or field-based projects (if the assessment team visits them) usually involves (1) messages conveyed by the project, including the portrayal of community leaders (for murals and sculptures), content addressed signs and messages displayed by the gardeners (for gardens), and plaques with dedications and the size and complexity of equipment (for playgrounds), (2) the state of a project (level of maintenance); (3) the location of a project (centrally located and prominent or not centrally located with limited accessibility to the public); and (4) the relationship or projects to each other (a garden and a mural in the same place). Is the project isolated from others? These and other questions determined by local circumstances help practitioners in their assessment.

Each of the four projects addressed in this book requires the development of criteria for assessing them. Murals are used to illustrate this point (Ochoa, 1997a). In addition to the location and size of a mural, its content must also be assessed. The practitioner must identify the predominant images, which are customarily placed in the center, and, in the case of large murals, multiple focal points. Each section of a mural must be identified, and the interrelationships of the sections noted. Since there may be a central message and a series of substories, a mural must be systematically examined for the central message to be uncovered.

Mapping. The process of mapping a community's indigenous resources is greatly facilitated if the organization that is undertaking this activity has used systematic assessment strategies and methods. The concept of mapping, whether cognitive, bioecological, cultural, or social, allows practitioners to gather information on a community and exercise empowerment principles in the process (Kretzmann & McKnight, 1996a, 1996b). The information gathered during an assessment phase gives practitioners a visual representation of a community's assets or needs, thus facilitating the analysis and planning of interventions. "Community mapping is, in the most fundamental sense, a method for visualizing a community on paper. . . . When used correctly with residents of low-income communities (including youth), community mapping is an exciting tool for empowerment and for giving voice to people whose opinions are seldom heard and acknowledged" (*Community Mapping*, 1996, p. 1).

The Academy for Educational Development's Center for Youth Development and Policy Research (1998) has made extensive use of community mapping as part of its work with urban youths. Community YouthMapping seeks to achieve four goals: (1) create age-appropriate avenues for involving youths and working with adults; (2) identify available resources (formal and informal) for use with youths and their families; (3) develop a mechanism for recording baseline information about youths; and (3) create a catalyst for influencing policy, practice, and resource allocation pertaining to youths.

A community-asset map can gather data on nontraditional settings, such as beauty parlors, barbershops, grocery stores, and houses of worship (Delgado, in press; Kretzmann & McKnight, 1993; McKnight & Kretzmann, 1990). Behavioral mapping, for example, can play an important role in helping a community better understand how a particular site is currently being used and by whom. Maps can also be constructed to identify places in a community that are dangerous to women, gays and lesbians, elders, youths, or any other group the community wants to protect.

Bioregionalism and mapping have offered community groups an exciting perspective on viewing a community, with a promise for community-enhancement projects, such as murals, gardens, playgrounds, and sculptures. As Berlin (1997, p. 141) noted: "Ultimately, bioregionalism is about taking back our home places. It's about the re-invention of democracy as ecological community. The major tool that's used to bring about the re-invention is the map."

Bioregional maps empower communities by providing them with a tool to gain a better grasp of their situation or context. These maps may be used in any context and so, are not limited to urban settings. The development of maps based upon local priorities and values helps community residents take back their area by identifying their indigenous (natural) resources, noting how development projects that are imposed on them by outsiders will affect their daily lives, and giving them a tool to communicate their priorities and concerns within and outside the community.

Maps are within the grasp of any community and can serve as an organizing tool (Berlin, 1997). They can be inexpensive or expensive, depending on the number of people who are involved in their creation. However, if mapping is to be carried out by volunteers, then the expense is restricted to photocoping and enlarging maps for the work to be displayed.

Kretzmann and McKnight (1993) developed a Capacity Inventory for identifying community assets. This inventory has four sections: (1) skills information (abilities that have been developed through work, recreation, volunteering, and so on, (2) community skills (abilities that can be translated into community capacity-enhancement activities), (3) enterprising interests and experiences (activities that address commercial needs and can generate remuneration, and (4) personal information (data that can be useful in further enhancing the capacities of residents).

Mapping for community capacity-enhancement interventions, however, focuses on locating indigenous resources and projects or identifying vacant lots and prime building walls that can be used for murals. This form of mapping can be undertaken by any group in the community and does not require a hugh expenditure of funds; access to a map, usually available at the city hall, and a photocopy machine that can copy a large map is all that is needed.

Factors to consider. The factors to be considered during the mapping phase are often dictated by the goals of the intervention and local circumstances. If the plan is to target an intervention to a subsection of a community, the process of mapping is much easier because only a limited amount of territory must be considered; a broader targeted intervention, however, entails much more time, energy, and resources.

Local circumstances also dictate the factors that must be taken into account. Communities with a history of welcoming outsiders will present different challenges from ones that are highly suspicious of outsiders. In addition, community capacity-enhancement assessment must build upon existing information. Although it is highly unlikely, there may have been previous efforts to assess assets whose results can be incorporated into a current effort. Despite the dynamic nature of local circumstances, there are at least four factors that will be manifest in a mapping effort: (1) the degree of desired specificity, (2) training and support, (3) extent of the distribution of the map, and (4) collaboration with other community-based interventions.

Degree of desired specificity. The actual recording of information on a map is not labor intensive. However, the gathering of the information can be labor intensive, particularly if it involves many interviews and elaborate recording mechanisms. Consequently, the degree of specificity that is needed will influence the labor intensity of the effort.

Mapping provides practitioners with a variety of ways of laying out a community. As a result, the nature of the mapping is greatly determined by the goals and the degree of specificity that is required to develop a functional map. For example, practitioners can create maps of all the murals in a community and may devise a method for classifying murals on the basis of their size, complexity, and messages conveyed; each of these domains can be placed on a map. Consequently, mapping is sufficiently flexible to include almost any form of information. This flexibility allows the organization and community that are doing the mapping to decide what kind of information is or is not important.

It is also possible to develop multiple maps of the same community, with each map recording a different type of information that can be used for different types of projects or for deciding which project is the most beneficial for a community at that point. Enhanced photocopies of a map can be made at a low cost, so the map can be used for multiple purposes.

Training and support. It would be unrealistic and unfair to hire or recruit residents to participate in the mapping phase without giving them the necessary preparation and support to do the work. Residents who have had training or experience in conducting field-based research will undoubtedly not require as much of an investment of time and energy as those who have had limited or no experience. Nevertheless, as stated repeatedly throughout this book, one of the primary goals of community capacity enhancement is to enhance community skills and knowledge. Consequently, social workers must actively involve residents in all aspects of mapping, including analysis.

Ideally, the same residents who were involved in the assessment will also be involved in the mapping. This phase of the framework would be greatly facilitated by the intimate knowledge the field interviewers acquired during the assessment. Knowledge that may not necessarily appear on any data gathering forms can be used in the analysis of the maps.

Extent of the distribution of the maps. Once a map is created, it does not have to hang on a wall or rest on a table. A well-designed map should be used in as many community gatherings as possible; the map can be photocopies and reduced and distributed to the residents for use in briefing the media or as an organizing-mobilizing tool in the community.

The goals that have been envisioned for the project will determine the extent to which maps are used in the community as a consciousness-raising tool. Since maps are a visual form of representing themes and issues, they can be used with external stakeholders and the media. For example, if the local media have focused almost exclusively on negative news about a community, a map of community-initiated projects, such as gardens and playgrounds, may provide a visual alternative that can be used by local newspapers, television programs, and the like.

Collaboration with other community-based interventions. Practitioners and the communities they work within must determine the extent to which the mapping-related activities and interventions are connected to other community-based initiatives. This issue takes on added significance when other community-based interventions are based upon a deficit perspective. In such a case, the decision to get involved, or not, is complicated and delicate.

No community-based initiative can exist in a vacuum, separate from other activities and the life of a community. These activities undoubtedly draw attention, energy, and other resources that could be used for capacity enhancement, but instead are used for interventions that are based upon pathological views of the community and its residents.

Mapping and its related activities will gain the attention of many other agencies and providers, which can result in efforts to develop collaborations with the agency and group undertaking this form of activity. Although collaboration always seems good on paper, it requires a considerable amount of time, thought, and energy to succeed. Therefore, the advantages and disadvantages of a collaboration must be weighed before a decision to collaborate is made. Although the author has a bias toward not collaborating at that point because conceptually different goals and demands are prevalent, some communities may determine that the benefits of collaboration far exceed the limitations.

Mapping strategies. As was noted, the actual mapping that transpires after an assessment is a straightforward process. Data, whether related to key institutions or artifacts, such as murals, gardens, and space, are located on a map. Different designations, in turn, can be identified through the use of different colored pins, for example (Delgado, 1998c). Murals in a clearly defined area can be designated by the use of red pins; community-built playgrounds, by blue pins; gardens, by green pins; and sculptures, by yellow pins.

Once the locations have been labeled on the map, then the practitioners can analyze any patterns in the presence or absence of artifacts or markers. When there are no markers, there may be empty spaces that can be used for a project. The location of these empty spaces may be strategic, so the project takes on greater significance for the community. It may be found that although there is no public land that can be used for a garden, some homes have sizable plots that are not being used (as evidenced by the presence of weeds) and can be converted into community gardens. Thus, strategies related to mapping can vary in a multitude of ways, depending on the goals of the projects; the nature of information gathering; and the feasibility of launching a project based on funding, time, accessibility to a community, and the willingness of a community to engage in this type of intervention.

Engagement

The process of engagement plays an extremely important role in any form of intervention, whether micro or macro focused. However, it is more significant and challenging in the development of community capacity-enhancement projects, which do not have to be deficit, or problem, oriented. Furthermore, because the involvement of human service agencies with murals, gardens, playgrounds, and sculptures is out of the ordinary, residents may have difficulty understanding it.

The benefits of participation in any activity that results in the creation of an artifact, such as a sculpture, mural, garden, or playground, goes beyond the achievement of a "product." As Breitbart (1998, p. 320) noted: "Often, with public art, it is the process rather than product of art production that generates the most significant benefits and lasting outcomes. . . . When young people are encouraged to re-examine the strengths and weaknesses of their surroundings and to then act creatively to transform them, the experience can alter young people's attitudes towards each other and their future; it can also provide a much needed outlet for the expression of feelings." Although Brietbart's comments relate to youths, they also apply to people in any other age group.

The engagement of community residents is a labor-intensive process that often involves numerous conversations; meetings; attendance at community festivals and other functions; and, in all likelihood, testing of the practitioner. The opportunity for the residents to see the practitioner in settings other than those associated with the provision of services and in many different lights allows them to view the practitioner as a colleague, rather than just a "provider."

Factors to consider. The importance of the engagement process requires practitioners to be keenly aware of numerous factors and circumstances to ensure the success of an intervention (Berlin, 1997). These factors can best be classified as environmental and interpersonal. Although it is impossible to separate these two areas, since there is a great deal of overlap, each has a primary thrust that includes a unique set of factors and considerations.

Environmental. Environmental factors and considerations play an immense role in the engagement process of community capacity-enhancement projects. Engagement is facilitated when community residents are open to sharing their hopes and pain with outsiders (Brown, 1995; Jason, 1997; Schwartz, 1997; Wuthnow, 1995). The extent of this sharing is dependent on a practitioner's interaction skills: how comfortable the practitioner feels meeting people on their own terms. Fluency in the languages spoken by community residents is also critical if a practitioner hopes to communicate effectively with those whose primary languages are not English. If a practitioner is not fluent in these languages, he or she needs to hire interpreters as part of the intervention team and develop skills in working with them.

Knowledge of the community residents' cultural histories and traditions is also necessary, although in this situation, the practitioner does not have to be bilingual. This knowledge is particularly important when working with newcomers to this country (Ryan, 1997). The circumstances leading to the newcomers' exodus from their home countries is important information in determining some of the following:

1. The histories of countries relating to each other, particularly if there is a history of antagonism between groups before they settled in the community.
2. How the newcomers view collective endeavors. For example, if collective efforts are associated with revolutions, these residents may be afraid to joining groups in this country (Delgado, 1997a).
3. The extent to which certain capacity-enhancement projects are attractive on the basis of cultural traditions. The groups may have a strong historical tradition of agriculture but no history of playgrounds or knowledge of what they are.
4. The traditions concerning men and women working side-by-side or youths working with elders?

To be successful, capacity-enhancement efforts must take into considerations these and countless other factors.

Interpersonal. Engagement is essentially a process of meeting and conversing with residents to learn about the history of events in a community. In short, it involves discourse with residents who represent a variety of perspectives, histories, hopes, and concerns for the future. Consequently, sufficient time, energy, and resources must be devoted to establishing relationships based on mutual trust and respect. Social organizations that launch community capacity-enhancement projects must be prepared to validate the importance of interpersonal relationships by providing practitioners with whatever support is requested to ensure that this important phase of the framework is not overlooked or underestimated.

Practitioners must be prepared to share of themselves, not just their professional credentials and training backgrounds, with the participants of a capacity-enhancement effort, since residents generally are more interested in knowing more about the practitioner as a fellow human being than about his or her professional qualifications. Furthermore, because community meetings often take place in people's homes, houses of worship, or other settings that lend themself to informality, practitioners must feel comfortable being part of such efforts and partaking of the food and rituals that are an essential part of many urban communities across the United States. In essence, the more a practitioner is a "human being" and less a "social worker," the greater his or her acceptance in the community. This is not to say that a social worker must stop being a social worker. However, the role of "expert" and all other roles associated with being a "professional" must not take center stage, minimizing the role of being a fellow human being and a colleague.

Engagement strategies. Capacity-enhancement interventions require practitioners to seek the advice, input, or suggestions of countless individuals, some of whom are used to be asked, while others are not. In essence, the best way to conceptualize engagement is as an interactional process in which the practitioner and the community, defined in its broadest sense, meet face-to-face and exchange ideas in search common goals and approaches.

In many ways, the importance of engaging consumers is not new to social workers, but the engagement of residents as colleagues is not always firmly established and accepted. Social workers may be comfortable in the role of provider or, more specifically, expert. Community capacity enhancement, however, requires social workers to be members of a team, along with other colleagues, who happen to be residents.

Intervention

The development of community capacity-enhancement initiatives is often the culmination of an extensive assessment and negotiation period for an organization. If they are to remain truthful to the spirit of capacity enhancement, practitioners must systematically and strategically involve those who will ultimately benefit from the intervention. There is still a valuable role for practitioners throughout the entire process. As Lakes (1996, p. 4) stated: "Sustainable development, then, is best orchestrated when grassroots groups welcome technical advisors and other outsiders to participate and collaborate in building up organizational infrastructures. . . . What this means is that indigenous groups desiring small-scale solutions to problems within their grasp will devise and implement projects or programs that make use of the human and material capital at hand. Resources external to the group . . . can be utilized in the development process as well, but should not be controlled from the top down."

The set of principles outlined in Chapter 5 must play an influential role in guiding a practitioner and his or her organization in developing interventions. However, practitioners should never lose sight of individual needs in developing group-community goals. Newstetter's (1980, p. 102) description of group activities during the 1920s, has implications for the development of community capacity-enhancement projects today: "Activities should aim: a. to be as representative as possible of interests held in common by group members, b. to be as appropriate as possible for meeting common needs. But, in accordance with the general purpose of individualization, division of labor in connection with a multiple activity or project may afford opportunity to develop the varied interests of different individuals simultaneously, and at the same time to meet specific yet different needs of particular group members."

Factors to consider. Countless factors must be carefully weighed in the process of creating community capacity-enhancement projects. However, seven factors stand out for practitioners that address both process and roles:

Time frame. As was already noted, the four projects outlined in this book involve different time frames. The longest, from a development perspective, are community gardens; the shortest, depending on the degree of complexity and involvement of community participants, are murals and sculptures. The time involved in developing community playgrounds (a few days) may be misleading because of the degree of planning that precedes the actual building period. The time frame will have short- and long-term implications, particularly with regard to funding sources. It is essential for funders to understand that the goals of capacity enhancement go beyond typical funding periods, especially when multiple capacity-enhancement projects are planned, each building upon the other.

Extent of collaboration to be attempted. The importance of collaboration, as was noted earlier, goes far beyond the immediate project; it has implications for future undertakings. Consequently, the time and effort invested in developing collaborative relationships should never be minimized, particularly when potential building blocks are involved. Collaboration always requires lengthy periods of negotiations, building mutual trust, testing, clarifying roles and responsibilities, and the like. Therefore, the more parties involved in the project, the more time needs to be invested; the greater involvement of parties that have historically not collaborated together, the greater the investment in dispelling stereotypes and strengthening lines of communication. Collaboration is never easy and necessitates careful planning to minimize potential future misunderstandings and hard feelings.

Role of the practitioner. There is little question that the roles of a practitioner involved in capacity-enhancement interventions should be those of a facilitator, broker, educator, consultant, and expediter. In essence, the practitioner must seek to create an atmosphere that is conducive to community residents taking responsibility for their decisions and actions.

As Lakes (1996) highlighted in discussing sustainable development, there is nothing wrong with a community tapping external resources in the pursuit of its goals. However, there is something wrong with an external player taking control and providing the leadership to an intervention effort. Thus, agencies and funders must be prepared to allow this bottom-up process to take shape without needing to control an intervention.

Cultural capacity of the practitioner. There is little question that social workers must have cultural competence if they wish to work successfully with multicultural communities (Daley & Wong, 1994; Delgado, 1998b: Rivera & Erlich, 1998a, 1998b). As was noted in the section on engagement, the language and skills that social workers bring to their community practice will play an important role in ultimately determining their roles and the likelihood of their success.

It is unreasonable to expect social workers to be equally competent with all groups in a community. However, it is equally unacceptable for social workers not to be proficient in working with groups that do not share their language or cultural backgrounds. In situations such as these, practitioners must be skillful at working with and enhancing the work of residents who can communicate with their respective communities. The topic of cultural competence goes far beyond the central thrust of this book. Nevertheless, successful urban practice requires practitioners to be comfortable and able to grow; learn new languages and skills; and be willing to play a supportive role to residents who can lead, communicate with, and work with their respective communities.

History of interrelationships among community groups. An in-depth understanding of the history of relationships among community groups of different ethnic and racial backgrounds is essential in planning community capacity-enhancement projects. It is much easier to accomplish community wide capacity-enhancement projects when there is a history of cooperation among groups and leaders who can bridge differences and conflicts than when there is a history of conflict and mistrust and no responsible leaders.

In the latter situation, intervention projects must be modest in scope and goals and build in a period of testing and building respect among groups. Much background preparation is necessary before a project is actually undertaken. There is no substitute for the development of a solid foundation among groups because even under the best circumstances, patience will be tested, disagreements will occur, and hard feelings will result. Community capacity-enhancement projects are just like any other interventions involving groups of people who come together for the first time. Thus, practitioners must be alert to any suspicions that groups may have about each other. Failure to plan for them will decrease the likelihood that a project will ultimately be successful.

Availability of funding. Capacity-enhancement projects, like conventional interventions that are practiced in the field, must take into consideration the amount of funding available for them. Consequently, the amount of money that can be used for a project will dictate the degree to which a practitioner can hire residents, invest in training and supervision, and ultimately influence the complexity and extensiveness of the project.

The wonderful aspect of capacity-enhancement interventions is the explicit need to involve as many people as possible, whether they are paid or volunteer their expertise and time. As a result, the lack of disposable funding is not a serious impediment to capacity enhancement. It just means that more time and effort must be devoted to obtaining in-kind donations and that it make take longer to complete a project. The project's impact, however, will not be compromised. The availability of funds, on the other hand, frees the practitioner to hire and circulate funds within the community by purchasing supplies, contracting with local establishments, and paying community residents. When funding is available, the project can be much more ambitious and have a dramatic impact on the community.

History of the organization undertaking the intervention. The practice of community capacity enhancement is relatively new to the field of human services, so there are probably few organizations in this country that have a history of work in this area. Consequently, it is important for an organization that is seeking to develop interventions with a capacity focus to provide practitioners with the necessary supports to do this type of community work.

These supports can vary, depending on local circumstances. However, at a minimum, capacity-enhancement work requires an organization (1) to allow the staff to be flexible in determining the type, time frame, and degree of complexity of a project; (2) to provide appropriate supervision or contract with consultants when the staff does not have the necessary expertise; (3) to understand that the success of capacity-enhancement projects can be measured only over the long-term and to ensure that this awareness and patience permeate all levels of the organization; and (4) to keep the entire organization abreast of the progress of capacity-enhancement projects and to clarify that these types of projects are significantly different from the "business-as-usual" types of projects. This latter point does not mean that capacity-enhancement projects are less or more important than the other types of projects; they are just different. Therefore, it is important that staff who work on capacity-enhancement projects are not made to feel that they are less worthy than the other staff.

Intervention strategies. Intervention strategies, such as the ones proposed in this book, can be conceptualized as consisting of the three critical arenas identified by McKnight and Kretzmann (1990): (1) primary building blocks (assets and capacities located inside the neighborhood, largely under neighborhood control), (2) secondary building blocks (assets located within the community but largely controlled by outsiders), and (3) potential building blocks (resources originating outside the neighborhood, controlled by outsiders). The primary area for conceptualizing and maximizing the impact of an intervention is where the three arenas overlap.

This is not to say that interventions cannot be developed strictly within one arena or mixed and matched according to local circumstances and an agency's goals. However, the maximum benefits to be derived from community capacity-enhancement projects fall within the overlapping arenas. Linkages that occur among the primary, secondary, and potential building blocks, although the most challenging to achieve, also yield the greatest benefits and are likely to result in change that goes beyond an immediate project. Furthermore, they establish the necessary foundation for future undertakings.

It is important to remember that the primary purpose of community capacity-enhancement intervention is to bring about a positive change in the physical and social environment of a community and to do so by enhancing residents' skills in the process. In so doing, interventions must also seek to increase ties within the community and with external sources. Communities cannot be expected to take on the entire burden of addressing issues and problems that largely are influenced by external forces.

Evaluation

The evaluation of an initiative is usually not the activity that an organization enjoys and looks forward to with great anticipation. There seems to be much mystery concerning how to measure the results of an initiative, whether it is deficit or asset driven. Consequently, the challenges of evaluating a community capacity-enhancement initiative are compounded by the need to evaluate the impact on (or benefits for) the general community or neighborhood, not just the participants.

The process and techniques associated with evaluating the impact of murals, gardens, playgrounds, sculptures, and other community capacity-enhancement projects will provide social service and other organizations with numerous challenges that go far beyond those usually associated with evaluation. These challenges, addressed in Chapter 8, raise important ethical, methodological, and practice issues for social work.

Practitioners must never lose sight of the primary goals of an evaluation of any kind, but particularly of community capacity enhancement: to improve, not prove, and to inform, and not judge (Kretzmann & McKnight, 1997b). Once these primary goals are understood and taken into account in the development of approaches and procedures, social workers and communities can then address the finer points associated with this type of activity.

Factors to consider. As with any evaluation effort that is community based, a multitude of factors must be taken into consideration in developing and implementing an evaluation. These factors can be classified as methodological-analytical, sociopolitical, and the degree to which the community's participation is actively sought.

Methodological-analytical factors involve questions of reliability and validity, sociopolitical factors involve questions of local politics, and the degree of community participation involves the issue of community ownership. Nevertheless, the design of an evaluation of a capacity-enhancement project include the creation of guidelines to help practitioners through all the decisions that must be made to ensure that the evaluation answers key questions and in a culturally competent manner.

Kretzmann and McKnight's (1997a) guidelines for asset-based evaluations are an excellent starting point for practitioners who are evaluating community capacity-enhancement projects to consider.

1. Evaluation questions must be developed by all significant parties, with particular attention paid to the input of residents, who are the ultimate beneficiaries of any intervention.

2. Residents must play an active and meaningful role throughout all stages of an evaluation, and every effort must be made to ensure that their contributions are taken seriously.

3. The results of an evaluation must inform community capacity-enhancement projects and not disrupt the community in the process.

4. The focus of an evaluation must always be on the immediate intervention, but attempts must be made to generalize beyond the project and local circumstances to other communities and interventions.

5. Evaluation methods must take into account funding, energy, and time and be flexible to local circumstances.

6. An evaluation must be process, outcome, and impact oriented, when possible, and document key challenges and unexpected benefits.

7. Every effort must be made to examine intermediate outcomes, which, in turn, can be followed throughout the life of the project.

8. The results of an evaluation must ultimately generate stories that highlight both the benefits and challenges, regardless of the success of the project.

9. Evaluation efforts must endeavor to integrate both quantitative and qualitative methods; both methods have value and, if properly conceptualized, can provide a richer, more descriptive, and analytical picture of the experience associated with community-based capacity-enhancement interventions.

The use of a participatory-normative approach to evaluation serves to engage communities in the design, implementation, and analysis of the evaluation; in the process, it empowers or enhances the capacity, (Lerner, 1995; Mercier, 1997). A participatory-normative approach is counter to the usual disempowering nature of most evaluation approaches used by human service providers. The degree to which the evaluator is willing and able to embrace empowerment principles, on the basis of such sociopolitical considerations as funders' inclinations, will play a crucial role in determining what the evaluation process, techniques, forms, and final product will look like and the degree to which results are accepted internally and externally (Graham & Bios, 1997).

Capacity-enhancement projects, as a result, must build into the evaluation a data-reporting system that incorporates participatory principles. To apply these principles, the project staff must pose and seek answers to three key questions: "1. Who decides what outcomes to assess given that multiple and changing goals are being framed? 2. Whose voice is being heard in framing expected outcomes and developing information management systems? 3. How can community residents contribute meaningfully to such technical decisions?" (Folkman & Raijk, 1997, p. 459). Thus, management information systems can not be "pre-programmed" before the initiative of a capacity enhancement project; community participation is critical in the setting of any information system.

Evaluation strategies. The hallmark of any evaluation design is paying close attention to stakeholders' perspectives, community assets, and the variety of approaches to evaluation methods that lend themselves to studying the intervention (Lerner, 1995). Thus, evaluation strategies must be based on two important considerations: (1) the primary approach to be taken in the evaluation (a combination of internal and external approaches is the one offering the greatest potential impact on a community) and (2) the extent to which the evaluation effort meets "scientific" criteria for rigor.

The approach an organization and community take toward evaluation can best be conceptualized as weighing the advantages and disadvantages of bringing an "outside" expert to evaluate the intervention. An internal-based evaluation relies on the resources (expertise) residing in the community. Clearly, there is much to be said for such an approach. However, few communities have people with such expertise living within their boundaries. Thus, an external-based evaluation is best characterized by an "outsider" coming into the community to evaluate an effort. Although common, this approach also has its problems.

Community capacity enhancement lends itself well to combining both approaches and thereby maximizing the advantages of each approach. Although this approach can operationalized in many different ways, it typically involes an outsider working closely, preferably in a collegial manner, with a committee composed of residents and other stakeholders. The outsider not only facilitates and convenes meetings, but strives to enhance the committee members' capacities through workshops, technical assistance, and other methods.

Such an approach is labor intensive and costly. However, it results not only in an evaluation that can withstand scrutiny by funding sources and other interested parties, but in residents developing research skills that can be transferred to other arenas. This collaborative partnership offers a tremendous potential for modeling how outsiders work with communities in other aspects of community capacity-enhancement initiatives.

As was already noted, practitioners must endeavor to create evaluation methods and tools that take into account local circumstances, rather than rely on outside methods and tools that were developed for projects and communities that are different from those being evaluated and that are based on different principles. As Kretzmann and McKnight (1997a, p. 7) noted, "A primary obstacle put before many local efforts is that they are held accountable for outcomes imposed upon them by others rather than for what they claim to be doing on their own."

In essence, these "foreign" methods may appear to be "scientifically" valid but are inappropriate for capacity-enhancement projects, which limits the relevance of the information that is gathered. Decisions concerning the "scientific" rigor, degree of innovation, and extent of community participation in all aspects of evaluation are all closely interrelated in the evaluation process, thereby making decision making complex and potentially contentious. Nevertheless, practitioners must endeavor to create the necessary atmosphere and mechanisms to foster discussions that will ultimately result in the correct decisions for the community.

A steering committee, composed of all the key stakeholders in the project, is one means of ensuring that proper representation takes place. This committee will be empowered to seek the advice of and input from community residents who are not on it, so it does not take action solely on the basis of its members' perspectives and preferences. Ownership of all aspects of a community capacity-enhancement project is an essential aspect of this type of intervention, and every effort must be taken to ensure that it happens.

Conclusion

This chapter has presented an overview of a framework for undertaking community capacity-enhancement interventions that are focused on murals, gardens, playgrounds, and sculptures that are built by the community. The principles addressed in Chapter 5 take on added significance in assisting practitioners in developing strategies that take into account local circumstances. The framework helps practitioners conceptualize and organize interventions and gain a better understanding of how the phases relate to each other and the overall goals for a project.

Practitioners will undoubtedly adopt some or all the principles recommended in this book and may substitute some of them on the basis of their value base, experiences, and goals. Nevertheless, principles are critical for navigating the rough waters associated with any form of implementation, let alone, implementation of a community capacity-enhancement project. Furthermore, it is impossible to separate principles from a framework because a framework does not exist within a vacuum and requires practitioners to be aware of the factors that influence their approach to presenting situations.

The proposed framework, too, can be modified to take into account practitioners' perspectives, preferences, experiences, and local circumstances. After all, the primary purpose of any framework is to be a tool that can aid a social worker in the development of any intervention, deficit- or asset driven. Thus, the combination of principles and a framework work well together in taking community capacity enhancement from a concept, philosophy, or ideology into practice.

5

Guiding Principles for Community Capacity-Enhancement Practice

Social work practitioners need guiding principles to assist them in analyzing and developing macro interventions. Guiding principles play important roles in helping practitioners decide how practice must be conceptualized and carried out. A lack of these principles will effectively render a practitioner "clueless" about how best to undertake community capacity enhancement. This chapter presents six key principles that the author believes are critical for bringing to fruition all the potential that capacity enhancement is capable of achieving.

Guiding Principles

Urban-based community capacity-enhancement projects have direct practice implications for those who are interested in community-focused work. The presence or absence of murals, playgrounds, gardens, and sculptures are indicators of a community's strengths. These types of projects also increase community exchanges and help strengthen a community's identity.

No book, course of study, line of research, or advice from colleagues can possibly prepare any social worker for all the possibilities inherent in urban-based practice, whether macro- or micro focused. But the use of guiding principles can help practitioners navigate the stormy seas they will encounter. Principles, although broad by nature, provide compass points to direct interventions. The manner in which they are operationalized is greatly determined by practitioners, the social organization that employ them, and the nature of the communities they wish to engage and work with.

The following six principles have served the author well as he has ventured into numerous urban communities across the United States. Some of these principles lend themselves to certain stages in an intervention; some are particularly relevant to assessment, others are much more specific to involving a community, and still others are more applicable to the development of services. Nevertheless, they all interrelate and fashion an approach toward urban community capacity-enhancement practice.

Principle 1: Create Community Participation Stressing Inter-Ethnic-Racial Relations

Bringing residents of a community together in pursuit of a set of common goals is extremely important in any form of community social work practice. However, when the community consists of many different ethnic and racial groups, many of which do not share same language, then these goals take on added significance. Community capacity enhancement offers the potential to unite groups in search of an agenda for positive change.

Murals. The painting of murals can involve anywhere from 1 individual (a commissioned artist) to a small group (3–10 people) or a large group (20–25 or more people). The larger the group painting a mural, the greater the meaning of the experience for the community. Community participation is a critical component or mural painting. As Morgenworth (1997, p. 10) noted, "The whole point of my work is collaboration. . . . This is the way I work—I don't put in my own ideas—I elicit ideas from the community and then orchestrate them."

Mural painting gives residents the opportunity to be constructive members of the community. As a result, murals make excellent projects for a group of youths (not to be confused with a gang) to work collaboratively together and with the community. The concept of "cultural explainers" was developed by the public art movement as a means of improving relations between racial and ethnic groups through the creation of art and encouraging dialogue between groups. The mural, or other art form, incorporates themes related to history, current presence, and future prospects and aspirations. Once painted, these art projects represent each culture to the others and stress inter- and intracommunity dialogue (Cotter, 1976).

Gardens. The activity of gardening is based on a universal language that allows groups from different backgrounds to work and share; this interrelationship is fostered when these groups had an extensive agricultural history before their arrival in the United States. The land, in this case a garden, represents a public space in a community where interethnic and racial contact is possible and even at close quarters. As Baker (1997, p. 21) noted: "Ethnic groups are constantly fighting for their share of a shrinking pie . . . with a garden like this [Green Oasis, Lower East Side of New York City] where all ethnicities come and work together, it helps a lot. It doesn't happen in a public park."

Newcomers to the United States, as was noted earlier in the book, can engage in gardening as a way of transitioning to their new community. Furthermore, this activity allows them to plant, when feasible, crops that are an essential part of their diets but may be difficult, if not impossible, to obtain in local grocery stores. The process of gardening also gives groups of different racial and ethnic backgrounds a period, often limited, in which they can interact in what is often perceived as a "safe place."

Playgrounds. There is little doubt that playground development provides all community residents, regardless of their abilities and time constraints, with an opportunity to plan, build, and maintain these structures. Franquemont (1995, p. 9) had this to say about the importance of this participation: "[C]hildren design their own 'play scapes' to be constructed by the adults of the community at a fraction of the cost of modular equipment. The community takes ownership of the structure, reducing problems with vandalism, graffiti and maintenance."

Although children are generally not allowed in the work area because of safety concerns, they can still play instrumental roles in building a playground. One of the exciting dimensions of playgrounds is the role of children in designing the structures. As an editorial in the *Buffalo News* ("A Place for the Kids," 1994, p. 2) commented: "Organizers were smart to let pupils at a nearby school say what they'd like to have in the playground." Youths can design playgrounds in a variety of ways: They can (1) draw pictures, which are then used by playground specialists in designing structures (Collins, 1996; Giasone, 1994); (2) participate in contests for naming the playground (City Editor, 1997); (3) help select the designers of the structure; (4) assist in generating funds to buy equipment and cover other costs (Daley, 1996); and (5) play an important role in helping to maintain the equipment once it is built by creating community expectations that the equipment must not be abused. In essence, community-built playgrounds must be built with, rather than for youths.

Another goal of participation in playground projects is to foster caring and relationship building among the participants. As Linger (1995, p. 2B) put it: "The projects are exciting and good for the community and its residents. . . . [They are] a way for people to make a difference, and out of working together, they may end up caring more about each other." Relationship building can also be facilitated by setting aside certain periods for specific groups, such as "Single's Night."

Sculptures. Sculptures, like murals, can provide communities with an artistic vehicle to facilitate interactions and communication and to raise important, if not controversial, topics. The process of creating a sculpture is no more demanding or intimidating than that of painting a mural, although sculptures involve different materials and take on different shapes.

Furthermore, since sculptures are found in all cultures of the world, they are easily recognizable to all groups. Consequently, sculptures can be created that foster interactions between different community groups. If they are sufficiently large, many groups can play a role in creating parts of them. In this case, the whole takes on greater significance than the individual parts, fostering a sense of community that is inclusive of all the members.

Principle 2: Adopt and Build Community Spirit as a Central Goal

The search for a "community spirit" is an elusive goal in many communities across the nation. Developing a "sense of belonging" and "connectedness" to neighbors is a critical dimension of community capacity enhancement. The creation of community has the potential to build a foundation from which multiple, ambitious projects are possible.

Murals. Murals give community residents the opportunity to stop, watch, and discuss the actual painting process and, when it the murals are completed and dedicated, to share their reactions. As Engle (1997, p. 15B) reported, "Yesterday's party [dedication] was for everyone who had walked by while the murals were in progress and wished they could share in the fun. . . . It became a neighborhood gathering. Adults stopped to watch young people make chalk drawings on the sidewalk."

It can be argued that a central goal of any mural painted within a community capacity-enhancement context must be to engender community spirit, in addition to other worthwhile goals. The subjects addressed in a mural must serve to bring the community together throughout all stages of the painting process, from selecting the subjects to researching them, painting them, and dedicating the mural. Murals, as a result, cannot afford not to generate a sense of community ("California Town Hopes," 1996; Delgado & Barton, 1998; Madden, 1996; Morgenworth, 1997; Treguer, 1992).

Gardens. In urban gardening there are numerous opportunities for community residents to develop a sense of community (Hinkemeyer, 1996; Miller, 1995). Obtaining land is one example. Obtaining land in urban areas necessitates having residents and interested organizations come together to achieve success As Holmes (1997, p. 18) stated: "The whole process of protecting and dealing with land is set up in the interest of private developers. . . . There is not a lot of institutional support for land-users to negotiate with sellers and the biggest hurdle was for the coalition to build these processes ourselves."

The process of gardening itself fosters the development of community. Numerous meetings are often required to establish an urban garden. In addition, there are countless opportunities to teach various aspects of planting. Each of these activities fosters a feeling of belonging. According to Hamilton (1996, p. 11), "Experience shows the greatest value of the garden may not be the vegetables or flowers produced, but instead the community building that happens when neighbors work together on a common project." And Lamb (1997, p. 7) noted that urban gardens "create a sense of cohesion, a sense of investment in a neighborhood, a sense of identity with, and belonging to, a place."

Gardens also encourage residents to become actively involved in their communities, and those who choose not to do so invariably know someone who is involved. The following description of one community garden (the Tenth Street School Mother's Club) in Los Angeles after the 1992 riots reflects the potential of gardens to foster community spirit: "In one neighborhood after the next, community gardens and parks somehow escaped the fury of the riots. 'The gardens are a source of pride for the neighborhood they are in. . . . People had cleaned up these lots themselves. We'd removed a lot of diapers and old Chevrolets, Anyone who has a history in the neighborhood remembers what these places looked like before, and the truth is everybody knows somebody who is involved with gardens.' " (Trust for Public Land, 1994, p. 1).

Gardens are excellent vehicles for involving new residents, individuals who are isolated, and newcomers from countries with an economy based on agriculture and where English is rarely spoken. As Negri (1992, p. 17) commented, "[p]lanting and growing 'just seemed to come naturally' to the seniors and others in the neighborhood who have gardens there. Most had once lived on farms or in places with a little land.' " Consequently, urban gardening can help integrate new residents into the neighborhood or even foster interethnic and racial relations. One urban garden project in Atlanta, Georgia, specifically fostered intergroup relations as part of its mission. As a representative (quoted in Puckett (1995, p. 7D) expressed it, "We hope that by working together, volunteers and residents can focus on their similarities instead of their differences."

Gardening can appeal to newcomers who wish to replicate their experiences with agriculture in their homelands. A number of urban gardening projects across the United States noted that Asian residents tend to be overrepresented in this movement (Hill, 1996; Holmes, 1997). In a Madison, Wisconsin, study, more than 50 percent of the urban gardeners were from Southeast Asia (Holmes, 1997). In some cases, gardening was either initiated or fostered by Asians (Hill, 1996). Thus, urban gardening may be one of the few types of initiatives that lends itself to involving different ethnic and racial groups. These sanctuaries provide a meeting place where everyone has a role to play and is accepted without bias. They serve as reminders of what is possible when different groups work together in search of a common community purpose.

Playgrounds. As would be expected with a community capacity-enhancement project, the act of building a playground is just as important, if not more important, than the actual use of a playground for developing a sense of community spirit. Community spirit is manifested in a variety of ways, ranging from pride in ownership to a willingness to identify with a community, a need to be able to volunteer on local activities, and a desire to raise children in the community and have them stay there, rather than leave to achieve "success."

In building a playground, teamwork is another important manifestation of community spirit. As a participant in a Dallas playground stated (quoted in City Editor, 1997, p. 1): "We are confident that this playground in North Oak Cliff will bring community members together and foster teamwork— all while creating an outlet for youthful energy." A participant in another playground commented (quoted in "A Place for the Kids," p. 2) that the playground helped transform an area that was a magnet for crime: "An abandoned field in the crime-ridden Genessee-Moselle neighborhood [was transformed] into a community playground . . . as a way of generating pride in the neighborhood."

A sense of ownership of a playground is essential in developing community spirit (As Daley, 1996, p. 33) wrote, "When you come to the park you overhear people saying, 'My husband built this' and 'I bought a brick for the walkway' . . . 'It brings us together.' " This ownership translates into a community influencing and deciding how the space is utilized. Community spirit, as a result, often represents the necessary foundation from which to bring about significant changes at the grassroots level.

Sculptures. The use of sculptures as a project for creating community spirit offers great potential for a community to come together. Depending upon the goals, one of which to what extent is it important to bring together significant sectors (including a large number of residents), sculptures can be effective in creating a community spirit.

The creation of mechanisms for generating ideas for a sculpture, its location, naming, dedication, and so forth increase the likelihood that the process of creating a sculpture is as important, if not more important, than the actual sculpture itself. Consequently, community spirit must play a central role in the creation of any sculpture if it is to maximize the potential of community capacity enhancement.

If multiple ethnic-racial community groups are involved in building a sculpture, communication processes must be established to minimize miscommunication, even if all the groups speak English. Trust building between groups must play a central part in any endeavor to develop a community spirit. In essence, building a sculpture that represents an entire community is no more or less challenging than painting a mural or creating a garden or a playground.

Principle 3: Systematically Build Intergenerational Activities into Interventions

Urban communities are not monolithic, even when they consist of one ethnic-racial group, since they comprise residents of all age groups. Community capacity enhancement can seek to bridge divides caused by age by actively creating opportunities for young and old residents to interact and work together—a typical process in "healthy" communities.

Murals. Although the actual painting of murals lends itself to youths, the process of mural painting must involve people of various age groups working together (Coleman, 1994a, 1994b; Dowdy, 1995). Elderly members of the community can play influential roles in the research portion of mural painting by interpreting cultural symbols and placing them within a historical context. The information that they provide takes on added significance in communities in which there has been a tradition of oral history, since elders are the primary, and often the only, source of information.

The intergenerational and community aspects of mural painting are well illustrated by the following quote: "A dignified elderly back women with a hat on the right side of the mural? That's Aunt Gert. Her daughter, in her 60s, came by one day when I was painting and said, 'If I bring my mother by, will you put her in? She's 90 and lived here all her life.' 'I met her, took her picture and put her in. Funny thing was, everybody seemed to know Aunt Gert, or to be related to her.' " (Morgenworth, 1997, p. 10). A community-asset perspective challenges practitioners to develop ways of tapping the resources of all community residents; fostering interactions along all dimensions, with age being an important factor, is one way of increasing the likelihood that a particular group's assets are not overlooked.

Gardens. Community gardening is an excellent mechanism for fostering intergenerational relations. Elders who have knowledge of gardening can work with youths in developing and maintaining gardens. Gardening lends itself to involving both men and women and people of various age groups One participant (quoted in Negri, 1992, p. 17) said: "It's a great way to encourage tenant participation, and it gives kids something to think constructively about." Another gardener (quoted in Puckett, p. 70) described a typical day in the life of a garden: "In the morning, the elder members of the community bring chairs out to the gardens so they can pull weeds and talk. After school, the children harvest potatoes and pick tomatoes. They watch in wonder as the fruits and vegetables grow riper each day."

In short, gardening is not restricted to any particular sociocultural, economic, or age group and can serve as an effective mechanism for bringing together age groups who do not normally interact or perceive themselves as having similar interests. Gardening is a nonthreatening mechanism for building upon the assets a community has in a society in which agricultural skills are often overlooked or undervalued.

Playgrounds. Planning and building a playground fosters intergenerational relationships and collaboration as few projects can. Communities are composed of individuals representing the entire life cycle; consequently, a community must endeavor to involve all age groups in an effort to build community spirit across the life span. People of all age groups have talents and abilities that must be identified and effectively used in the building process.

However, such a noble goal is difficult to achieve through projects without a conscious attempt to do. Construction of a playground is one vehicle for bringing together multiple generations. Several participants in playground construction (quoted in J. B. Collins, 1996, p. 1) commented on this dimension: "It will not only serve the small children of many communities but it will bring the adults in these communities closer together." Consequently, playgrounds, to a greater extent than the other projects addressed in this book, facilitate interactions between children and adults. There are few arenas in which elders, for example, can naturally come together with young children. A playground can be built to encourage elders to come and sit and watch and, it is hoped, interact with young children and their caretakers.

Sculptures. As was noted, the process of sculpturing does not require the active participation of a large number of people, although many people can be involved if that is the goal of the community. Hence, any attempt to encourage intergenerational involvement must be carefully planned by creating jobs that lend themselves to particular age groups.

Some phases of sculpturing lend themselves to involving elders, for example. The designers and builders of a sculpture can easily tap the expertise of elders in construction and materials, for instance, by having them act as consultants and advisers. Elders who have the physical ability and desire can also be involved in the actual building of a sculpture. In addition, they can play active roles in fund-raising, preparing and issuing public relations announcements, greeting guests at the dedication ceremony, and so forth.

Principle 4: Implement Interorganizational (Formal and Informal) Collaborative Goals

The professional literature on social work intervention in urban areas is strong and emphatic that collaboration must play a central role in the development of any initiative (Barton, Watkins, & Jarjour, 1997; Dupper & Poertner, 1997; Page-Adams & Sherraden, 1997; Spergel & Grossman, 1997). To be successful these collaborative relationships, must be part of a comprehensive approach (Page-Adams & Sherraden, 1997).

Murals. The painting or murals does not require extensive collaboration with formal or informal community institutions (Lauerman, 1998; Lueck, 1997). Nevertheless, murals provide an excellent opportunity for the organizations that sponsor them to collaborate with other interested parties. Collaboration, it should be noted, does not mean that every interested party must participate to the same degree and make the same commitment.

Thus, collaborative partnerships must be sufficiently flexible to allow the parties to participate according to their abilities and time requirements. The process of developing a partnership can result in multiple benefits that go beyond just the painting of a mural by laying the groundwork for future opportunities to collaborate. Collaboration can open the door to a community's full appreciate of the advantages of working together—this experience may be contagious! (Doss, 1995; Lotozo, 1998; Lubrano, 1998; McRorie, 1997; Shapiro, 1997).

Gardens. The development of urban gardens is an excellent opportunity for social and recreational organizations to become active in community life beyond the provision of their usual services and activities. Social service organizations, for example, can help community groups obtain funding to purchase land (Holmes, 1997), serve as fiscal conduits for grants (Hinkle, 1997), or utilize garden projects for leadership, economic development, and community revitalization.

Social and recreational organizations are often in the unique position to broker between community residents and governmental offices, funding sources, and private developers. It is rare for these disparate parties to come together without the help of a broker. The process of finding a common ground and a willingness to compromise is not easy. Consequently, by taking this position, social service, recreational, and other organizations can take the initiative in fostering and developing urban gardens.

Playgrounds. Community playgrounds are excellent vehicles for bringing together public and private organizations such as construction companies, suppliers, houses of worship, city and state authorities, and community-based organizations, that usually do not work together because they are sufficiently complex and can benefit from tapping a wide range of expertise (Collins, 1996; Landscape Structures, 1998; Landis, 1994). These relationships, in turn, can foster the development of future partnerships that can result in greater benefits to the community.

Sculptures. The central nature of collaborative partnerships in the development of sculptures may be similar to that of the other projects addressed in this book—fund-raising activities involving donations, expertise, and the like. However, the specifics may vary according to the type of sculpture and the materials to be used.

Sculptures made of wood, for example, may entail the creation of collaborative agreements with lumber yards, and those made of cement may, depending on their size, involve local cement companies. Consequently, the nature of the materials will dictate the best sources of supplies and expertise. Nevertheless, it would be surprising to find a community with a long history of collaboration with either of these types of businesses. Therefore, projects must be highly flexible in choosing the principle collaborative parties that best meet local goals and circumstances.

Principle 5: Have Community Capacity Enhancement as a Central Goal

Community social work practice is not restricted to enhancement-type work. In fact, it is safe to say that most community social work practice is deficit driven and attempts to meet or redress some wrong. A focus on enhancing community capacity, however, requires a clear vision, will, and set of strategies. Thus, community capacity enhancement does not generally happen by accident; it requires a purposeful approach and considerations.

Murals. Capacity enhancement involving murals can transpire in a variety of ways and address a variety of areas, including research, making public presentations, work-related factors (work habits, exposure to the processes of starting and completing a project, consciousness of safety), communication, and academic subjects (particularly mathematics and chemistry). Clearly, all these factors are rarely in the foreground of community residents' wishes to paint a mural. However, a mural cannot be painted without knowledge of these areas. In essence, learning transpires without the participant feeling that "this is like school."

Research and communication skills (public speaking) are an integral part of the development of murals. A muralist must spend a considerable amount of time undertaking library research and interviewing residents about cultural history. Since few public education systems in this country give people of color an opportunity to learn more about their history, ethnic pride may be an important secondary gain of mural painting (Ochoa, 1997a). These research skills (reading and interviewing) have great promise for participants in this process to be transferred to others areas of their lives.

After the muralists conduct research and interview residents, they must then organize and present their ideas to a community decision-making group and explain why a certain design has historical and cultural meaning. The communication skills involved in this process are both verbal and written. The failure to communicate effectively can create misunderstandings or hard feelings about a mural's purpose and content. Needless to say, communication skills are transferable to other arenas.

The work-related skills enhanced during a mural project are extremely important to the participants and ultimately to the community. The development of a mural must be thought of as fulfilling as both an art project and a job. The development of good work habits enhances the value of murals as a capacity-enhancement activity. The group nature of this activity requires members to be able to count on each other in order for the project to be successful. Thus, attendance and punctuality are critical factors in mural painting; participants who are unable to attend or who expect to be late must inform the supervisor, so the team can make the necessary adjustments.

Murals must never be thought of as individual projects; truly successful community-initiated murals involve a countless number of people (Fishman, 1996). However, teamwork, although often talked about in group-oriented projects, is never easy to achieve. With murals, teamwork plays an instrumental role throughout all phases of the painting. A team approach to murals allows the participants to find their individual voices and use their unique talents and abilities.

The experience of starting and finishing a project is another important aspect of mural painting. The ability to start and finish a project provides a wealth of knowledge and appreciation of the importance of planning and the compromises that are often associated with implementation. The awareness of what goes into a project gives muralists a perspective that is often overlooked in community-focused interventions.

Consciousness of safety must also be central to any mural project. Mural painting, particularly a mural that covers a large portion of a wall and requires scaffolds, can prove dangerous if a muralist does not follow established rules of conduct. There are just too many junctures in a mural project at which the participants can get hurt if they do not follow safety procedures.

Finally, successful mural projects require the participants to have a solid understanding of mathematics and chemistry, subjects that are often not well taught to or fully grasped by students in schools. Mathematics (primarily geometry and the use of scales) and chemistry (the mixing of paints) are important subjects in a mural project (personal communication with N. Abbate, November 13, 1996). As a result, murals, are an excellent medium for teaching and demonstrating the importance of academic subjects in the "real world." Thus, the enhancement of knowledge and skills is well integrated into the painting of a mural.

Gardens. Gardening, like mural painting, is an activity that requires lessons to be learned that can easily be transferred to other arenas (Sprott, 1996). The knowledge of chemistry (soil), crop selection, and mathematics (optimal spatial planting), combined with communication skills, teamwork, finances, and cooperation, are indispensable for an excellent education. Additional lessons—about pricing, supply and demand, marketing, and distribution—can be learned when the primary goal of gardening is to sell food in the marketplace. Many schools in urban areas have land that can be converted to gardens, thereby eliminating a major barrier to these types of projects—the acquisition of land.

One elementary school in Massachusetts developed a classroom curriculum on gardening themes As Milmore (1997, p. B14) reported, "Each class designs and plants its own plot . . . offering students a natural sequence of gardening experiences by the time they graduate from the fifth grade. To enliven classroom curriculum, teachers chose garden themes involving wildlife, butterflies and caterpillars, windflowers, herbs, vegetables, mixed flowers, alphabet, Early American, prairies, and plants for dyeing." There are an endless number of possibilities for youths in and out of school to use gardens as learning experiences.

Playgrounds. Individuals involved in planning and building playgrounds develop organizational and planning skills that they can apply to other community-focused projects, including helping other communities build their own playgrounds (Langhenry, 1997). The transfer of skills, knowledge, and experiences to other or similar arenas enhances a community's capacity to help itself. This concept takes on added significance when youths are involved (Delgado, 1996b). Youths not only benefit directly from the playground, but they take the experience of planning and building into future community-focused projects, from the construction of gardens, sculptures, and murals to community organizing efforts that are focused specifically on achieving institutional change.

Community capacity enhancement stresses the acquisition of additional knowledge and skills in the process of building a playground. Consequently, every effort must be made to match residents with activities that tap both their abilities and wishes. In addition, assignments must be carefully thought out to enhance the acquisition of skills and knowledge that can be translated to other arenas—employment, for example.

Thus, skills learned in constructing a playground—translating the community's ideas into reality, mathematics, the importance of communication and motivation, and researching and negotiating with appropriate parties, to list a few—can all be transferred to other arenas of life. The coordinator and others who play leadership roles must make every effort to help the participants transfer these skills because participants do not automatically make this connection; many may think that participation is just a nice experience in community building and do not realize how their talents can be used in other areas of their lives.

Sculptures. The use of sculptures as community capacity-enhancement projects offer all the same advantageous as the other projects by providing participants with experiences that result in increased abilities. However, with the exception of construction experience, which is heavily involved in building playgrounds, the skills and knowledge areas learned can serve participants well in future endeavors.

If the sculpture project is of sufficient size and complexity to require dozens or hundreds of participants, then the translation of experiences into other arenas is of even greater relevance. For example, a leadership role that requires a person to recruit, screen, and supervise participants is a worthwhile experience that can prove attractive to potential employers or community organizations. Thus, the larger the project, the greater the benefits of participation.

Principle 6: Stress Grassroots Funding When Possible

The importance of funding is well understood in the field of human services. However, funding must be examined from three perspectives: (1) the amount, (2) the source, and (3) the conditions. Community capacity-enhancement projects, as a result, must be broad based and pay particular attention to grassroots efforts. In addition, it would not be wise to think that resources equal money. A capacity-enhancement perspective takes a broad approach toward conceptualizing resources, conceiving of them as individuals, space, organizationals, and so forth. In essence, assets are much more than money; thus, fund-raising may involve donations of time, expertise, equipment, and space.

Murals. The costs of painting murals can vary substantially, depending on the size and complexity of a painting. A large mural that covers a significant portion of a building's wall, for example, typically costs over $20,000 to paint and requires approximately eight weeks to complete (Fishman, 1996; personal communication with N. Abbate, November 13, 1996). The costs can be reduced if every effort is made to comparison shop for materials. However, the major portion of the cost is for labor, namely, the individuals who have been employed to plan and paint the mural.

As a result, the high cost of a mural project requires a community to develop funding strategies. These strategies are usually multifaceted and involve grants (governmental or private), grassroots efforts, donations, and volunteers. Grassroots efforts are particularly important in this regard because they give the community an opportunity to contribute to the cost of a mural, thereby increasing the residents' sense of ownership of the final product.

Gardens. Gardens, unlike murals, playgrounds, and sculptures, are not expensive to develop, once land has been acquired. Unless the land needs extensive preparation, in which case heavy equipment may be needed and extensive work accomplished, funding of such a project is not outside the realm of most communities.

Thus, for this type of project, donations can be obtained from local businesses and community fund-raising events that publicize the garden, as well as generate funds. For a garden, a variety of sources, both profit and nonprofit, can be tapped for donations. For example, local botanical gardens (nonprofit) and nurseries (profit) can donate plants, expertise, and equipment. This flexibility allows the community to maximize its internal resources—for example, tapping botanical gardens, if available.

Playgrounds. Community playgrounds require a huge expenditure of funds, in addition to obtaining land. Fund-raising, as a result, is a major component of any initiative. It is estimated that a playground can cost anywhere from $30,000 to $165,000, depending on its size and design (City Editor, 1997; Giasone, 1994; Langhenry, 1997; Linger, 1995; Salter, 1996). Consequently, few communities, particularly those in primarily low-income areas, can afford to develop a playground without extensive fund-raising.

In all likelihood, fund-raising will involve multiple approaches and activities: Nurseries can donate mulch and flowers, local hardware stores can donate building supplies, and local grocery stores and restaurants can provide food and beverages (Daley, 1996). In addition, foundations and corporations can initiate special programs by providing money to purchase equipment and building supplies; Kimberly-Clark recently donated $2.6 million to build thirty-six community playgrounds across the United States and Canada (City Editor, 1997; Giasone; 1994). Still other activities can include grassroots projects, such as dances and penny collection derives ("A Place for Kids," 1994; Daley, 1996; Langhenry, 1997), to raise money, applications for government grants (Collins, 1996), and requests for private or public entities to donate land.

No one person has all the necessary capabilities to reach out to all these arenas. Thus, the development of a coordinating committee, with appropriate subcommittees, is a viable approach to obtaining funds. This decision-making vehicle ensures a more equitable distribution of work and "ownership" of the project. Furthermore, it facilitates the assignment of roles based on abilities, willingness, and accessibility to funding sources.

Sculptures. Community-targeted capacity-enhancement projects, regardless of the funding required, must actively seek grassroots sources of funding. Sculptures are no different from any of the other projects discussed in this book. The average cost of a sculpture can range from less than one hundred dollars to well into the thousands, depending on its size and complexity. Consequently, this flexibility makes sculptures excellent projects that can be used within funding constraints.

The major portion of the cost, regardless of size and complexity, however, is often for paying the artist and the acquisition of materials. Although it may be tempting not to undertake a fund-raising activity for a small project because the costs can be paid by an organization, it is advisable that an event be planned. A fund-raising event, such as a raffle or bake sale, gives the community an opportunity to share in the costs and is an excellent mechanism for raising public consciousness about the goals of the sculpture project.

Conclusion

The six practice principles outlined in this chapter and applied to murals, gardens, playgrounds, and sculptures are not new to the field of social work and other helping professions. A search of the literature will uncover numerous scholarly references to each principle. However, when combined and applied within a community capacity-enhancement perspective, they take on added meaning for practitioners and communities.

These six principles interrelate well and form the foundation from which to conceptualize capacity enhancement in urban communities. The continued demands on space in urban communities require practitioners to develop creative ways of operationalizing these and other capacity-enhancement projects to maximize space, time, and resources. Practice principles, as a result, help social workers consider the types of enhancement projects that best lend themselves to local circumstances.

II

MURALS, COMMUNITY GARDENS, PLAYGROUNDS, AND SCULPTURES

Section 2 specifically focuses on four types of community capacity-enhancement projects (murals, gardens, playgrounds, and sculptures) and consists of two chapters. These projects are not the only types that can be initiated, however, the creation of community banners, food cooperatives, credit unions, and various kinds of businesses, for example, can also be conceptualized as community capacity-enhancement projects.

Chapter 6 (Four Types of Urban Community-Enhancement Projects: Murals, Gardens, Playgrounds, and Sculptures) presents a detailed description of each of the four community-based projects, along with a step-by-step understanding of the process leading to their creation. Chapter 7 (Analysis of Common and Unique Development Tasks) analyzes the developmental tasks that are common to and different for the four projects.

6

Four Types of Urban Capacity-Enhancement Projects (Murals, Gardens, Playgrounds, and Sculptures)

This chapter describes four community capacity-enhancement projects and places them within a historical context, so the reader can gain a better appreciation of their significance in the lives of urban communities. The concept of community-built projects is defined, and data related to these types of projects are presented to highlight their importance to urban-based communities across the United States. In addition, the various dimensions and tasks associated with each project are defined and described in detail. However, since Chapter 7 analyzes these projects and compares them, this type of analysis is not presented here.

To some extent all four community-built projects provide a community with an opportunity to enlist volunteers in the pursuit of common goals. When they are completed, these projects symbolize a concrete achievement that the community can use to honor itself and those who played an active role in bringing them to realization.

Community Built

The term *community built* has many different meanings, depending on the context in which it is used. For some, it means built in the community and makes no reference to the process used; in short, it means built by outsiders for the benefit of a community. However, as used in this book, the term refers to both process and outcome and incorporates many of the values that are central to social work practice with oppressed groups, such as empowerment, participation, and capacity enhancement.

As a result, the term must be examined from the viewpoint of the degree to which residents are involved in all facets of a project. With playgrounds, for example, *community built* can mean that the community plays a decisive role in all facets of the project, including the actual design and construction of the play equipment. However, it can also mean that the community actively participates in all facets of a project, but hires an outside firm to assist and provide the necessary equipment. With murals *community built* may signify both that the residents are active in all aspects of the project and that the community acts as close collaborators with an outside artist.

Consequently, it is important for communities and practitioners to operationalize the concept of community built/community created according to local circumstances and the goals of capacity enhancement. Clarity about the meanings of key concepts like community built is essential to avoid misunderstandings between the community and the practitioner. This book has purposefully provided examples of various degrees of community built and capacity enhancement to familiarize the reader with their potential for achieving change at the local level.

For a project to be labeled community built, it must meet a set of criteria that stress participation and result in an environmental change. According to Arie-Donch (1991) the criteria are as follows: (1) A concrete product is the end result, (2) the project is built primarily by volunteers, (3) successful completion is dependent on the participation of a wide sector of the community (the wider the better), (4) the project's scale corresponds to the size of the community to increase accessibility, (5) the project has distinct phases (a beginning, middle, and end), (6) the project develops in the community a sense of ownership, (7) the project is spatially defined, (8) the project has significance (social, political, and psychological) for the community, (9) the final form of the project reflects the needs of the community, (10) the final project can last long enough to be enjoyed by future generations, and (11) the project is permanent and creates a sense of permanence and long-term community commitment.

Data and Community Capacity-Enhancement Projects

A practice model must be grounded theoretically and empirically if it is to be useful for practitioners. There is no question that ideology plays an important role in the development of a model. However, if the model is to be applicable in "real" practice, it must be solidly based on empirical evidence of its effectiveness.

New paradigms of practice, nevertheless, rarely, if ever, have a well-grounded body of empirical evidence from the beginning. The greater the innovation resulting from the paradigm and the more it is grounded in the community, the greater the challenge in gathering data. As Malakoff (1995, p. 8) noted, "The idea that greening activities create a friendlier, more cohesive community that is better able to tackle the many problems of mod-

ern life is hard to 'prove,' researchers say, because the evidence is often anec-
dotal, incomplete, or tantalizingly subtle."

Consequently, it is not unusual for a model to have certain components
that are well grounded in empirical data and minimal or no empirical data
on other components. This is particularly the case when there is an overem-
phasis on quantitative data (Layder, 1993; Stanfield & Dennis, 1993). The
inclusion of qualitative results, particularly those that are based on ethnographic premises and methods, can help a model achieve wider acceptance
because these results increase the model's relevance (Facio, 1993).

Studies that stress outputs and impacts on the community are lacking,
particularly for mural, playground, and sculpture projects. Gardening, however, has been the subject of several studies. The nature of gardening, which
generally stresses an activity, such as the generation of food, opens up possibilities for output and impact evaluation studies.

A 1988 Gallup public opinion survey found that 88 percent of those
surveyed believed that gardeners were important "beyond their beauty or
pleasing appearance (Malakoff, 1995). In reporting the results of a 1994 national probability survey by National Gardening Association, Malakoff
(1995) noted that of the approximately 50 million households in the United
States that are not involved in gardening, 13.5 percent (6.75 million) would
be interested in participating in an organized community gardening program
if it were accessible within their communities. Furthermore, of the approximately 30 million households that are involved in gardening, 300,000
(1 percent) of them do so through a community gardening program.

The amount of money that is generated or saved by growing food in a
garden has been well documented and lends itself to quantification. Evaluators can determine the average yield production per acre or other geographic unit. In addition, a 1992 study of 361 community gardeners found
that 48 percent of the unemployed people who were surveyed saved at least
$150 by gardening; nationally, the U.S. Department of Agriculture esti-
mated that urban gardeners involved in department-sponsored programs
grew an estimated $16 million worth of food in 1993 (Malakoff, 1995).
Small gardens can generate $350 to $600, depending on their location in
the United States (Hill, 1996). A 1995 survey of a section of Madison, Wisconsin, with a high concentration of urban gardens found that 75 percent
of the vegetables that the clients consumed came from community gardens
(Holmes, 1997). Many of these gardeners were newcomers and low-income
residents.

The results of two additional studies summarized by Malakoff (1995)
lend further credence to the impact of gardening on participants. In addition to the creation of food, nutritional intake is also felt to be a benefit.
One study of community gardeners found that 35 percent of those surveyed
believed their diets were improved as a result of eating freshly harvested vegetables; another study found that Philadelphia gardeners significantly increased their consumption of vegetables.

Studies related to the prevention and control of crime across the country reported positive results pertaining to the reduction in crime rates. In Philadelphia, an initiative to clean up vacant lots and plant gardens resulted in a 90 percent decrease in thefts and burglaries and a decline in the number of crimes per month from 40 to an average of 4 (Trust for Public Land, 1994). San Francisco's Mission District (Dearborn Street) documented a 28 percent drop in crime after the first year of a garden project; when the residents formed a neighborhood-watch group after their success in creating a community garden, crime went down 78 percent (Trust for Public Land, 1994).

In Philadelphia, a city-sponsored mural-painting program has proved successful. As Gardner (1997, p. 9) stated: "The murals not only benefit the young artists—they also build a sense of community and pride in neighborhoods. Only a handful of the 1,400 murals painted since 1984 have been marred by graffiti. And there's a waiting list of 3,000 individuals who want murals painted. Residences get to know each other at meetings called to decide a mural subject. They organize cleanups, plant gardens, and lobby police to crack down on drug dealers. 'It's a domino effect in a positive way.'"

Murals

Description

A mural is an art form that is expressed on a building's walls as opposed to a canvass (Barnett, 1984). Murals represent a community effort to utilize cultural symbols as a way of creating an impact internally and externally. Murals should not be confused with graffiti. A mural represents an artistic impression that is not only sanctioned by a community, but often commissioned by it ("California Town Hopes," 1996; Madden, 1996) and invariably involve a team of artists. Graffiti, on the other hand, represent an artistic impression (sometimes referred to as "tagging") that is individual centered and manifested on subway trains, doors, mailboxes, buses, public settings, and other less significant locations. Their content generally focuses on the trials and tribulations associated with urban living, issues of oppression, or simply a "signature" of the artist (Baez-Hernandez, 1995; Ferrell, 1995; Nwoye, 1993; Tumin, 1971).

Murals represent a much higher level of organization, and the community often participates in their design and painting; their location within the community also reflects the degree of community sanctioning—those that are prominently located enjoy a high degree of community acceptance, whereas those in less prominent locations do not (Blue, 1997; Cooper & Chalfant, 1984; Kurlansky, Naar & Mailer, 1974; Lawrinsky, 1997; Walsh, 1996). Murals have added significance because of the limited market for artists of color in the United States (Delgado & Barton, 1998; Weitz, 1996).

Some cities in the United States are fortunate to have organizations that are devoted to mural painting. These organizations not only accept commissions to paint murals, but use community capacity-enhancement strategies by actively soliciting, training, and employing residents in the design and painting of murals. As Delgado and Barton (1998, p. 348) noted: "Some geographical areas of the country are fortunate, as the case in Chicago (Chicago Public Art Group), Los Angeles (Social and Public Art Resource Center), and San Francisco (Precita Eyes Mural Art Center) where there are centers devoted to this art form. However, these centers are rare in other cities across the United States. This art form provides many artists with an opportunity to earn a living and serve as socially constructive outlets for their art. Artists have a community sanctioned medium for expressing their emotions and communicating them to the community."

As an artistic communicative genre, murals "date back to the cave paintings of pre-history and they are a durable art form—many cave paintings and Renaissance frescoes still survive. Murals have traditionally presented a forum for the political and social concerns of the people—often their only forum. Thus they have become a valuable historical record and an important tool for community expression" (Dunitz, 1993, p. v).

The roots of murals in urban communities have been traced to early mesoamerican culture and evolved over the centuries. Furthermore, this art form found favor during the New Deal art projects of 1933–43, when they received national attention, in large part because of the artistic talents of three prominent Mexican artists—Diego Rivera, Jose Clemente Orozo, and David Alfaro Siqueriros (Pasmanick, 1997; Romo, 1996).

The social movements of the 1960s provided an important impetus for communities of color to embrace murals as a medium, since people of color were not positively represented in the history books; mass media; or "established" art venues, such as museums and galleries (Dunitz, 1993; Dunitz & Prigoff, 1997). The Chicano rights movement of the 1960s further enhanced this medium nationally. Themes of identity, conflict, culture, and politics are commonplace in Chicano murals and express the muralist's sense of self and community as Cockcroft and Barnet-Sanchez (1990, p. 10) wrote: "Nowhere did the community-based mural movement take firmer root than in the Chicano communities of California. With the Mexican mural traditions as part of their heritage, murals were a particularly congenial form for Chicano artists to express the collective vision of their community. The mild climate and low, stuccoed buildings provided favorable physical conditions, and, within a few years, California had more murals than any other region of the country."

In murals, artists could share cultural traditions, raise critical social and political themes and issues, and reaffirm ethnic and racial identities. One mural artist (quoted in Morgenworth, 1997, p. 10) described the importance of this art form for the community as follows: "The mural is the ideal form for the community. . . . It's larger than life; you see your community on the wall and the kids who work on a project feel empowered."

It would be simplistic to think that murals can be easily classified according to Holscher (1976, p. 25), "One is impressed by the heterogeneity of the mural styles and locations. The typical mural does not exist. There are too many of them, depicting numerous ideas and themes, painted in literally hundreds of different places, to allow us to form an unsophisticated conclusion about the reasons for their existence." Holscher's (1976) analysis of Chicano murals during the 1970s in Los Angeles, noted that these paintings covered (1) a search for identity, (2) an affirmation of Chicano culture, (3) a concern for social problems, and (4) a variety of topics related to the first three themes.

Although murals play an increasingly important role in urban areas and communities, the professional literature has largely ignored the significance of this art form for community-based practice (Delgado & Barton, 1998). Mural painting must be appreciated from a multifaceted perspective, since it encompasses much more than just painting on a wall. Delgado and Barton (1998) identified the following seven dimensions of murals that address their goals, content, and location: (1) symbols of ethnic and racial pride, (2) religious-spiritual symbols, (3) themes of social justice in the United States and abroad, (4) decoration, (5) homages to national and local heroes, (6) memorials commissioned by local residents, and (7) location of murals within the community.

Dimensions

Symbols of ethnic and racial pride. Murals provide communities of color with an important outlet for expressing their cultural pride (Coleman, 1994b; Drescher & Garcia, 1978; Gomez, 1998; Holscher, 1976–77; Laird, 1992; Treguer, 1992). Undervalued communities, particularly those whose backgrounds are rarely projected in a positive light in this country, have few ways of communicating their pride within and outside their communities (Dunitz & Prigoff, 1997).

Among Latino groups, for example, murals allow subgroups to express the uniqueness of their history and culture. "Pre-Columbian themes, intended to remind Chicanos of their noble origins, are common. There are motifs from the Aztec codices, gods from the Aztec pantheon, allusions to the Spanish conquest and images of the Virgin of Guadalupe, a cherished Mexican icon" (Treguer, 1992, p. 23).

Murals, particularly those painted by residents, provide communities with an opportunity to project their own symbols of pride onto the external community. As one muralist (quoted in Valdes, 1995, p. 54) noted, mural themes are influenced by whether the artist is internal or external to the community: "There's a certain stereotype perpetuated by some white artists doing public works projects. . . . You see the same thing over and over again: Say no to drugs, stop the violence. I wanted to do a mural that reflects us as we really are. We don't just kill each other and sell drugs. We have other aspects to our lives. We need a variety of murals and public arts projects."

Religious-spiritual symbols. Spirituality and its various manifestations continue to play an important function in undervalued communities, particularly those of color (Cox, 1995; Kostarelos, 1995). Thus, the use of spiritual-religious symbols must be expected to figure prominently in murals (Coleman, 1994a; Cooper & Sciorra, 1994; Treguer, 1992; Ybarra-Fausto, 1990). Murals can both depict important spiritual-religious themes and figures and be painted on interior and exterior walls of houses of worship.

Themes related to religious beliefs, persecution, and interpretation of heaven are not out of the ordinary. The Virgin of Guadalupe (patroness of Mexicans), for example, is often found on murals in Mexican American communities (see Photograph 6.1).

The following description of a mural painted in the interior sanctuary of an African American church (First A.M.E. Church of Los Angeles) in South Central Los Angeles does a wonderful job of illustrating how religious themes are interwoven with racial-ethnic pride and suffering as the result of persecution. "In the upper left corner are images showing the cultural legacy and achievements of Africa. Below that is the enslavement of blacks in America. In the lower right corner is Biddy Mason, a slave who won her freedom in a Los Angeles court, then went on to become a suc-

Figure 6.1. "Guadalupe Diosa de las Americas." Chicano Park, San Diego. Painted by the Golden Hills Mural Gang and Mario Torero.

cessful businesswoman and philanthropist. What became First A.M.E. Church initially met in her home." (Dunitz, 1993, p. 210).

Themes of social justice in the United States and abroad. Murals have the potential to tell a community's story (narrative) from a community's perspective. There is no disputing the impact of oppression on undervalued communities in this country. It would be rare for a social worker working with residents of these communities to go through a day without hearing a story of oppression in action. Consequently, murals in urban communities often depict scenes related to social justice in the United States or, as in the case of newcomers who are refugees, in their homelands (Chalfant & Prigoff, 1997; Coleman, 1994a; Dowdy, 1995; Holscher, 1976; Valdes, 1995).

Murals are a natural form for the expression of protest by communities with limited access to mass communication outlets as Holscher (1976, p. 27) noted: "The concept of art as a revolutionary tool, as a weapon in a propaganda campaign against the oppressor, or as revolution itself has been carried over into the murals by Chicano artists in Los Angeles today." Kunzle (1995) made a similar observation about Nicaraguan murals depicting the Sandenista revolution in that country. Mural scenes depicting social problems, unresponsive institutions, and police brutality are common themes in urban murals. "These neighborhood billboards are used to elicit critical examination of the root causes and solutions to the daily onslaught against inner-city youth . . . [to document] community life and . . . to kindle discussion on the untimely deaths of neighborhood residents" (Cooper & Sciorra, 1994, p. 14).

The messages transmitted by murals can also be controversial in the community, touching on sensitive political and emotional topics (Woods, 1996.) As a result, murals can cause community residents to stop daily activities to debate or discuss these topics, as evidenced in the following example in Venice, California: "Artists love to pull on the chain of convention. . . . The painting that is causing all the trouble is a life-sized picture of a pig in a police uniform whaling away with a billy club at a spray-paint artist. . . . [Whatever [the mural artist's] intent, the painting and the tarp have sparked a ruckus over public art, censorship and respect for the police in a part of town where, ordinarily, almost anything goes" (Terry, 1997, p. A16).

Decoration. Murals can also serve the rather "mundane" goal of decorating unsightly places in a community and making these spaces memorable. As Treguer (1992, p. 24) reported, "What had been a hideous forest of concrete pillars soon became a pleasant and attractive place, a park decorated with paintings of remarkable beauty whose subject-matter was critical, even subversive." Beautifying a community, or decoration, also serves important psychological and political functions for a community (Gold, 1996). It conveys to the internal and external communities that pride in the surroundings is evident and that outsiders must think twice before making disparaging comments or even dumping unwanted trash in the community because it will not be tolerated (Kasrel, 1997; McCoy, 1997).

The decorative aspects of murals have not been lost on countless communities across the United States. A case in point is Twentynine Palms, California, which considers itself the Mural Capital of America, although in 1996, it had 7 murals (with 3 more planned) and Los Angeles had more than 1,000 ("California Town Hopes," 1996). Twentynine Palms currently has a public works campaign to make the town more attractive to tourists and considers murals the "windows" to the town's history.

Homages to national and local heroes. Murals can be vehicles through which oppressed communities can openly pay homage to local and national leaders. Undervalued communities rarely have their heroes validated by the nation. Consequently, murals provide important outlets for communities to validate the contributions of their own. The Philadelphia mural, "Wall of Neighborhood Heroes" (see Photograph 6.2) is an excellent example of how a local community can honor its heroes.

Other than the African American hero Dr. Martin Luther King Jr., and, the Latino hero Cesar Chavez, heroes of color are rarely openly acknowledged in the United States. Thus, communities of color must actively seek mediums through which their heroes can be validated.

A mural on Florida Street in Los Angeles does a wonderful job of illustrating a community's homage to national and local heroes. The upper section of the mural depicts famous leaders from history, and the bottom shows Cesar Chavez leading a protest. The protesters are "everyday" type

Figure 6.2. "Wall of Neighborhood Heroes." Painted by Philadelphia Mural Art Staff. Photo credit: Don Springer.

of people—teachers, priests, mothers, fathers, and students—and are represented by real people from the community. Escobar (1997, pp. 1–2) described the heroes depicted in the mural this way:

> Kateri Tekawitha helped northern native tribes unite and make peace with Canadian native tribes. Fray Bartolome de las Casas, a Spanish priest, spoke out against the injustices that were being committed against the Indians during the invasion of the Americas by the Spanish. Sister Ines de la Cruz, a Mexican literary genius of the late 17th century, argued for women's rights. Her mystical poetry was very influential among later generations of Latin American writers. Oscar Romero, Archbishop of El Salvador, spoke out against his government because of the injustices being done against the poor. He was assassinated in church. Miguel Hidalgo was a great leader in the Mexican independence movement. He inspired many Native Americans to stand up and fight the injustices from the Spanish government. Martin Luther King was the great African American civil rights leader who struggled for equal rights for African Americans not only in the United States but in Latin America too . . . he was killed for his efforts on behalf of justice.

Local heroes (individuals who have transcended their roles and captured the imagination and gratitude of a community) are rarely recognized by the local press, which is often more concerned about identifying "criminals" of color. Consequently, it is not unusual to see faces of local heroes mixed in with cultural and historical images. The showcasing of local heroes also individualizes a mural, allows the community to relate to its content, and increases its acceptance and validation by residents.

Memorials commissioned by local residents. Murals can provide local residents with a medium to honor deceased relatives, friends, and prominent residents and a mechanism to help them grieve. Murals have even been commissioned in honor of a dead pet (Gonzalez, 1998). Residents can commission a mural to be painted. As Gonzalez (1994, pp. 67–68) described them, "[T]he walls, sometimes playful in spirit and other times dripping with menace, are also a visual chronicle of each beleaguered neighborhood's history. Played out from block to block, the results of bad luck, bad health, or just plain badness are etched onto brick and concrete looming as a cautionary backdrop for those who survive another day, an uneasy reminder of how chaotic city life has become . . . death is the ultimate scene-stealer."

Cooper and Sciorra (1994, p. 17) commented on the juxtaposition of images and symbols of memorial artists in New York City as follows: "Drawing from sources sacred and profane, memorial artists creatively juxtapose an array of images and symbols in their work. Their innovative mix allows for individual input while establishing the parameters of this recent genre of graffiti art." These murals are extremely colorful and generally consist of portraits and names (sometimes nicknames) of the deceased and scenes depicting how they died, as well as their likes, special talents, and messages from loved ones. These types of murals also have a community perspective. "[T]he idea of honoring the dead and remembering is very visual. . . . People watch while the murals are painted; they have a ceremony at the end. It's a way for the community as a whole to deal with these losses" (Gonzalez, 1994, p. 64).

Location of murals. The literature on murals understandably focuses on the content and process of the actual painting. However, there is an equally, and often overlooked, aspect, namely, the location of a mural in the community, which is influenced by the community (Dowdy, 1995; Drescher & Garcia, 1978; Fishman, 1996; McRorie, 1997; Plaisance, 1996). The example of memorial murals highlights the importance of the artist and his or her relationship with the community. "Many admirers of subway graffiti found the appropriation of city property a particularly alluring and provocative feature of the art form. Memorial artists, on the other hand, are more inclined to seek permission for coveted wall space" (Cooper & Sciorra, 1994, pp. 12–13).

Delgado and Barton (1998) analyzed the location of murals and noted three dimensions that have important implications for analyzing a community: (1) limited audience exposure—infrequently traveled areas and small public spaces, such as alleys; (2) targeted audience exposure—located inside highly visited buildings like police stations, hospitals, clinics, schools, and other public settings; and (3) maximum audience exposure—located in public areas and outside public buildings with a significant flow of traffic.

Elements of Mural Painting

It is not possible to become a successful muralist without being willing to learn, grow, share, and care about a community. The competencies developed or enhanced in painting a mural not only benefit those who are directly involved, but are shared by the community. Once a mural is painted, it can serve as a valuable teaching tool for youngsters. Classes can visit murals and use them as subjects for discussions and historical lessons and as a means of helping students gain a better understanding of their community (Engle, 1997; Milmore, 1997; Negri, 1992; Sprott, 1996). In essence, murals serve as excellent mechanisms for teaching and learning.

Mural painting, however, is quite complex and often involves a great deal of background research, preparation of the painting surface, and interactional aspects that often go unseen by the public. Although all age groups can paint murals, mural painting lends itself to work with youths and the development of their competencies: (1) research, (2) negotiation, (3) consciousness of safety and following rules, (4) teamwork, (5) exposure to aspects of starting and completing a project, (6) work habits, (7) communication skills, and (8) knowledge of mathematics and chemistry (Delgado & Barton, 1998).

Community's decision to paint a mural. There are many different kinds of murals and just as many reasons for a community to paint them. A community may wish to use a mural as a "signature," or identity-displaying sign to showcase itself to the external community. In instances such as these, murals will be prominently located and represent an entire community through consensus-driven themes and symbols (McRorie, 1997). This type of mural involves a lengthy period of research, discussion, and negotiation. Its importance warrants serious discussion and the allocation of much time, energy, and other resources.

Murals can also take on a less important role within a community as indicators of specific locations, like those painted on public buildings, such as schools or houses of worship. These murals may be directed toward a specific audience (women, children, or newcomers, for example) and involve only a sector of the community, rather than the entire community. Thus, the reasons for painting a mural dictate the goals, and every other decision flows from this initial decision.

Researching and negotiating content. This phase in the mural-painting process usually covers three interrelated, yet equally important, aspects: (1) the goals of painting a mural, (2) the location of the mural, and (3) the content to be addressed in the mural. Murals, particularly those that use historical figures, events, and symbols, require extensive research, using library materials and interviewing community "historians." The researching of historical events and figures allows the muralist to develop investigative skills that can easily be transferred into other arenas, such as school and work.

Muralists are often called upon to interview longtime residents and senior members of the community to gather information on the meaning of cultural themes. Oral history is an excellent mechanism for increasing a community's involvement in the creation of a mural. Furthermore, when there is little or no literature on topics related to the history of communities of color, it may be the only way to capture information on key historical events in a people's and community's life (Doss, 1995).

Fund-raising. Murals can vary widely in cost. However, it is generally estimated that a "typical" mural costs approximately $20,000 (Fishman, 1996; personal communication from N. Abbate, November 13, 1996). This seemingly high cost, however, covers the hiring of painters and paying them weekly wages and thus often requires a community to get funding from any one or combination of the following sources: (1) a grant from a governmental agency, foundation, or corporation; (2) donations of funds and supplies from local businesses and community leaders; or (3) the development of grassroots fund-raising projects that involve a wide sector of the community.

The latter effort offers the greatest potential for community involvement and ultimate ownership of a mural. However, it is also the most labor intensive of all the revenue-generating activities. In this instance, the process is as important as the product (a mural). A combination of efforts represents a compromise for organizations that are seeking to sponsor murals. The involvement of government, foundations, or corporations, however, bring a different dimension to the process, namely, negotiation of the mural's content.

Preparing the wall. Almost all walls in a low-income community, unless they are in public buildings, have to be restored or undergo extra preparation before murals can be painted on them. The degree to which a wall is properly prepared is just as important as any other phase of the project.

Preparation of a wall generally entails several steps: wire brushing, caulking, and priming (Shapiro, 1997). Consequently, the preparation of the wall is critical, particularly if the muralist has high expectations that the painting will last for a long time.

Painting the mural. The painting phase will prove challenging for any community or team of painters, particularly when youths are playing a central role in the project. Depending on the nature and size of the mural, this phase can take up to two months. The success of the painting is greatly dependent on the participants' degree of teamwork, communication skills, and consciousness of safety on the job.

Teamwork is essential for a large team of painters to interact effectively and efficiently (Delgado & Barton, 1998). The painting of a mural requires careful planning, since many people are painting at the same time. Thus, excellent communication skills are essential because various people are painting at different heights simultaneously, which increases the likelihood of accidents occurring if communication is poor. Proper work habits such as getting to work on time and letting the team leader know when one will be absent, are also important, since every member of the team is valuable and interdependent.

Dedicating the mural. The dedication of a mural, like the premiere of a major play or motion picture, can have a great deal of fanfare and flair. The fact that a mural is on a wall, preferably a large and strategically placed one, facilitates the creation of a ceremony that promotes the involvement of a large number of people, not to mention the media. Thus, a community should not be inhibited from seizing the opportunities that such an event presents.

The dedication of a mural is a golden opportunity for a community to pause and celebrate. It also gives the residents the chance to meet and exchange thoughts and feelings with the artists. The residents can ask the artists about the symbols and themes represented in the mural, and the artists can share with the residents their hopes for the painting.

Maintaining the mural. To last a long time in relatively good condition, a mural must be painted with a solution that helps protect it against the elements. In addition, the community must make every effort to ensure that the mural is not defaced, although vandalism is rarely a concern when the community has a sense of ownership of the mural. Nevertheless, the community's ability to maintain a mural is often an indicator of the community's solidarity and the residents' commitment to each other.

Summary

Although Holscher's (1976, p. 28) comments were specifically on Chicano murals, they sum up the importance of this art form for other undervalued communities in cities: "In a sociological sense, it is difficult to assess the murals from the artist's perspective. . . . What does exist in the murals by Chicano artists is a common bond based on language and on points of view which have been tempered by direct and indirect experiences with Mexico and by the situations that Chicanos have encountered in the United States." In essence, murals play an important role in allowing communities to tell their stories to the outside world—stories that, unfortunately, are rarely heard without considerable distortion by external sources.

Gardens

Description

The importance of gardens in urban areas and other contexts has been well documented (Hynes, 1995; Kirschbaum, 1998b; Landauer & Brazil, 1990; Lewis, 1996; Monroe-Santos, 1998). The international literature refers to community gardens as "home gardens," which are defined as "an assemblage of plants which may include trees, shrubs, and herbaceous plants or vines growing in or adjacent to a homestead. These gardens are planted or maintained by members of the household and their products are intended primarily for household consumption. They hold promise . . . as a means of providing for a range of basic human needs: food, fuel, medicines, animal feed, and building materials, as well as social, aesthetic, and cultural functions" (Landauer & Brazil, 1990, p. vii).

The presence of gardens in urban areas of the United States opens up a new arena for the study and development of initiatives to bring together groups in a community in search of common goals, even when these groups are racially and ethnically diverse. Urban gardens are an essential part of an ecological system that fosters the development of community, relationships, and capacity enhancement. There is a trend, for example, for institutions, such as hospitals, hospices, and residences and nursing homes for elderly people to have gardens attached to them (Raver, 1994). These gardens not only contain medicinal plants, they also provide space for reflection and, if possible, actual gardening by the patients.

Hynes (1995, p. x) had this to say about the multifaceted roles that community gardens can play in the United States: "Community gardens in American cities are not altogether new. However, their purposes today—neither charity, nor philanthropy, nor war relief—are. Their goals include teaching children horticulture and diverting them from the streets; cleaning up overgrown neighborhood eyesores and pushing out drug dealing that, like weeds, overtakes neglected vacant lots; growing and preserving food from seed to shelf; restoring nature to the industrial city using heirloom plants and bird and butterfly gardens; and, in one instance, bringing the farming tradition of rural Mississippi to urban Philadelphia. . . . At its core, the community garden movement in the late twentieth century is about re-building neighborhood community and restoring ecology to the inner city."

Hynes (1995, pp. xv–xvi) then analyzed why community gardens are much more important than parks for inner-city residents: "Late twentieth-century cities . . . may need local community gardens even more than they needed grand central parks of the late nineteenth century. For the give-and-take of working in gardens attaches their gardeners to a particular place through physical and social engagement. Community gardens create rela-tionships between city dwellers and the soil, and instill an ethic of urban en-vironmentalism that neither parks nor wilderness—which release and free us from the industrial city—can do. Gardens offer a more intimate and local space than the large landscape parks can offer."

Victory gardens played an important role during World War II and have increased in popularity in recent years (Hamilton, 1996). They are so pop-ular today that there is a national organization devoted to urban gardens (the American Community Garden Association). It is estimated that between 300 and 500 cities in the United States have nonprofit organizations de-voted to urban gardening. Urban gardens have evolved into social inter-ventions over the past three decades from the initial appeal of growing veg-etables to using gardens to improve relationships and neighborhoods. As Miller (1995, C8) reported, "During the 1992 riots in South Central Los Angeles, the seven community gardens there escaped the barrage of dam-age. It is this attitude that has made the popularity of community gardens grow in recent years."

According to the American Community Gardening Association (1997, p. 2): "Community gardening is an international movement bringing to-gether neighbors of diverse ages and backgrounds to create new community resources. Neighborhood gardens serve as a catalyst for community devel-opment, beautify local areas, reduce food costs, and provide valuable recre-ational and therapeutic benefits." The following comments by researchers who studied community gardens (quoted in Malakoff, 1995, p. 8) highlight the community development dimension of gardening: "[T]here is plenty of evidence that greening can help pull together and improve community. . . . Among other things, . . . gardens that are built and maintained by commu-nity residents have 'unique social and economic benefits. The spaces provide opportunities for neighborhood residents to develop and control part of their neighborhood, an advantage not afforded by traditional parks.' . . . 'Gardens are active places that people make themselves, use for work and socializing, and can love.' " Another researcher noted: " 'A community activity such as gardening can be used to break the isolation, creating a sense of neighborliness among residents. . . . Until this happens, there is no community, but rather separate people who happen to live in the same space.' "

Home and community gardens are not new to Africans (Asare, Oppong, & Twum-Ampofo, 1990; Okigbo, 1990), Asian and Pacific Islanders (Christanty, 1990; Thaman, 1990), Latinos (Ninez, 1990), and Native Americans (Budowski, 1990). Consequently, with the migration to or dispersal within urban areas of the United States of newcomers from these ethnic and racial backgrounds, gardens can be used as community-enhancement projects because of these newcomers' untapped expertise and familiarity with gardens.

Contrary to common perceptions, there is more than one type of community garden. The type of community garden that is planted is determined by the community's purpose. There are at least twelve different types of gardens (Minnesota Green, 1992): (1) intensive food production (for personal consumption or donation to the hungry, (2) an urban oasis (sanctuary), (3) a gathering place (designed to encourage interpersonal exchanges), (4) a horticultural demonstration center (for aesthetic purposes), (5) small-space sites (for aesthetic as well as practical purposes), (6) edible landscape (for food production in addition to beautification of the community), (7) a public parkland (a recreational and relaxation site), (8) urban permaculture (hedges to offer security and provide a cool, shady area), (9) a community farm (a large plot of land at least one acre in size for the development of multiple crops), (10) a children's garden (to encourage exploration and the acquisition of skills and knowledge), (11) a horticulture therapy market garden (gardening as a therapeutic or rehabilitative intervention), and (12) community welcome (floral greeting located in sections of the community).

For the purposes of this discussion, gardens can be divided into three types based on their primary goals: (1) aesthetic (beautification); (2) recreational, and (3) practical (growing food). However, these distinctions are not as clearly defined, garden can sometimes serve several purposes (Fishman, 1998b; Griswold, 1997; Herbert, 1998; Holloway, 1993; Reicher, 1995; Vallongo & Mackey, 1998; Vasey, 1990).

For example, gardens are increasingly being used to aid people who are disabled (Fishman, 1998b). The following example clearly illustrates how gardening can be both rehabilitative and a community service at the same time: "The vegetables grown in the jail's fields are all donated to San Francisco's soup kitchens. . . . 56 jailhouse gardeners, including five women, feed thousands of poor while learning self-respect. About 2,000 inmates have participated in the farming program since it began in 1986" (Leary, 1991, p. A15). The next description of how vacant lots in Manhattan, New York City, were transformed into vibrant, important spaces in a community highlights the potential power of gardens for creating positive community change "Until the mid-80's, the four vacant lots on 11th Street between Avenues A and C were dumping grounds for old furniture, car parts, even bodies. Then, fed up with the unsightly mess, neighborhood residents began to spruce up the lots, getting rid of the refuse, planting flowers, vegetables and herbs and building makeshift shelters called casitas. The lots were turned into gardens, and the gardens into unofficial community centers where countless weddings, birthday celebrations and block parties were held. On hot and muggy summer evenings, Lowest East Side residents fled their cramped apartments to relax with friends in the casitas" (Lii, 1997, p. A17).

To the uninitiated, an urban garden is just that: a garden in an urban area (Lewis, 1996). However, the type of garden provides an important message about a community's goals and economic needs as Herdy (1997, p. 7) noted: "Some gardens are for looks, with ornate flowers splashing color in a sea of green. Others are for recreation—nothing fancy, just a few plants here and there to give a reason for digging the earth. But the 'Good Luck' garden, tucked away in a neighborhood known for high crime and apathy, is strictly for the hungry, and it's worked for free by people whose only agenda is a selfless one."

When the primary role of a garden is to beautify the community, as is the case of flower gardens, it does not mean that the plot of land is used strictly for this purpose (Bellisle, 1996; Carrier, 1997; Hamilton, 1996). Spencer's (1995, p. D6) description of a flower garden in Stockton, California, illustrates the multiple purposes such a garden can play: "[The flowers] surround and beautify the playground for children enrolled in the St. Mary's Interfaith Transitional Learning Center. They provide a floral vista to alleviate the wait for treatment at the Dental Center, and they brighten the prospects of those lined up for an evening meal. . . . As we all know, the beauty of a flower garden lifts the spirit of the viewer. How fitting that these gardens are available to those whose spirits are in such great need of lifting. Most St. Mary's clients have very little beauty in their lives; these flowers can add some color to the pervasive gray hues of their existence." This garden relies on donations of plants from local nurseries and the work of community volunteers. So what appears to be a singular purpose is much more ambitious.

A review of the literature on community gardens uncovered few scholarly publications. In one of the few scholarly books on the topic of urban gardens, Hynes (1995, p. x) highlighted their nature and importance: "At its core, the community garden movement in the late twentieth century is about rebuilding neighborhood community and restoring ecology to the inner city. Some gardens are linked to housing projects, others to local markets; still others employ people who are incarcerated or newly released from jail." Lewis (1996) identified a series of psychological, sociological, and physiological responses that people have to gardens and gardening and noted the importance of plants and gardens in people's lives.

Community gardens, like the other projects described in this book, fulfill multiple instrumental and expressive purposes for urban-based groups. They represent (1) efforts to personalize and beautify surroundings; (2) a mechanism for establishing control over an environment that, at times, may seem hostile and beyond control; (3) a means through which residents can come together in pursuit of a common goal; (4) a method for learning and teaching in a multicultural context; (5) a mechanism for obtaining donations and channeling volunteers; and (6) a symbol of hope and pride that is conveyed to the external and internal communities. Gardening, incidently, has been shown to raise property values (Swift, 1996).

Urban gardens can also play an instrumental role in helping communities deter crime (Bellisle, 1996; Carrier, 1997; Malakoff, 1995; Miller, 1995; Sprott, 1996). Open spaces in high-crime areas are often areas where individuals who are involved in criminal activities congregate. Consequently, turning these spaces into gardens represents a community effort to exercise control as Hill (1996, p. 1) explained: "The reason we purchased that lot was that there were a lot of drug dealers and prostitutes hanging out. It was county owned. We didn't have a lot of ways of monitoring it. . . . But if we purchased it, then only certain people could use it." Carrier (1997, p. B-05) made a similar observation: "Keeping her street safe was what Anna Baez hoped for her North Baker [Denver] community's new mini-garden planted by 100 volunteers. 'I feel more comfortable because of fruits and vegetables,' she said."

Elements of Gardening

Creating a community garden is a complex process involving important decision-making along a continuum that can best be conceptualized as consisting of seven steps (Minnesota Green, 1992): (1) deciding to create an urban garden, (2) acquiring the land, (3) recruiting volunteers, (4) establishing the organizational structure and responsibilities, (5) fund-raising, (6) planting (site considerations and preparation), and (7) caring for the garden.

Deciding to create an urban garden. There are generally at least four primary reasons for a community to decide to create a garden: (1) a local leader-stakeholder decides to convert a vacant plot of land for productive use (Berlin, 1997); (2) a local institution, such as a church, school, college, or nonprofit organization, makes a plot of land available to the community for gardening (Hinkle, 1997; Silvern, 1997); (3) a community wishes to generate food to donate to a local food pantry or soup kitchen (Herdy, 1997); or (4) funding is provided by external private or public sources, such as city-run community gardening programs (Breslau, 1995) or federal-state initiatives like Urban Resources Partnerships (Lyon, 1989; Monroe-Santos, 1998).

Acquiring the land. The process of obtaining land can prove to be a rewarding experience for a community. As Hair (1996, p. 16) pointed out, "Not that reclaiming vacant city land for gardens is easy. It takes hard work, constant care, and commitment. But organizers say that messages, taught through the garden's cycle of death and renewal, are lessons they want young people to learn from the senior gardeners. By taking responsibility, even in the face of threats or failures, they can claim a stake in the future of their neighborhoods."

There are numerous urban-based initiatives to encourage urban gardening (Bellisle, 1996; Herdy, 1997; Leary, 1991; Monroe-Santos, 1998; Raver, 1994; Silvern, 1994; Stocker, 1989). The most common involve a municipal government's issuance of permits for extended periods (five to twenty years) to community groups or establishment of a land trust (a nonprofit organization that owns the land on behalf of a community) through which a city government can transfer land (Bellisle, 1996; Hair, 1996; Hinkle, 1997; Miller, 1995; Minnesota Green, 1992; Negri, 1992). However, in an alarming number of instances, permits have not been reissued when they have expired, and city governments have sold vacant lots to generate tax revenues (Baker, 1997; Kinzer, 1994; Kirschbaum, 1998a; Lii, 1997; McKinley, 1997; Monroe-Santos, 1998; Raver, 1999; Stone 1998; Trust for Public Land, 1994). In one distressing case (New York City), more than three hundred community gardens were scheduled to be destroyed over the next several years (Baker, 1997).

Community gardens can, if they have sufficient space, also be conceptualized as small neighborhood parks. Small neighborhood parks, according to Arie-Donch (1990, p. 1), serve multiple community functions: They "help define a community's edges, create a sense of neighborhood identity, provide opportunities for neighbors to meet one another, offer recreational activities and provide visual rest areas that break up the relentless rhythm of residences and businesses."

Recruiting volunteers. Volunteers are a crucial ingredient in any community gardening effort. Although plots are gardened by volunteers, a wide range of expertise is needed that the volunteers may not have. Therefore, sometimes a community garden has to seek expertise outside the group, preferably for free. Expertise is easier to obtain once a community garden is thriving According to Minnesota Green (1992, p. 8), "Whenever possible, rely on experts who can assist your project as part of their job responsibilities. Once the community garden is underway, public relations becomes an important strategy for finding volunteers. Prospective volunteers and supporters will begin to find you once they know your group exists."

Establishing the organizational structure and responsibilities. Any project, enhancement oriented or otherwise, that actively seeks widespread community participation, must develop a mechanism for channeling participants on the basis of their skills, time constraints, interests, and other considerations. One mechanism that is often used in community gardening is a steering committee that is either appointed or elected (Glentzer, 1996).

This committee, as would be expected, fulfills a variety of important organizational functions. It (1) sets policy pertaining to all aspects of gardening, (2) holds special events to draw volunteers and increases the visibility of the garden as a means of acknowledging special friends and volunteers, and (3) develops and conducts fund-raising activities.

The composition of the steering committee must be carefully thought out and must include various types of individuals, not all of whom are gardeners or community residents. However, it is important to ensure that the committee is heavily weighted toward residents to ensure community ownership of the garden. Possible nongardening members can be representatives of the sponsoring agency (if applicable), community stakeholders (elected and nonelected leaders), representatives of supporting organizations, and persons with gardening expertise who do not work in the community garden (Minnesota Green, 1992).

Fund-raising. Raising money to purchase or lease land, planting equipment, seeds, and water and to hire a part-time coordinator takes on added significance in low-income communities. A steering committee is often entrusted with this responsibility. Although the generation of money is a primary goal of fund-raising, it is not the only one. Local hardware stores and nurseries can donate equipment, plants, and other supplies that are just as good as hard currency.

Fund-raising plays a variety of critical roles in addition to generating money. Community-centered activities, such as dances, picnics, and raffles, not only bring a community garden money, they serve excellent public relation functions and can arouse widespread interest in gardening, identify potential volunteers, and open up avenues for the donation of plots of land.

Planting (site considerations and preparation). There are a number of dimensions to planting that go beyond selection of the crops to be harvested. One of the most overlooked factors of community gardening is the condition of the soil. Soil is to a garden what paint is to a mural: It is not possible to have a healthy garden without proper soil. Gardeners must make sure that the soil is rich in organic matter and that it has the pH level that plants require (Guest, 1997).

Consequently, in cases where the soil is not adequate, which is usually the case in urban areas, a considerable amount of time and energy must be devoted to enriching it. Like murals, the foundation is critical if a garden is to thrive and fulfil a multitude of community-enhancement functions. As a result, site considerations and preparation, must be seriously considered before a community makes any other decisions.

Caring for the garden. In many ways, this phase is probably the most rewarding because of the opportunity to interact with other gardeners. The care of a garden usually entails simple tasks, such as watering and weeding, unless there is some form of infestation. Weeding is often mentioned as the most frequently defined task for a gardener. Weeds, incidently, are usually defined as anything you did not plant yourself (Guest, 1997)!

Other aspects of garden care must be attended to if a community garden is to thrive. Abandoned plots can create serious problems in community gardens. The advice provided by Minnesota Green (1992, p. 23) highlights the need for gardeners to develop clear procedures and consequences in the case of abandoned plots: "Schedule weekly weed checks. Violators are called and sent a postcard if not contacted. If the plot is not weeded within ten days, clean, roto-till and re-plant a cover crop. If the vegetables are already growing, then weed and maintain the garden and donate produce to the local food shelf. Those leaving on vacation and others who are unable to care for their gardens are expected to contact the coordinator and make arrangements with a fellow gardener to weed and water while away."

Summary

The role and importance of gardens in urban life has generally escaped the attention of practitioners and scholars. Urban gardens have tremendous potential for directly or indirectly reaching a wide sector of a community in an empowering and capacity-enhancement manner. Hinkle's (1997, p. 01N) observation sums up the importance of urban gardens for communities: "What Louisville [Kentucky] desperately needs is for one group to spearhead this effort [help solve the economic and social ills that neighborhoods face]. . . . Community gardens work because they build a sense of community and can even create a few jobs. . . . [S]uch projects cause property values to go up, lesson the cultural gap between urban dwellers and rural neighbors, provide participants with a sense of ownership and increased self-esteem, promote civic mindedness, and improve nutrition."

Those who are actively involved in gardening no doubt experience the greatest benefits; those who choose not to participate are also affected by the garden's presence. Urban gardening provides the social work profession with an approach that views gardens as nontraditional settings that are accessible geographically, psychologically, and culturally to residents. If conceptualized correctly, gardens can be empowering, nutritional, economical, and can build community.

Community Playgrounds

Description

Although community playgrounds primarily target the recreational needs of children, they also fulfill other functions that rarely get noticed in the everyday life of a community. The structures can play a central role in connecting residents with each other and provide an outlet for families to do some activity together that does not require the expenditure of funds. In essence, they have become an accepted part of life in the United States, in both small rural communities and urban areas (Erickson, 1994; Toufexis, 1996).

The professional literature, although limited in scope and quantity and, with some exceptions, generally dating from the late 1970s and early 1980s, provides a variety of perspectives on community-built playgrounds. Birkeland (1994) highlighted the importance of parents joining together to build playgrounds in the face of major obstacles placed by public officials, bureaucrats, and businesspeople. The author argues that the opposition to community-built playgrounds has its origins in a patriarchal-capitalistic culture that devalues women and children's needs, unstructured learning and play, and a shared sense of community.

Brower and Williamson (1974) concluded that playgrounds play significant roles in urban areas and that their significance increases as open space becomes scarcer and there are fewer opportunities for neighborhood children to interact, share, and learn from each other through play. They stressed the need for playgrounds to reflect the values and priorities of the communities in which they are situated. Hayward, Rothenberg, and Beasley (1974) emphasized the importance of open spaces in highly densely populated communities and noted playgrounds should provide recreational-interactional opportunities for all age groups and reflect the activities preferred by local residents.

Nicolaidou (1984) documented how the massive urbanization of cities has severely disrupted interactions between residents and reduced the free space available for groups to share activities. When playgrounds have been developed to occupy spaces that were traditionally child focused (roads, paths, and courtyards), there has been an impact on "free play." Strict and inflexible organization and poor maintenance of equipment make playgrounds less attractive for play. Finch's (1983) study of playgrounds in a working-class community in England found that these settings were more fully utilized, maintained, and integrated into the community when parents' groups played active roles in supervising play.

The movement toward community-built playgrounds is not new in American history. As Daley (1996, p. 33) noted, "The recent popularity of community playground construction is reminiscent of a similar movement in the early 1900s, when municipal reformers touted playgrounds and parks as a 'school for citizenship.' . . . The idea was that playgrounds would promote a spirit of neighborliness and cultivate civic virtue." McArthur (1975) also placed playgrounds within a historical context and focused on one city (Chicago) to illustrate key points. He noted that one of the major priorities that cities faced at the turn of the twentieth century was inadequate play areas for children. The collaboration of social workers, civic organizers, and local businesses was instrumental in creating an extensive network of playgrounds in Chicago and served as a model for other cities across the United States.

Cavallo (1981, p. 1), too, placed the movement to develop playgrounds within a historical context, specifically within the "child-saving" reform movement of 1880 to 1920. This movement targeted city children, especially those from working-class and ethnic backgrounds, as a means of buffering them from the social and economic hazards associated with city living at that time.

The popular media has recognized the importance of community-built playgrounds in the life of a community ("A Place for Kids," 1994; City Editor, 1997; Collins, 1996; Daley, 1996; Franquemont, 1995; Giasone, 1994; Langhenry, 1997; Linger, 1995; Salter, 1996). Newspaper articles have extolled the virtues of communities coming together to help children, highlighted the need for public-private partnerships, and stressed the importance of "community spirit" and how it can influence other dimensions of community life.

Community playgrounds are structures whose sole purpose is to meet the recreational needs of children of various ages and physical abilities. The nature of these playgrounds will vary according to the size of a lot, the design, and the equipment. However, a central purpose of community-built playgrounds is to involve as wide a sector of a community as possible in their design and building. Historically, playgrounds have rarely been designed and built by the community they are situated in. As a result, they have rarely, if ever, reflected the needs of the community or been maintained by the community because the parents and children who use them have never been asked for their input (Franquemont, 1995). Seeking input is just the first step in developing community ownership of a playground; the building of these play structures is influenced by the opinions and desires of those who will utilize them.

Barn raisings have had great appeal throughout this country's history (Kemmis, 1996). Simply described, a barn raising brings all members of a rural community, regardless of age, gender, and skills, together for a concentrated period (usually one or two days) to help a fellow neighbor who has suffered some tragedy, like a fire, to build a barn. It serves to help a neighbor in need, reaffirms a community's definition of itself, and ensures the members that they do, in fact, belong to a community that cares.

An urban equivalent of a barn raising is the community-initiated building of a playground. This activity, has unfortunately, generally gone unnoticed in the professional literature, although its significance to an urban community is equivalent to that of a barn raising to a rural community. Nevertheless, building an urban playground presents challenges unlike those of a barn raising. As Linger (1995, p. 2B) observed, "A public playground is a lot more difficult to build than a barn. There are myriad government regulations and always an intensive search for money, equipment and of course, volunteers."

Elements of Community-Built Playgrounds

The undertaking of a community-built playground, as was already noted, can be the result of a wide range of concerns or hopes. However, when a community builds a playground with minimal reliance on outside assistance, the cost can be 50 percent to 80 percent less than if it is commercially built

(Leathers & Associates, 1996; Wolkomir, 1985). These savings can put a playground within the reach of most communities in the United States.

When a community decides that it wants to develop a playground, there are essentially nine steps to bringing this goal to fruition: (1) the community's decision, (2) establishment of a committee or task force with elected leadership (to serve as a coordinating body), (3) selection of the site, (4) contracting and negotiating with appropriate parties (landowners, the builder, and contributors), (5) publicity, (6) obtaining volunteers and assigning roles, (7) the actual building of the playground, (8) the dedication, and (9) maintenance.

Community's decision. The decision by a community to build a playground may be prompted by various considerations or events. These considerations may include children getting seriously injured in the street while playing, the need to take ownership of vacant land that is used for drug selling, the quest for a project that will unify the community, and the availability of funds through governmental foundation grants. Another consideration may be that a playground represents a logical extension of other community projects, such as gardens, murals, or sculptures.

According to Frost and Klein (1979, p. 132), community-initiated playgrounds are built as a result of "an expression of the unique ideas and needs of the adults and children who build and play on it. The playground typically grows out of a desire to do something positive for children, an economic need, and unwillingness to leave something as important as providing a play space for children to the bureaucrats." However, regardless of the motivation, this initial step conveys a sense of organization and leadership that is present in a community.

Establishment of a committee. The decision to build a playground cannot be the sole responsibility of one individual but must rest squarely in the hands of the community (including children), regardless of whether an external source (such as a governmental agency or foundation) is eager to fund such a venture (Leathers & Associates, 1996). Generally, a committee is established that has representatives from all the key sectors of the community, including its children.

Since playgrounds specifically target children of various ages, it is recommended that this steering committee consist of anywhere from twelve to twenty-five members with representatives from the following areas: (1) schools, (2) youth-oriented nonprofit organizations for children under age twelve, (3) parents, (4) the general coordinator of the playground, and (5) other key stakeholders (Leathers & Associates, 1996). It is also recommended that at least half to three-quarters of the committee consist of parents with children under age twelve and that no segment of the community is larger than one-third of the committee (Leathers & Associates, 1996). It is essential to include children in the process (Cundy, 1998; Ham, 1998).

The involvement of children in the design of the playground is a natural extension of any community capacity-enhancement project (Iltus &

Hart, 1994). Children, after all, are capable of engaging in design work on the basis of their experiences—both positive and negative—with playgrounds. The creation of a playground without the requisite input from children can result in a playground in which children do not play. As Arie-Donch (1990, p. 3) noted: "Playgrounds are too often the result of compartmentalized thinking by adults. Because a space has been designated a play area does not mean children will necessarily play there. . . . The reality is that children will choose to play everywhere. One of my favorite pictures is of a large group of children playing in a junk pile while a new pristine playground lays abandoned next door."

The steering committee makes the appropriate decisions and appoints subcommittees to carry out assignments and recruit residents. The steering committee members must have responsibility for some aspect of the project; it is not usual to have the title of coordinator attached to their roles—coordinator of volunteers, of tools, of the design and special needs, purchases of materials, of food, of child care, and so on (Leathers & Associates, 1996).

The committee ensures that any decision that affects the project reflects the sentiments of the community. It also ensures the fair distribution of work and provides the community with an "official" body to engage in brokering, contracting, and the like.

Selection of the site. There is little question that the selection of an appropriate site for the playground is one of the earliest and most important decisions for a community to make. Numerous considerations are involved in choosing the site in addition to whether the land is available. Some of these considerations are physical access (a central area with access to transportation); high visibility from the street (to discourage vandalism); a flat area with good drainage; access to parking but not near a street, so children do not run out into traffic; and complementarity to the surrounding community (to encourage use) (Leathers & Associates, 1996).

Contracting and negotiating with appropriate parties. Building a playground often involves negotiations with numerous parties, public and private. However, three essential parties are invariably involved: the owner of the land, the builder, and major contributors. Although it is possible to negotiate with the owner of privately held land, it is probable that the land the playground will be built on will be owned by a public entity (Collins, 1996; Giasome, 1994; Salter, 1996).

The consequences of a city taking over gardens to be used for other purposes, most likely housing, can prove painful to a community. As Lii (1997, p. A17) reported: "Driven by the demand for affordable housing, the city (New York) recently gave a private developer . . . the go-ahead to clear the four gardens to make way for 98 condominiums. . . . Yesterday, as the police watched and about 20 gardeners and their supporters stood in the raw cold and chanted 'Shame on you' and 'Get out of our gardens!'

bulldozers scooped out desiccated vines and brittle shrubs." Thus, when negotiating with public entities, communities must be strategic in selecting appropriate sites and negotiating favorable terms to their agreements, including the length of the contract.

Publicity. There are two key aspects to publicity regarding playground construction: (1) the recruitment of volunteers for all phases of the project and (2) the announcement of the dedication of the playground. Publicity, however, must be conceptualized broadly and creatively. This, it should be noted, is an excellent opportunity for a community to make a "positive statement" to the external community.

Neighborhood schools need to be targeted—through announcements at general assemblies, notes sent home, school organizations, and teacher-administrator forums. Houses of worship, local recreational agencies, and community-based organizations should also be targeted, in addition to the usual print media and radio and television stations.

Obtaining volunteers and assigning roles. The actual building necessitates hundreds of participants, depending on the size and complexity of the playground. Volunteers are also needed for planning, publicity, and fundraising. Roles can vary according to abilities, interests, and amount of time that can be volunteered (Langhenry, 1997). There are roles for all age groups: staffing the tent to check the volunteers' credentials, providing child care, cooking and serving food, providing first aid, providing nails and equipment, and handling press releases and meeting with the press, to list but a few.

It is advisable to have a member of the steering committee designated the coordinator of volunteers (Leathers & Associates, 1996). This individual must have the necessary ability to recruit, screen, supervise, and validate the work of volunteers. In essence, volunteers are a tremendous resource, but they require attention, time, and effort if their services are to be meaningful to a community playground.

Building the playground. The planning for a playground may take anywhere from three months to a year, but the actual building may take several days, depending on the size of the playground and the number of volunteers who participate—thus, the analogy to a barn raising. The planning phase involves extensive research on safety procedures, accessibility for handicapped people, building standards, and so forth (Salter, 1996). Consequently, much work and time must be spent before the construction begins.

The building of the playground takes on an atmosphere that is difficult to describe. However, the actual event has been compared to festivities associated with a parade, circus, community block party, or celebration and the seriousness associated with a major building project that has drawn the attention of external authorities. In short, participants often describe the experience as "once in a lifetime," "unforgettable," "a happening," and "sensational." Frost and Klein (1979, p. 132) summed up the "feelings" associated with community-built playgrounds well: "The authors, who have been involved in over 100 creative, community-built playgrounds, never cease to wonder at the excitement generated before, during, and after construction. The excitement comes from a sense of pride in doing something assertive to improve the quality of life. It comes from a feeling of déjà vu: of reliving pleasant childhood memories or of fulfilling unrealized childhood dreams. It comes from the joy of children as they explore the newly constructed equipment."

The process of building a playground allows an entire family to participate together alongside other families, friends, and strangers. This experience unifies families, neighborhoods, and newly made friends in common pursuit of community-centered dreams. There are precious few activities in this society that allow an entire family to undertake an activity together that welcomes participation from all regardless of age, abilities, and backgrounds.

Dedication. The dedication represents both the end and the beginning—the end because it is the culmination of a lengthy and arduous process, and the beginning because it represents a new dimension to a community with tremendous potential for other, future activities. Thus, a dedication ceremony gives the entire community an opportunity to come together and celebrate an accomplishment. It is rare for a dedication not to attract representatives of the media, public officials, and other stakeholders.

The dedication also serves to validate the community to the city. This validation is particularly important in communities that have less-than-"stellar" reputations. Thus, an event, such as a dedication of a "community built" playground, sends a message to the external community that there is a concern for children, there are residents who have capabilities, and there is a sense of community spirit that is often not identified by the local press.

Maintenance. Although the actual building of a playground gets the greatest amount of publicity and volunteers, maintenance must never be overlooked. There is no denying that the building phase generates the greatest degree of excitement and participation. However, the maintenance phase is no less important, even if it is not glamorous. The greater the use a playground gets, the greater the need for a maintenance program that is systematic and actively addresses potential problems with the the equipment.

A community must decide who will service the playground and when it is to be serviced. These decisions may entail the establishment of a committee whose sole responsibility is to ensure that the maintenance is kept up. Frost and Klein (1979, p. 168) made the following suggestions based on their experiences with community-built playgrounds: "Children's ideas should be actively solicited concerning playground improvements. A committee of parents and teachers with rotating membership should perform periodic preventive maintenance and make modifications."

Summary

Community-built playgrounds have a far greater significance than just as places where children play. They reflect a community's desire to claim their own space and control the activities within this area. Thus, the presence of such playgrounds can serve as excellent indicators of a community's capacity to rally for a common good. One participant (quoted in Salter, 1996, p. D1) summed up the experience in building a playground as follows: "I think it's because it was just so personal for us building it. . . . It was like summer camp, when you have this real intense experience that you never forget. Kids can't destroy it, because they helped build it."

The building of playgrounds, as conceived of in this book, is an urban version of an old-fashioned barn raising, with all the attributes of such an activity. Playgrounds can be complex to build and maintain and reflect a high level of community commitment and capacity. As Frost and Klein (1979, p. 168) stated: "The creation of a community-built playground is a bold act requiring a great deal of time and hard work. However, the end results are well worth the effort."

Social work practitioners can help initiate the development of playgrounds as vehicles for community development, increasing intergenerational exchange, and converting vacant land from criminal to recreational (and community-controlled) activities. Playgrounds, when developed with minimal or no assistance of professionals, can also serve as indicators of a community's strengths in asset assessments (Delgado, 1996b). One playground builder (quoted in Franquemont, 1995, p. 9) summarized the importance of these structures as follows: "Our goal is [to] help build effective, powerful communities through the construction of meaningful and useful monuments to the collective spirit."

Sculptures

Description

Urban sculptures, like their murals, represent a community's effort to express to the internal and external world a message; this message, in the form of an artistic representation, conveys both social and political ideas. However, with rare exceptions, community-built sculptures rarely stand alone in a community space. They are often a part of another project like a playground or garden and enhance an environment and hence are generally overlooked by the media and other parties if they are well integrated into these spaces. For example, because children may play on a sculpture that was created to be a part of a playground, they and adults may not think of it as a decorative object because it is so functional.

The creation of sculptures, like murals and gardens, does not require special equipment if the materials used (such as concrete, wood, and earthworks) are readily available in the community or easily accessible. Materials that are not easily accessible increase the difficulty for the community, particularly if building the sculpture requires specialized equipment. Unlike murals, sculptures can be durable and less likely to be damaged as a result of weather. When wood is the material used, specialized treatment can enhance the life of the sculpture and reduce the need for elaborate maintenance procedures.

Sculptures are a form of artistic expression that can be traced back to the beginning of recorded history and can be found in virtually all cultures of the world. Traditionally, sculptures in the United States have been located in museums, office complexes, or the homes of wealthy individuals who have purchased or commissioned them. Consequently, they are not usually found in communities, especially low-income communities. Therefore, it is not surprising that a search of the literature did not uncover many scholarly or popular publications on community-built sculptures, unlike the other projects addressed in this book.

That sculptures have not received their due attention from the scholarly or popular media may be the result of an interplay of several factors: (1) there is a paucity of community-inspired and initiated sculptures; (2) there have been minimal efforts to publicize sculptures that are present in communities; (3) well-conceptualized sculptures blend into the landscape of a community and escape notice by residents and outsiders; (4) sculptures have been viewed primarily as an art form that is best appreciated in museums, not in communities; and (5) sculptures do not lend themselves to the same level of community participation as do murals, playgrounds, or gardens. Sculptures can be in different shapes, sizes, styles, and materials; they may stand alone or be a part of an existing structure, such as a wall (Vogel, 1997). Like murals, sculptures can also be controversial and generate discussion (Kimmelman, 1993).

Sculptures often fulfill a variety of goals for a community that initiates and sanctions them. These goals are to be (1) decorative—a means, like murals and gardens, of beautifying an area in desperate need of beautification; (2) functional—to play an important role in the community, for example, a sculpture that is an integral part of a strategically placed bench that encourages residents to sit and talk; and (3) symbolic—a vehicle for conveying a community's past, present, or future.

The following example of a sculpture in New York City highlights the multiple roles of sculptures in a community: "The bronze statue of Confucius has dominated the landscape in Manhattan's Chinatown since 1984. . . . Yesterday, Confucius got some company: a statue of a Qing Dynasty official from Fujian Province, whose role in 19th century history . . . helped ignite the Opium War by banning the drug, to the chagrin of British officials. Those who brought the Lin statue to Chatham Square say they did so to deliver a strong anti-drug message. But the statue carries a strong political message as well: it underscores the ascending power in Chinatown of immigrants from mainland China, particularly the Fujianese" (Chen, 1997, p. A32).

The concept of sculptures as "community markers," which convey the ethnic or racial composition of a community to the outside world, is not new in urban areas of the country (Mays, 1997). However, such community markers are not without controversy. As Mays (1997, p. C5) commented: "And why must we have . . . huge monuments . . . spelling out, in writhing dragons and other mythological creatures, the Chinese ideogram for 'gateways?' It's a community marker that falsifies Spadina, by suggesting that the neighborhood has always been Toronto's Chinatown. In fact, waves of immigrants have come and gone through the crowded lanes off Spadina over the last century—Jews, Portuguese and Italians. Chen's piece seems to specify the intersection . . . as a kind of Oriental theme park forever—when, historically, no part of downtown Toronto has been more ethnically mercurial."

Elements of Sculptures

A community-initiated sculpture generally involves eight stages: (1) the community's decision to commission a sculpture, (2) selection of the site for the sculpture, (3) selection of the artist, (4) a design contest, (5) fund-raising, (6) the actual sculpturing phase, (7) dedication of the sculpture, and (8) maintenance.

Community's decision to commission a sculpture. In a similar fashion to the other projects addressed in this book, the community engages in a process that ultimately results in a decision to commission a sculpture (Glentzer, 1996). The process may be facilitated by an outside source that is willing to provide funds to cover the costs of the project.

This decision will be greatly influenced by the goals the community wants the sculpture to achieve. As was already noted, the sculpture may be decorative or functional or meant to convey an important message about an event in the community or the hopes the community wishes to articulate for the outside world. Sculptures, depending upon their size and purpose, can easily be added to gardens, playgrounds, and murals, which can serve as backdrops to sculptures that encourage residents to come together.

Selection of the site for the sculpture. The choice of a site for a sculpture is just as important as the commissioning of the sculpture. A similar set of circumstances to those of murals emerges in the decision about where to locate the sculpture. The size and purpose of the sculpture play an important role in the decision. A community may wish to create a large sculpture (Chen, 1997) to attract attention from within and without the community, but the greater the size of the sculpture, the greater the amount of work and the greater the restrictions on where it can be located.

A large sculpture will be located in a prominent section of the community, preferably where there is constant foot and automotive traffic. Needless to say, such a project must enjoy wide sanction in the community, including its stakeholders. The example of the Lin statue in New York's Chinatown brings this important point to life: "Lin faces northeast and East Broadway, which some people call 'Fuzhou Street' because of the prevalence of Fujianese. His back is to One Police Plaza and the Manhattan Detention Complex (Chen, 1997, p. A32).

A sculpture that is small can be well integrated into a garden or playground. As a result, it does not need to have the approval of an entire community, since its impact is much more at the neighborhood level and it is meant to reflect the priorities of a much smaller group of individuals.

Selection of the artist. The choice of the artist may be relatively easy when the sculptor lives in the community and is well respected. However, when the artist is not from the community, a process involving residents must be developed to solicit their input in the selection process. It is important for the selection committee to develop clear guidelines for judging the merits of the artists to avoid any hard feelings should there be differences of opinion.

Some of the criteria may be the artist's (1) knowledge of the community or willingness to learn, (2) philosophical stance on community participation, (3) experience with similar types of projects, (4) fee, (5) availability during a specified period, and (6) ability and willingness to use materials that are readily accessible to the community. Clearly, the artist must be able to represent the wishes of the community regarding the nature of the sculpture and the degree of community involvement in all phases of construction.

Design contest. The design of a community sculpture can be an excellent method for raising communitywide issues and concerns and involving the residents. Maximum involvement of a community in the process of sculpturing is possible when a content is used to solicit designs. A contest also generates publicity and increases the likelihood of community ownership.

A design contest, as was noted for playgrounds, can generate a great deal of interest and result in a design that reflects the community's values, interests, and priorities. The contest can target the primary audience the sculpture is trying to reach. For example, a sculpture that is to be located in a playground and is intended to reach children would benefit from a contest in which children participate. A sculpture targeting elders, in turn, can easily result in a contest stressing elder-designed sculptures.

Fund-raising. The cost of a community-built sculpture can range from several hundred to thousand dollars, depending on the design, size, materials used, and cost of hiring an artist-project coordinator. The costs may be even higher if the artist pays residents to help construct the sculpture.

However, community-built sculptures are financially within the reach of most communities, particularly if the materials are donated by local businesses and volunteers are used extensively throughout the process. It may be possible to involve local schools in a community-built sculpture project, with the activity serving an educational goal and reinforcing classroom material. Similar approaches can be developed with other settings, such as senior citizens' residences.

Actual sculpturing phase. The process of sculpturing can easily involve numerous volunteers from the community. Participation is further facilitated when materials, such as concrete, wood, and earthworks are used that can be worked without elaborate preparation and equipment. The typical process of building consists of at least five phases: (1) planning, (2) obtaining materials, (3) preparing the site, (4) building the sculpture, and (5) applying of a protective substance (if necessary).

The actual building phase may last anywhere from one to several days or weeks, depending on the time required for the previous phases. Complex projects necessitate extensive planning, preparation, coordination of volunteers, and the like. In those instances, community-built sculptures resemble the effort involved in developing large community murals, gardens, and playgrounds.

Dedication of the sculpture. The goals and processes related to the dedication of a sculpture are the same as for the dedication of a mural, garden, and playground. The dedication ceremony will reflect the goals for the sculpture and thus target the primary constituencies.

When a sculpture is part of a broader project, such as a community garden, it may be possible to have two dedication ceremonies so the dedication of the sculpture is not lost in the fanfare over the dedication of the larger project. Unfortunately, when a sculpture is part of a broader project, it tends to be overlooked in the excitement and its potential contribution is minimized.

Maintenance. Community-built sculptures are never maintenance free and are subject to vandalism. Much of the nature of maintenance is determined by the amount of traffic the sculpture receives and the materials used in building it. Nevertheless, it is important to note that there is no such thing as a maintenance-free sculpture.

Playground-based sculptures invariably are made of wood that can be easily treated to minimize the impact of the elements. However, the wear and tear associated with children climbing on a sculpture may require considerable work, particularly to avoid accidents and injuries related to splinters and the like. As a result, communities must think of what will happen to the sculpture after it has been dedicated and plan accordingly.

Summary

The role of sculptures in galvanizing a community to work together is just as strong as the role of murals, gardens, and playgrounds, although sculptures generally do not get as much publicity as do the other projects. Sculptures can be small or large and require little or a great deal of labor; if they are labor intensive, they will involve a wide sector of a community.

Sculptures lend themselves well to being integrated into other community capacity-enhancement projects, such as gardens, playgrounds, and murals. This flexibility enhances their attractiveness to a community and brings a different perspective. Nevertheless, sculptures have a potential contribution to make to community capacity enhancement, but in a more specific and directed manner. The conventional way of looking at sculptures—historical pieces made of marble or bronze located in museums, may have biased many against basing this form of artistic expression in the community. However, the same principles involved in creating murals, gardens, and playgrounds are also applicable to community-built sculptures.

Conclusion

It is amazing how a shift in paradigms, in this case from a deficit to an asset perspective, changes how practitioners view community murals, gardens, playgrounds, and sculptures. These outlets for artistic, recreational, and creative energies once seemed only interesting or prosaic to the average outsider to a community. The new set of lenses provides a "picture" of a community that has talents, political will, and hopes for the future.

Like any other form of building, much time, thought, and effort must be expended in planning and organizing before a project comes to fruition. This aspect of the experience is often overlooked by the public and the media. However, it represents the foundation of any community capacity-enhancement project. The process of undertaking a capacity-enhancement project is even more important than the outcome, although the outcome should never be minimized for any community.

The projects described in this chapter fulfill a multitude of important roles in urban-based undervalued communities and can serve as stepping-stones to more ambitious change-related projects. None of these projects is mutually exclusive with the others or with any other form of capacity-enhancement activity. Nevertheless, the amount of time, energy, and level of community participation limits the number of projects any community can successfully carry out.

Social work practitioners can view these projects as important indicators of community assets or as vehicles for creating community solidarity and addressing key community needs. The author has provided detailed information on the nuts and bolts of community-enhancement projects not to overwhelm readers or make them expert builders, but to inform them of the complexities involved with these projects, and the level of commitment needed by all parties before such projects are undertaken.

7

Analysis of Common and Unique Development Tasks

The primary goal of this chapter is to present an analysis of what makes an urban setting attractive for macro social work practice using an assets paradigm. The chapter is divided into two sections. The first section analyzes what makes murals (Delgado & Barton, 1998), gardens, community-built playgrounds, and sculptures important to urban communities and identifies the common developmental aspects of these community capacity-enhancement projects.

The second section addresses the unique developmental tasks associated with each of the four community capacity-enhancement projects and highlights their key conceptual and practice differences, and discusses what makes them important to the community, any aspects that are culture specific to a group, and the implications for social work education and practice.

Common Developmental Tasks

The social needs and problems of urban communities cannot be identified and addressed in isolation, as if they there was no relationship between the various needs and problems (Weisbrod & Worthy, 1997). Murals, gardens, playgrounds, and sculptures must also be linked and coordinated, when possible. These four projects overlap and have common core elements, yet each individual project has unique qualities and thus implications for practice. This analysis identifies the critical elements common to all these types of projects and identifies the aspects that are unique to each. In addition, it discusses applicable practice principles and uses these principles to develop a macro-practice model.

Common Core Features

On the surface, murals, gardens, playgrounds, and sculptures appear to have little in common other than that they can be found in urban communities and take up space. Each of these community capacity-enhancement projects ostensibly has different goals: murals, to convert unsightly walls into colorful ones; gardens, to generate food; playgrounds, to provide recreational areas; and sculptures, to decorate spaces. A community's use of frameworks also differs according to the type of project, although the frameworks may share some common phases.

It may seem strange, for example, to think of the arts and social services as being more than an idealistic partnership. As Glentzer (1996, p. 64) noted: "It all works together . . . to address the issues that are foremost in this community [Houston, Texas]. . . . One of the things we forget is the real essence of art: It has the power to transform. . . . If you take that creative impulse . . . and apply it with the same aesthetic sensitivities toward neighborhood problems, the same kind of transformations can take place." In fact, it is not unusual for cities to foster the arts as a means of rebuilding downtown sections (Weber, 1997). Murals and sculptures can play important social roles within communities by making residents think and act in communal, responsive ways.

Upon closer examination, these types of projects share a great deal in common and complement each other. All these projects can serve as excellent alternatives to issue-based organizing, act as mechanisms to enhance community capacities, and control open spaces, as well as beautify urban communities. They can reflect cultural practices of everyday life in a community (Ybarra-Fausto, 1990). At least the following twelve dimensions unite them.

1. They involve physical space in the community.Although the amount of space required for each project can differ dramatically, with murals requiring the least amount of space (building walls) and playgrounds requiring the most, all four projects are dependent on open physical space. The location of these projects in the community dictates the amount of space that is needed.

Inattention to the importance of open spaces in a community often results in the use of these spaces by individuals who do not share the values and goals of the community. As a result, these open spaces can be a source of disruption for a community. "The disorder of a junk lot or graffiti-splashed park can contribute to a sense of permissiveness that fosters criminal behavior. The theory explains, in part, why cutbacks in park maintenance [open spaces] have contributed to making parks unsafe and why community efforts to clean public spaces have so successfully reduced crime. . . . The key is to bring the community into the decision-making process about where gardens, playgrounds, and recreational facilities should be located and how they are managed. Too often, parks and recreational programs have been developed without community input" (Trust for Public Land, 1994, pp. 18–19).

The physical condition of a community sends a message to both the outside world, as well as the community. As Lewis (1996, p. 54) stated: "The physical condition of a community, its buildings, streets, and vacant spaces, makes an enormous difference in the way members of that community feel about themselves. What we see often tells us what we are. . . . The physical condition of a community, therefore, plays a double role. For the community, it is a measure of itself; for outsiders, it creates an impression of community quality and character."

2. They require active participation and sanctioning by the community: For murals, gardens, playgrounds, and sculptures to have the impact on a community they are capable of achieving, they must be sanctioned by the community and actively seek the residents' participation (Bush-Brown, 1969; Glentzer, 1996; Sommer, 1994). Murals or sculptures, for example, that are commissioned by the city government do not have the same impact as do those that actively and systematically provide communities with a voice and decision-making responsibilities about the location and significance of the projects as Doss (1995, pp. 52–53) explained: "Many government-sponsored artworks can be described as localized extensions of the elite culture dominating modern museums, especially because the experts who initiate public art often look to museum collections for evidence of cultural authority. However, the contemporary art museum tends to focus on blue-chip artists of established 'professional excellence' rather than local artists who might collaborate with their communities (or outsiders who might do the same)."

In the field of playground development, active participation by children and their parents is called the "participatory design process." According to Eriksen (1985, p. 39), there is a difference between giving a community a voice and having the community design a playground: "Many participatory design plans have been used around the country in recent years to give community members a voice in how their community is to be built, but people designing places is a truly different model. It carries the people involved through the entire planning and design process, from gaining awareness of the built environment to analyzing needs to developing the architectural or landscaping program and designs."

Community gardens can thrive only when the community is actively involved in all facets of their development (Lewis, 1996). Hynes (1995, p. 6) made this point clear in describing the gardens of Harlem in New York City: "The Greening of Harlem rises from and thrives on neighborhood involvement. The seventeen grassroots gardens—designed, built, and tended by neighborhood people and community institutions . . . are a small but potent symbol of local love and labor. This community reclamation of abandoned lots, parks, and playgrounds; the modest reversal of neighborhood disintegration; and pride in the greening of Harlem, is largely based on begging, borrowing, and bartering."

The greater and more widespread the participation, the greater the influence. It should not be lost on practitioners that these projects are much more labor intensive, costly, and time demanding than nonparticipatory projects. However, if the primary goal is to involve and enhance community capacities, then the process of developing the project is equally, if not more important, than the actual project. Finally, all these projects lend themselves to incorporating intergenerational activities as a means of breaking down stereotypes related to age, race, ethnicity, and class (Henkin, Santiago, Sonkowsky, & Tunick, 1997).

3. There is an inherent flexibility about the amount of space and funds that are needed. Although each project requires space in a community, there is sufficient flexibility that each project can be developed within the constraints of available space and funds. The flexibility inherent in the community capacity-enhancement projects addressed in this book increases their attractiveness for community intervention. For example, it is not unusual to find a small garden consisting of several square feet, a mural painted on a small wall, or a sculpture in an entrance to a building.

There is little question that the significance of the project must be placed within the context of its feasibility. In Oakland, California, for example, a community could not develop a garden because of the lack of available space in the neighborhood; the only large lot could not be used because the owner refused to allow access. Then the owners of a medium-sized vacant lot made it available to the community. They were gracious enough to allow the community residents to plant a garden and essentially turned over their privately held parcel to the community (Berlin, 1997). Thus, in planning a garden, mural, playground, or sculpture, the community needs to take into account local circumstances, one of which is the availability of space.

4. Projects can be developed in three out of the four seasons (except winter). Other than mural painting, which is usually undertaken during the summer months, the projects addressed in this book can be developed nine months of the year, depending on the section of the country in which the communities are located. It is possible, depending upon the type of garden, to plant and harvest during spring, summer, and fall. Although the construction of playgrounds is best undertaken during the spring and fall when children are in school, it is possible to build them in the summer. Sculptures can be constructed year-round indoors; it is preferable not to prepare the site and hold the dedication during the winter.

This does not mean that a community does nothing related to enhancement projects during the winter. A well-planned capacity-enhancement project requires planning, recruiting volunteers, obtaining donations, and other tasks that can be accomplished during the winter months. In addition to providing a respite for the participants, which should never be underestimated, this period allows the community residents sufficient time to reflect, plan, and validate their experiences.

It is difficult for a community to undertake a capacity-enhancement project and simultaneously plan other projects; usually, that practice is an invitation for both the current and future project to fail. The availability of a "down period" can be reframed into a period during which important work can be accomplished in doors and hence is not subject to the vicissitudes of weather.

5. Learning is integral to all the projects. Community capacity-enhancement projects must actively seek to identify, enhance, and utilize indigenous talents and resources. The learning and teaching aspects of interventions are often overlooked or lost in the quest to achieve results, such as the reduction of some risky behavior. However, educational dimensions must be systematically built into any form of intervention for the entire community to benefit (Bicho, 1997; Ham, 1998). The artist or builder can be viewed as a visual educator (Ybarra-Fausto, 1990).

This goal, however, necessitates the development of certain skills that can be categorized as research, teaching, and communication. When purposefully addressed, learning is made relevant for the student and the community. Schools are excellent sites for using murals, gardens, playgrounds, and sculptures.

Gardening, for example, has slowly found its way into schools and become an integral part of the curriculum in some. According to Cook 1997, p. 9, "The whole inspiration is to create food and ecological security by setting up schools as centers for that kind of learning. . . . [O]ur vision has to do with changing consciousness and awareness. . . . [I]f we can make change at the school level (especially in primary public schools), we can affect larger changes in the community, the state and the country." Educational goals must play an integral part in any community capacity-enhancement project and, when possible, involve residents in carrying out teaching activities (Cundy, 1998).

6. Diversity of roles allows for the participation of individuals with various abilities and commitments. Success in the creation of murals, gardens, playgrounds, and sculptures is possible only when the participants are encouraged to assume responsibilities that are closely matched with their abilities and interests. Community capacity-enhancement projects must have a wide range of roles to facilitate this matching process. Thus, proj-

ect coordinators and committees need to develop assessment mechanisms to ensure that matching does transpire, to encourage maximum participation and contributions.

Community gardening, for example, consists of multiple stages, some of which entail labor-intensive efforts while others do not. Elders, for example, can provide advice, maintain the garden, and harvest crops; those who are physically capable can help clean up lots and do soil preparation and planting; others may be able to provide consultation. In essence, there is sufficient flexibility in roles to allow everyone to feel a part of the experience (Negri, 1992).

Although murals can be physically demanding, elders can contribute by providing information about cultural symbols or posing for the artists. Playgrounds and sculptures, too, require the undertaking of multiple tasks that allow for the maximum participation of residents, regardless of their time commitments, abilities, and interests. Consequently, these projects must enhance the contributions of all the community's members.

7. Each project necessitates implementation considerations: Flexibility in planning and implementing a community-based project is essential: To plan is human; to implement is divine. Namely, a capacity-enhancement project must never be conceptualized as an all-or-nothing endeavor. Thus, goals and local circumstances, including timing, require social workers to select and adapt each project. For example, the four enhancement projects addressed in this book can appeal to a cross-section of community groups, regardless of gender, age, ethnic-racial backgrounds, and source of income (Hurt, 1998).

Each project, however, has the potential to be specifically targeted to certain age groups. Murals lend themselves to involving youths; gardens, to elders; playgrounds, to children of all ages; and sculptures to all age groups. Thus, the age group being targeted must be determined by the goals of the community and local circumstances, such as a high concentration of an age group in the community. The ability to tailor the project to local circumstances increases the likelihood that the community will be involved and thus that a maximum degree of success and benefits will be achieved.

8. Projects lend themselves to sponsorship. The appeal of community capacity-enhancement projects is the opportunity they provide for communities to establish partnerships with a wide range of organizations, public and private. These partnerships, which, it is hoped, are multi-sponsorship in nature, will not only help with the existing project but could also be used in future projects.

Community capacity-enhancement projects can bring together organizations businesses, houses of worship, and non-human service-oriented organizations, that would not normally have a chance to work with each other. These forms of partnerships, however, may be subject to conflicts because of possible biases among the parties. Nevertheless, if they are properly planned, they have a tremendous potential for benefiting the community. Collaboration, as a result, significantly expands the possibilities for undertaking community capacity-enhancement projects.

9. Projects serve decorative as well as other important community functions. Community capacity-enhancement projects fulfill a multitude of important goals for a community. They not only brighten a community and turn areas that can be considered eyesores into productive or decorative areas, but help a community take stock of its assets. The physical changes that result from these projects must never be minimized because of the psychological implications for residents and the outside world. In discussing the role of projects focused on urban youths, Breitbart (1998, p. 324) stressed how capacity enhancement can result in products and physical changes in a community's environment: "The actual physical products of these young people's efforts—the greenhouses, community gardens, murals, designs and banners—were envisioned or placed in public spaces that had meaning for youth. Ideas were put out for others in the neighborhood and beyond to draw strength from. As such, they provide a stark contrast between what is currently in place and what could be there instead."

The attractiveness of community capacity-enhancement projects rests in their ability to change an environment physically, as well as achieve important social and political goals. The change in environment will often offer the community an opportunity to provide a "cultural signature" through the creation of an artifact. Like any artifact, community capacity-enhancement artifacts can be understood and admired only if they are viewed from multiple perspectives.

10. Projects serve an important role as indicators of a community's assets and problems. Murals, gardens, playgrounds, and sculptures can be effectively used to assess the degree of hope and involvement in a community. The significant presence of these projects can be a strong indicator of a community's assets. Urban communities, particularly those that have historically welcomed low-income groups of various ethnic and racial backgrounds, have generally been viewed from a deficit perspective—namely, how much graffiti, abandoned cars, vacant lots (with broken glass, discarded trash, and discarded tires) and buildings, can be found in the neighborhoods. However, an assets perspective focuses on how many murals (nature of their narrative), gardens, playgrounds, and sculptures can be found in the community.

It can be argued that in communities where graffiti (Cooper & Sciorra, 1994; Walsh, 1996), a popular art form also known as tagging, is commonplace, lots left vacant for extended periods without construction and broken windows left unrepaired may represent signals to the community that it has been targeted for "disinvestment" by external sources. As Miller (1995, p. C8) stated: "An empty lot breeds problems. . . . People dump bodies, cars, tires, mattresses, old refrigerators and rat-attracting trash. Drug dealers often see them as 'turf' and drug users sometimes claim them as shooting galleries." In addition, empty lots may also be indicators of the extent to which the community residents have internalized feelings of hopelessness and are not organized to fight external and internal forces. In essence, acts of vandalism and disrepair can test the determination of a community to make progress.

Nevertheless, the presence of a mural or sculpture, for example, does not necessarily translate into a community asset or an indicator of capacity. "Many government-sponsored public artworks can be described as localized extensions of the elite culture dominating modern museums, especially because the experts who initiate public art often look to museum collections for evidence of cultural authority. However, the contemporary art museum tends to focus on blue-chip artists of established 'professional excellence' rather than local artists who might collaborate with their communities (or outsiders who might do the same)" (Doss, 1995, pp. 52–53).

Murals, gardens, playgrounds, and sculptures can serve as indicators for determining the state of a community from an assets perspective (Delgado, 1995; McKnight & Kretzmann, 1990). The mapping of a community's assets allows for the systematic identification and location of indigenous resources that can be tapped for other endeavors. Residents who are responsible for developing and maintaining murals, for example, have the potential to take this leadership role into other arenas within the immediate or broader community. They can be enlisted to serve on agency boards, advisory committees, and task forces or even hired to work in social service organizations.

11. Projects lend themselves to political activism and the celebration of accomplishments. All the projects addressed in this book can be used to mobilize communities to bring about social change. One community gardener summed up this point as follows: "Greenling [turning the term redlining into a positive] . . . also brings together groups that might have passed in the night: political activists and gardeners. 'There are people who have political savvy, but don't see gardening as a valuable forum for social change. . . . Then there are gardeners who don't really see a need for political activism until their garden is threatened'" (Malakoff, 1995, p. 9).

Dedication ceremonies are opportune times for community residents to celebrate their accomplishments. As Arie-Donch (1991, p. 346) noted: "Dedication day served many important functions. It provided deadlines for the community to rally around (a positive crisis) and offered an opportunity to acknowledge the community's accomplishment and the individuals who made it possible. With the ceremony, a rite of passage takes place whereby everyone in the community takes ownership in the project. Through this celebration, the continuity of the project remains unbroken when the project directors leave."

12. Community capacity-enhancement projects have therapeutic value. These projects make excellent conjunctive therapeutic activities for residents in need of physical and psychological help. The professional literature has highlighted a number of highly successful programs that used horticulture as a therapeutic tool with elders (Beckwith & Gilster, 1997; Hazen, 1997; Kaplan, 1973; McGuire, 1997; Sarno & Chambers, 1997; Simon & Haller, 1997; Smith & McCallion, 1997; Stein, 1997; Stoneham & Jones, 1997; Wells, 1997). Mural painting, too, has been used as a form of art therapy for residents who have experienced severe emotional problems (Shapiro, 1997).

Thus, projects, such as murals, gardening, playgrounds, and sculptures, can use the concept of community capacity enhancement in a therapeutic manner. In these cases, the community benefits from the participation of individuals in therapy because the projects are still community based and sanctioned.

Organizing does not have to be based on issues. According to Malakoff (1995, p. 9), "'the simply human neighborly process of community gardening is ultimately a political activity. . . . [Greenling could provide communities with] greater understanding and success than some other more costly, more displacing, more abrasive forms of community political action.'"

Specific Developmental Tasks

Although these projects have common elements, there are differences that are specific to each. These differences must be taken into account in determining which project will be the focus of macro practice. Locally determined circumstances dictate how and whether these types of projects are feasible and recommended, combined or phased in, as part of an initiative.

Murals

Diego Rivera, one of the most famous muralists on this continent, summed up the importance of murals for communities: "[M]ural painting must help [a person's] struggle to become a human being, and for the purpose it must live wherever it can; no place is bad for it, so long as it is there permitted to fulfill its primary functions of nutrition and enlightenment" (Rivera & Wolfe, 1934, p. 13).

Vergara (1995, p. 2) touched on the importance of murals in communicating with both the internal and external world: "Ghettos are pervaded by abandonment and ruin; they openly display crude defenses and abound in institutions and facilities that are rejected by 'normal' neighborhoods. In these communities the walls have become surfaces on which to vent anger, to display models of worthy emulation, to represent African American and Latino culture, and to remember the dead." In short, murals are much more than artistic expressions when viewed within the context in which they are created. Context serves to inform the audience of key themes, areas of tensions, and concerns of the community. Murals must be studied as a sociopolitical phenomenon, not just an artistic work. This analysis provides a perspective on a community that is all too often overlooked by the external community. In essence, no two murals are ever alike; the stories shared through the pictures represent an important message that must be integrated into any community asset or needs assessment.

Project-specific aspects. A method for raising consciousness. There are few descriptions in the literature that capture both the essence and importance of murals in urban-based communities as well as the following: "San Francisco has more murals per person than any other city in the country, maybe even the world. In the sunny Mission district, the city's oldest neighborhood, large mythic images rise up from the concrete surroundings, on buildings, walls, and storefronts. The mission . . . became, in the 1960s and 1970s, a hub of the political and cultural Chicano movement. Part of that movement was the telling of a survival history demanding to be told, in intensely visual, and highly visible, murals covering the walls of the neighborhood" (Lawrinsky, 1997, p. 20).

These murals were not restricted to any particular types of walls or places, but could be found throughout the community, big and small in size, addressing various issues of ethnic pride, cultural history, and social justice themes. "Over the entrance of an elementary school, Cesar Chavez, leader and farmworker in a plaid shirt, stands more than two stories tall, welcoming in the children. On the front of a bookstore, farmworkers of every ethnicity participate in a perpetual and bountiful harvest. At a taqueria, a crop duster spews pesticide onto a field of lechugueras, or women lettuce pickers, including one who is pregnant with new life. . . . On the rectory of St. Peter's Church, angry faces of the oppressed look out onto the street, but the corn goddess rises, and a brown Aztec fist radiates strength in the blue sky above. These concrete canvasses tell the story of life, liberty, and the pursuit of happiness. They tell the story of people, of workers, of the struggle for freedom and justice. And they tell this story in big pictures where everyone can see it" (Lawrinsky, 1997, p. 20). None of the other community capacity-enhancement projects described in this book can approach murals as a medium for telling stories.

Degree of upkeep as an indicator of a mural's importance. By the nature of their location, murals, except for those painted indoors, are exposed to the elements. Their durability, as a result, can pose a challenge for communities, particularly those that are low income. Vergara (1995, p. 135) commented on the precarious nature of murals: "Exposed to time and the elements, the existence of murals is precarious from the start. Typically they are painted on the exposed side of abandoned buildings, and destroyed with the demolition of their host structures. Those rare ones that survive become eroded—their paint fading, their bright colors muted, the plaster behind the painting showing, the composition breaking down into fragments, softening the stern faces and whitening the Afros." Thus, unlike playgrounds and sculptures, murals are fragile. Their survival and maintenance can attest to their importance to a community.

The Social and Public Art Resources Center of Los Angeles (SPARC) systematically cataloged nearly 1,000 murals, assessed their condition, and made repairs when necessary. They noted that approximately 25 percent (about 80 out of 326 murals) of the murals examined in the initial three months of the survey were classified as in extremely bad condition and worthy of being designated "emergency cases" by a mural-maintenance panel consisting of artists, scholars, and community activists.

Degree of flexibility. The degree of flexibility that murals provide makes them attractive for communities and practitioners. The location, size, costs, and level of complexity vary, allowing communities latitude in designing and painting murals. Murals can be designed "community" projects, employing a sizable number of residents (20 or more) and covering a wide area of a centrally located wall. Their flexibility gives local merchants an opportunity to hire a small group of muralists to paint the outside walls of an establishment.

Although it is always preferable to employ a well-established muralist to help in the design and implementation of a mural project, it is not necessary to do so. Murals have been created with chalk, for example, although their longevity is short lived (Engle, 1997; Lawrinsky, 1997). These types of murals lend themselves to be "painted" by school-aged children as part of a community-centered project.

Extent of library research. To a greater extent than the other projects addressed in this book, murals require participants to undertake library research on history and culture. This research serves as a backdrop to the creation of themes and symbols that will become part of the mural's content. The research skills that the participants acquire in the process can easily be transferred to other arenas.

Murals make excellent projects for youths of color to explore their cultural heritage and learn about the heritages of other groups; fostering ethnic and racial pride can often be major goal of murals, with implications that go far beyond just learning about cultural heritage. The process of creating a mural can easily be conceptualized as the process of reclaiming an identity deeply rooted in ancestral origins. This reclaiming of history has numerous benefits that go beyond the immediate goal of painting a mural.

Importance of symbols that are culturally and historically based. Murals provide communities with a mechanism through which to uncover and discuss painful experiences. Sometimes these experiences are buried deep in a community's history, and the painting of a mural serves as a vehicle for a community to discuss and come to terms with its past. As Doss (1995, p. 195) reported: "During the process of making the mural, Guadalupe's [Guadalupe, California] historical baggage was dragged out of the closet and dusted off. Townspeople analyzed their social and political histories and confronted Guadalupe's legacy of interracial struggle. Newly attentive to issues of race and class, they openly discussed the dynamics of their past, present, and future relationships."

The lengthy process involved in painting a mural provides numerous opportunities for a community to come together and discuss, challenge, formulate, and possibly answer questions. Topics may be too controversial at first to facilitate discourse. However, as a painting unfolds, the community may have had sufficient time to think about the consequences of an event and be willing and able to open up old wounds for the benefit of healing and moving forward.

Art as a form of communication. Murals provide communities with a voice through which to articulate issues of oppression and social justice. Therefore, their content must be seriously studied for its symbols and messages as an artifact reflecting community priorities and hopes. Art as a vehicle for the expression of desires and fears is not new, but murals, through their larger-than-life size, present a picture of a community that is rarely shown in the public media.

Expressions of issues related to social and economic justice rarely receive airtime on local television news programs or appear in the print media. Consequently, undervalued communities must find outlets for their expression of rage. Murals, like billboards, are usually centrally located in a community, allowing all sectors to read their messages.

Mural-specific implications for social work education and practice. Mural projects can be initiated, maintained, and fostered by social workers and provide community-based organizations with intervention projects that can accomplish multiple community capacity-enhancement goals. As was mentioned earlier, few cities have organizations that are devoted exclusively to public art projects like murals. When these organizations are present, collaborative opportunities between them and social workers who engage in community practice are endless. When these organizations are not present, social workers can use murals as a means of organizing communities.

The Great Walls program, developed by SPARC, although not staffed by social workers, serves as an excellent example of the potential that murals have for low-income communities of color. The Great Wall of Los Angeles details the history of California from a perspective of women and people of color and is considered to be the largest mural in the world (located on Coldwater Canyon Avenue and stretching for approximately half a mile).

The mural, which was painted over a seven-year period (1976 to 1983), represents the collaborative effort of artists, teams of youths, and community residents. "Scattered throughout the Great Wall are the names of those who helped plan and paint it. Although Baca is often given sole artistic credit for the Van Nuys mural, hundreds aided in determining its narrative structure and overall aesthetic. In addition to a handful of arts professionals and consultants, Baca recruited 215 teenagers to work on the wall. . . . Treating the Great Wall as an educational project and a vehicle for 'the rehabilitation of self-esteem,' she hired kids ranging in age from fourteen to twenty-one as artistic contributors and collaborators. Their ethnic and racial backgrounds varied; many were gang members or on probation" (Doss, 1995, p. 178).

The goals of SPARC's Great Walls program are not unlike those typically stressed in community practice based on an assets perspective: (1) to foster pride and a sense of community, (2) to beautify communities through public art that is based on community symbols and themes, and (3) to provide youths with opportunities to learn artistic skills. Although it is not explicitly stated, community capacity enhancement plays a central role in the organization's thrust toward community participation.

To have meaning for a community, art must arise from it, rather than be imposed on it; public art is a mechanism for enhancing community capacities and a form of memorializing important messages for future generations. Dunitz and Prigoff (1997, p. 18) did an excellent job of placing murals within a realistic context and summarizing their importance for low-income urban communities: "While it is true that mural art is achieving broader recognition and acceptance, those murals that include self-expression and self-definition by artists in impoverished neighborhoods, whose work seldom has been valued by the formal art community, are the heart of the mural movement. Murals are certainly no panacea for cities. . . . But community murals can be an empowering force, giving visibility to community issues and serving as a means of communication between people and cultures."

Gardens

Urban gardens have evolved into social interventions over the past three decades as Miller (1995, C8) noted: "The initial appeal of urban gardens used to be a simple desire for home-grown vegetables. Now, it seems however, community gardens are becoming a way to improve relationships and neighborhoods. During the 1992 riots in South Central Los Angeles, the seven community gardens there escaped the barrage of damage. It is this attitude that has made the popularity of community gardens grow in recent years." Urban gardens, as a result, can be used to help people and communities grow. Urban-garden interventions provide social workers with an avenue to engage in community capacity enhancement and the creation of community spirit.

Project-specific aspects. Financial considerations: generate money, save money on food, or contribute to the hungry. Urban gardens, unlike the other projects addressed in this book, can serve economic goals by saving or making money for gardeners. They can be devoted to growing food for personal consumption, income generation, or donation to food pantries (Herdy, 1997; Sprott, 1996). Recent shifts in national policy on welfare will have a profound impact on communities with sizable concentrations of poor and low-income residents, increasing the importance of communities developing alternative sources for food. "As poverty and hunger intensify and public assistance evaporates, urban communities are coming together around gardening and food security—cultivating neighborhood gardens and urban farms alike as centers for community cohesion, nutritional sustenance, and economic opportunity. These local efforts are part of a grassroots national movement that's uniting urban gardeners, small farmers, environmentalists and anti-poverty groups around the concept of community food security. The goal is to create proactive, sustainable solutions to the interrelated crises of unequal food access, poverty and hunger" (Cook, 1997, p. 3).

One gardener (quoted in Puckett, 1995, p. 7D) commented on the difference between the goals of consumption and beautification: "You'd be surprised at what you can grow in a small space. . . . Some people grow flowers in their gardens, but I need all mine for food." One garden in Denver, Colorado, is devoted to growing food for the hungry. As Hinkemeyer (1996, p. 3D) reported: "Like gardeners at many of the sites, Conant [a gardener] shares what he grows with others in need and takes surplus to food banks. Other gardeners share their time and produce with food canning projects, Project Angel Heart and shelter."

It is difficult to make a profit with produce from an urban garden (Fiffer & Fiffer, 1994; Hynes, 1995). However, the money that is saved from grocery bills can be significant, particularly for low-income groups "In addition to giving low-income residents access to land to raise nutritious food, community gardens can deliver excess to local pantries. Gardeners know the value of being able to put their hands on soil. Community gardens can give this opportunity to people who lack access to land and in so doing help build stronger communities and more attractive neighborhoods" (Hamilton, 1996, p. 11). There are other practical advantages to growing food as well. Many low-income people do not have easy access to grocery stores in their communities. This situation is compounded by the lack of access to public transportation and the difficulty of carrying large quantities of food back home using public transportation (Malakoff, 1995).

Spiritual-social role. Although murals are a mechanism for a community to display spiritual, or religious, themes, gardens can fulfill a unique role in bringing groups together in pursuit of spiritual values and social relationships As Baker (1997, pp. 21–22) described: "Many . . . Lower East Side residents use the gardens as open-air chapels and spiritual centers. An Hispanic church holds its novena, nine-day period of prayer and singing. . . . Some gardens function as healing centers for people with AIDS. And in others, gardeners practice rites of Catholicism mixed with the indigenous practices of the islands; plots often include Santeria shrines, with their attendant candles, religious medallions, and fragrances."

Lewis's (1996) research on green nature in cities through use of gardens and trees, noted eight benefits for residents and communities: (1) social harmony (a mechanism for bringing people together in a cooperative venture), (2) communication (a process of neighbors sharing and getting to know each other), (3) friendship (places where residents share values and appreciate each other's contributions), (4) self-esteem (feelings of success and pride), (5) patience (a slower pace to urban life resulting in less stress), (6) learning (greater knowledge about people's role with nature and the interconnectedness of these two spheres), (7) grounding (development of a better sense of the environment), and (8) healing (gardens serving physical, emotional, and spiritual functions).

Social interactions can be facilitated or enhanced by creating garden spaces with this purpose in mind. One gardener (quoted in Hinkle, 1997, p. 01N) put it this way: " 'The garden has meant a lot to me. . . . We have fifth graders from Byck Elementary School come and learn about horticulture. We even have a Sunday school class from Joshua Baptist Church [Louisville] that occasionally meets at our garden. We have picnics and other activities, too. It's just a good place for people to meet.' "

Upkeep and vandalism as indicators of community ownership. The physical appearance of a garden can be an important and telling indicator of how the community views the garden. Gardens are often located in public areas of a community and are easily visible from a street. Their location facilitates the process of observation. Gardens require active upkeep to eliminate weeds that destroy plants and make it arduous to plant. Depending on the size of a garden, weeding may be time and labor intensive.

The degree to which vandalism is operative is another indicator of community ownership, and thereby respect, for the garden and the individuals who work the land. As Hair (1996, p. 16) remarked: "The issue comes up in the community gardens—are the bad elements going to come around and ruin the garden, or is somebody going to take the produce, or go through and stomp everything down. . . . Just as in life, there's always a possibility that can happen, but it rarely does." As a result, the degree of damage caused, particularly in the case of graffiti (the extent and nature of messages), can provide clues about community tensions and fractions.

Seasonal considerations. Although the winter months have a severe impact on all the community capacity-enhancement projects described in this book (unless they are located in warm climates), gardens are, without question, the most affected. The suspension of active gardening, however, does not mean that gardeners disband until the spring and there are no important tasks that need to be accomplished until then.

A community gardening association noted that activities must continue year-round if a garden is to flourish: "The biggest challenge in the group's ability to grow comes during the winter months when the continuity of the garden season is broken. Winter is an excellent time to do planning and evaluation, volunteer recruitment and training, fund raising and socializing" (Minnesota Green, 1992, p. 8). Thus, there is always something that must be accomplished to have a productive and well-maintained garden.

Length of time before a garden is fully developed. Unlike the other projects, community gardening cannot generate fast results. It often requires a lengthy period (possibly several years) before food can be generated or plants and flowers grow sufficiently to beautify an area. The first year is usually devoted to site preparation and cleanup, as well as to improving the soil and increasing the access to water (Minnesota Green, 1992).

Site preparation may require an extraordinary amount of work if the lot, which is not unusual in many urban areas, had been used for the disposal of garbage and building materials, such as bricks (particularly in cases where a building has been torn down). Consequently, this phase can prove labor intensive. Thus, gardens must be thought of as long-term projects that will provide excellent benefits to a community but will take a great deal of time and effort before they do so.

Facilitating intercultural communication and relations, particularly for groups from farming backgrounds. There is something wonderful about gardening that, in itself, is a universal language. "Cultures and languages of different lands may vary, but plants are universal. Plant growth proceeds in stages familiar to gardeners all over the world. Although the names may differ, the process can be a focus for communication with others; people often resist instruction less when the medium is a nonthreatening plant rather than another person. The gift of a carefully tended plant carries something of the spirit of the one who grew and nurtured it" (Lewis, 1996, p. 105).

Most newcomers to urban areas of the United States have had agriculture in their background. Thus, gardening represents an excellent mechanism for tapping this experience. However, just as important, one of the major challenges in developing a sense of community in many cities is overcoming the barriers that the lack of a common language presents. Consequently, any activity that fosters people of different cultural backgrounds coming together takes on added significance in cities.

The amount of land is dependent on its availability and the goals for the garden. Gardening must be flexible to flourish in urban areas. The amount of land available often determines the nature of the garden. A small plot may lend itself to planting flowers and a large plot, to planting crops. However, there is no denying that the larger the plot, the greater the potential for a community to achieve impressive goals.

A large parcel of land offers the community an opportunity to involve a wide sector, grow sufficient food to help the hungry, and make a substantial impact on a blighted area. Nevertheless, large tracts of land are rare in most communities. Thus, a small parcel of land is still usable for a garden, although it limits the goals that can be achieved and the number of gardeners who can participate in the experience.

Garden-specific implications for social work education and practice. There are numerous community practice implications for using gardens in asset assessments and capacity-enhancement interventions. The process of gardening, after all, lends itself to achieving many different goals. Baker (1997, p. 17), for example, views community gardening as a mechanism for creating relationships, generating food, and bring community residents together in a place where they can feel safe: "What's at stake is more than the opportunity for neighbors to get acquainted as they share in the basic human impulse to turn the soil and make things blossom. These grassroots ventures play a crucial role in times of dwindling social services, as places for kids to keep busy after school, as sanctuaries and silent shrinks for the poor who cannot afford psychological counseling, and as recreation spots for those who cannot journey to places like Florida and Vermont."

There are tremendous similarities between gardening and macro-focused skills and knowledge areas. "Building community gardening organizations requires a broad range of skills from horticultural knowledge to community organizing, fiscal management to ecological expertise, as well as administration, fundraising and multifaceted program development" (Annual Report, 1996–97, p. 4). A job description for the coordinator of a gardening association could easily be found in a social work organization that employs macro-social work practitioners.

The Louisville Coalition for Community Security has an initiative to rent or buy approximately 1,500 vacant lots in Louisville and convert them into community gardens for the cultivation of food. Most of these lots are owned either by the city or by the U.S. Department of Housing and Urban Development (Hinkle, 1997).

Much can be learned about community gardening by looking at how this movement is faring in other countries. As Moskow (1997, p. 19) stated: "In the United States, community gardening is primarily a recreational activity and a community event, but as welfare cuts are instituted . . . more and more people may find themselves turning to community gardening and urban agriculture as a means of feeding family and neighbors. Havana [Cuba] provides an interesting context for urban agriculture both because of the enormous scale of urban agricultural activities and also because of the involvement of the government."

It would not be too much of a stretch for a social worker to facilitate the creation of a coalition of different stakeholders, residents, and educational-human service organizations. This brokering role can be instrumental in attracting external resources for such a project. Furthermore, the benefits will not be restricted to the present; this coalition can expand to include other sectors of a community and other types of projects.

Community-Built Playgrounds

The recent popularity of playgrounds is not new in this country's history. A similar movement occurred in the early 1900s when many municipal reformers viewed playgrounds as a means of promoting neighborliness and "civic virtue" (Daley, 1996). Community-built playgrounds can play instrumental roles in bringing together community residents in search of a project that serves children and unites the community in a common pursuit. Playground construction is a nonstigmatizing activity that taps a community's skills and knowledge of construction; these abilities can be easily translated into other forms of building.

Project-specific aspects. A considerable expenditure of funds. Although it is possible to build a playground in stages because of funding limitations, it is preferable to do so all at once, if possible. Donations may be in the form of money, supplies from local businesses (such as food and lumber), and volunteers (builders and planners).

Despite the flexibility, it may take a long time to build a playground. Supplies may be expensive, particularly if high-quality, pressure-treated wood is used. A large number of volunteers are needed all at once for the construction to be cost efficient. Expertise related to the planning and building of these structures is not easily or cheaply available. If a community relies on volunteer experts, it must be flexible and patient about their availability. Thus, a project may take much longer to build if volunteers are used.

Intensive construction over one or two days. Community-built playgrounds can be built in a short, but intense, period, such as a weekend or three-day holiday. In this case, volunteers do not have to take time out from work or school to participate.

However, the intensity of the activity necessitates that the event be well planned and coordinated to avoid delays, which can be disastrous, or accidents, since the building often involves hundreds of individuals. Thus, a condensed period of activity offers advantages and disadvantages for a community. To maximize the advantages and minimize the disadvantages, a planning period must be built into the entire process.

A considerable number of volunteers. The construction of a playground requires the involvement of numerous individuals performing multiple tasks. Consequently, the amount of planning and screening that goes into selecting and assigning volunteers can be formidable. However, the need for various roles facilitates the recruitment and assignment of volunteers and increases the likelihood that the entire community can contribute and feel a sense of ownership of the final outcome.

Roles may vary to allow volunteers of different abilities, ages, and interests to participate actively and meaningfully. Although children are often not allowed in the construction site, they can still help by carrying food, nails, and other supplies to the builders. They also play an instrumental role in designing and naming the playground. In essence, the viability and success of a community-built playground rests on the ability of the organizers to involve all sectors of the community; there is no such thing as not having a role for someone who wishes to participate!

Community playgrounds can be low maintenance. Although a playground like a mural and a sculpture, requires little daily upkeep, it still needs to be maintained. Thus, the community must be willing to undertake periodic maintenance that is normally associated with day-to-day use.

As a result, the community has to set up a mechanism for enlisting and deploying residents to perform maintenance tasks. The failure to take these tasks into account in the planning and implementation process may result in the playground becoming unsafe for children; such a playground will become a symbol for a community of "how good things were back then".

Careful consideration of liability issues. Unfortunately, the community does not have the luxury of focusing exclusively on the building of a playground. It must, for example, contend with liability issues arising from children getting hurt while playing in the playground. Consequently, insurance must be purchased and funds set aside to pay for it. The failure to purchase insurance may cause severe financial hardship for the community if a child is injured and his or her parents file a lawsuit.

In essence, once the playground structures are built, they become the responsibility of a community organization that can apply for and obtain the necessary liability insurance. However, the planning committee cannot wait until the playground is built to investigate the costs of such insurance, so it can determine whether it is desirable and feasible to build the playground. Fundraising mechanisms must be established and systematically built into the process of upkeep to ensure that the play structures meet the community's needs.

Accessibility: for disabled persons. Ensuring that the playground is accessible to all sectors of the community is essential in building a playground that is welcoming to both able-bodied and physically challenged residents. In fact, physical accessibility takes on added significance in low-income areas of a city because of the limited options that residents who are physically challenged have in gaining access to playgrounds and other recreational areas. Thus, if a playground is to be truly community built and used, it must be accessible to all, and this factor must be taken into account in planning a playground.

Consequently, unlike the other community capacity-enhancement projects discussed in this book, a number of regulations concerning physical accessibility must be considered in all phases of building a community playground. This technical knowledge may be obtained by soliciting volunteers with this type of expertise or purchasing it. However, the community does not have the option of ignoring accessibility or assuming that a playground is accessible because it looks like it is.

Playground-specific implications for social work education and practice. A playground has tremendous potential for reaching out to children and their families and can serve as a powerful socialization vehicle for a community with few outlets for such interaction. Since parents may take their children to the playground at specific times of the day or on certain days, these periods may lend themselves to the development of various types of groups, workshops, information sharing, and so forth.

Playgrounds, if sufficiently large, can be used to host fairs of various types, particularly those that target children and their parents. They can also serve as places where practitioners can go to observe how well children from different ethnic-racial backgrounds interact and play with each other. In essence, community playgrounds not only make excellent projects but are excellent places to observe a community.

Sculptures

Although sculptures offer great potential for community involvement, they do so to a much lesser extent than the other projects addressed in this book. These structures, however, can be built to take into consideration the goals of the community, the availability of space, and the amount of available funding. In addition, community resources can be utilized in all aspects of their design and construction. Sculptures are complementary to the other projects addressed in this book.

Project-specific aspects. Physical challenges in creating sculptures. Sculpturing, particularly large pieces, present artists and communities with a unique set of challenges, as was the case in Toronto, Canada. As Mays (1997, p. C5) reported, "When asked to do public commissions, it sometimes turns out, our best and most accomplished artists [sculptors] are unable to cope successfully with the peculiar demands of working in the city's open air, with its rush of traffic, looming buildings, hard light and moving shadows, spaces often too empty or too crowded. The years of working in quiet studios and showing in sanctified, climate-controlled museums, it appears, have taken their toll . . . leaving only a few nowadays . . . capable of taking charge of a public place and leaving a powerful, indelible mark on it."

However, sculpturing does not have to result in large art pieces. One of the many advantages of sculptures is that they can be created with a keen understanding of the goals and amount of space that is available. Thus, sculptures can be relatively small.

Little open space. Of all the projects discussed in this book, sculptures require the least amount of public space. The size and shape of sculptures lend themselves to the size and shape of the space that is available in the community. Because of this flexibility sculptures can either stand alone or, as is common, be a part of other community projects, such as gardens.

However, when they are part of an existing area, such as a garden or playground, sculptures may blend in too well and not be recognized as an artistic artifact. As a result, the goal of the sculpture must be thought out carefully: Is the sculpture making a "stand-alone" statement, or is integration the hoped-for goal? The flexibility that sculptures provide communities makes them attractive for areas with limited space.

Access to machinery and expertise. The creation of a sculpture is not an easy process, particularly if the sculpture is designed to be placed outdoors and hence will be subject to the elements. Thus, the sculpture needs to be built from materials that can withstand heavy traffic and weather. This does not mean that community capacity-enhancement project sculptures can be undertaken only by communities with access to the necessary resources, machinery, and expertise.

However, community-built sculptures should use materials that are accessible to the community. Access refers to materials and tools that can be obtained and worked with relatively easily. Concrete is often used in community sculptures for these very reasons. Therefore, a community should not shy away from building a sculpture because sculptures are associated with massive statues that require expensive materials, equipment, and expertise. Sculptures come in all types, so a community can pick and use the appropriate type to match its goals and local circumstances.

Cost. The cost of creating a sculpture can vary widely, depending on its size, location (indoors or outdoors), and the need for specialized equipment. The Lin Zexu state in Chinatown, New York, which was built out of bronze and is 18 feet, 5 inches, cost was $200,000. It was financed by numerous individuals and civic associations with Fujianese ties (Chen, 1997).

Not all sculptures need to be that expensive and can be built within the budgetary requirements of the community. Instead of paid staff, sculptures can be totally dependent upon volunteers, including the artist. Artists who are just starting their careers may be more likely to volunteer their time and talents to develop a portfolio and enhance their reputations.

Symbolic message. Sculptures can depict real-life figures, as in the case of statues; be functional; or convey symbolic messages to a community. In the former, the statue may ostensibly appear to be a decoration. However, on closer examination and reflection, the message may have to do with the figure that was selected, the location of the statue, or even the sponsoring committee.

Sculptures can be functional if they are conceptualized to be part of an area of the community that is highly visited. For example, a sculpture in a playground can be functional by being part of the "equipment." A strategically located bench, in turn, can serve as a place for residents to meet and converse. Thus, sculptures can enhance a community by providing residents with an opportunity to meet and interact, whether in a playground, park, or area near public transportation.

When the sculpture is abstract, the statement will depend on the goals the community had in erecting it. Even when it is abstract, the community must not have difficulty understanding its message. The community, however, may have to interpret the message to the outside world. This action may prove important in situations in which the outside world has not understood a community.

Upkeep is limited. If upkeep is an important consideration for a community, a sculpture offers tremendous advantages over a mural, garden, and playground, in that it requires minimal maintenance and upkeep if it is constructed out of the proper materials. Obviously, this consideration must be taken into account during the planning phase of the project because it will dictate the kind of sculpture that will be and the materials that will be used in its construction.

When a sculpture is constructed out of bronze, for example, upkeep will not prove labor intensive, although the building of it will. A sculpture made out of wood can be treated to minimize the impact of weather. Consequently, the upkeep of sculptures is just as important as the upkeep of murals, gardens, and playgrounds and must be taken into consideration by the community residents when they decide to build one.

Opportunity for wide community involvement. Community-built sculptures provide the same options for community involvement as any of the other projects. Community residents can play an active role in all phases of sculpturing, from selecting and naming the design to building the sculpture. Depending on the size of the sculpture, its development may involve only a few individuals, unlike playgrounds, for example.

The multiple phases of sculpturing lend themselves to involving groups of different ages, backgrounds, abilities, and interests. Elders, for example, depending on their physical abilities, can play active roles in the selection and design phases: those who are physically able can mix cement, and others can play important roles in fund-raising, publicity, and recruiting volunteers.

Sculpture-specific implications for social work education and practice. Community-built sculptures offer great opportunities for fulfilling many goals that social workers who work with communities often seek to accomplish. The conceptualization of sculptures as having community capacity-enhancement potential may be foreign to most practitioners, however. Although sculptures do not have to be highly visible (one of their goals is to blend into the environment), they still provide practitioners with a mechanism for enhancing the capacity of communities and bringing the residents together.

The flexibility that they offer, including cost, allows sculptures to be created with a clear sense of the communities' needs and resources. In addition to beautifying an area, sculptures can fulfill abstract goals in conveying a message concerning a community event, hero, or situation. Sculptures can also be practical and fun and fit nicely into playgrounds or gardens. Because of their flexibility, local circumstances play a critical role in shaping their function.

Conclusion

This chapter provided the reader with an understanding of the complexity, challenges, and rewards of four community capacity-enhancement projects. These projects share many similarities pertaining to their primary goals, the importance they place on community participation, and the benefits they can realize for communities. The potential of community capacity-enhancement projects goes far beyond creating physical changes in the community, in that important social, economic, and political goals may also be realized.

These projects, too, have unique features that must be taken into account in the development of goals and during the assessment and planning phases of macro practice. Their unique features, however, require practitioners to exercise caution and judgment in determining, in collaboration with the community, which ones are feasible and will have a maximum impact depending on local circumstances. No one project is "perfect" for any given community and issue. Thus, the selection of a project is based on the consideration of a series of factors, events, and conditions.

III

APPLICATION OF THE FRAMEWORK TO PRACTICE AND LESSONS LEARNED

Section 3 consists of six chapters that ground the reader in community capacity-enhancement work involving murals, gardens, playgrounds, and sculptures. Chapters 8 through 12 utilize the framework for practice (assessment, mapping, engagement, intervention, and evaluation) presented in Chapter 4 and make extensive use of case illustrations to highlight key points and considerations. Photographs provide a visual perspective on many of the cases and help the reader better appreciate the complexity and beauty of the projects. Chapter 13—Reflections on Practice (Lessons and Recommendations)—summarizes what the author considers to be important trends and considerations for urban-based, community social work practice focused on capacity enhancement.

The numerous case illustrations indicate how community capacity-enhancement practice involving murals, gardens, playgrounds and sculptures gets operationalized in urban communities across the United States. They provide the reader with an opportunity to "see" how theory translates into real-life practice situations, an important dimension of social work education. In so doing, they provide practitioners with both the necessary context and specifics related to interventions to foster application to the practice arena.

The case examples provide sufficient "description" as well as "prescription" to facilitate the development of practice skills related to urban-centered projects. In addition, every effort was made to include case examples involving community- and agency-initiated projects to illustrate their similarities and differences. Some of the cases do not fit neatly into a category, and some may even describe projects that had limited success; not all community capacity-enhancement projects can achieve all their lofty goals.

Case illustrations are used of all phases of the framework and are drawn from the following sources: (1) the media (particularly newspapers), (2) modifications of existing case studies, and (3) new case studies based on fieldwork with select communities across the United States. Cases that were drawn from the literature have been followed up to provide supplemental material.

The case examples, unfortunately, sacrifice depth to illustrate a variety of perspectives on key practice and theoretical points. The author prefers short cases, rather than lengthy ones, because the reader can more easily and quickly read, analyze, and draw implications from them. Delgado's (1998c) framework for analyzing the various stages of planning collaborative partnerships with nontraditional settings lends itself to use with community capacity-enhancement initiatives: (1) goals of the stage, (2) key theoretical concepts, (3) key practice challenges, (4) description of the stage, (5) case illustrations, and (6) key practice skills. Special emphasis is placed on the intervention phase to explicate aspects of practice that are particularly important in operationalizing community capacity-enhancement projects.

The reader is advised that every effort was made to include case illustrations of a variety of projects, situations, and communities. At times, however, the cases reflect the author's success with certain communities and projects more than others. Some cases have been selected that do not neatly fit into the general types of cases used throughout the book. These case illustrations illuminate a different perspective on community capacity enhancement that may be of interest to the reader and may provide a viable alternative for practitioners.

One of the cases (San Diego's Chicano Park) receives additional attention in this section because of its richness, incorporation of multiple community capacity-enhancement projects, abundance of documents detailing the process and results (including its own web site), and the accessibility of one of the park's original organizers to be interviewed. All these factors allowed the author to draw extensive lessons from the experience of the community and the role gardens, murals, sculptures, and playgrounds in the change process.

When a case was previously reported, a citation is provided. However, when a case was developed specifically for this book or additional material was obtained on a previously published case, no citation is included. The author hopes that this approach will facilitate the reading of the case examples. Finally, the reader will find case illustrations of particular projects reflected throughout most of the chapters. By providing continuity of subject and context, these cases allow the reader to witness most, if not all, the phases of the framework.

8

Application of the Framework to Practice: Assessment

As with any form of intervention, assessment is the foundation upon which a project or service rests. Thus, like a foundation of a house, if it is not properly executed, the structure upon which it is built will not be stable. Community capacity enhancement, too, is in tremendous need of the information gathered through a systematic assessment. This chapter provides the reader with a variety of perspectives on and approaches to assessment from an assets viewpoint.

Description of the Phase

The assessment phase generally consists of multiple strategies, activities, and tasks and is greatly influenced by the goals of the organization that undertakes the assessment. Consequently, no "magic" formula can be recommended because local factors dictate the nature of the assessment. Social workers who are searching for a "cookbook" on assessment for the development of community capacity-enhancement strategies are doomed to failure. "There is little room for formula or 'cookie-cutter' thinking in community capacity building. What works well in one community may not work well in another. Recognizing the difference, then creating a unique response to each local situation, demands the exercise of judgement" (Poole, 1997, p. 168). This judgment, in turn, necessitates an in-depth assessment of the community to take into account local values, history, culture, and expectations.

Goals

Community capacity-enhancement assessment must generally address five primary goals: (1) to identify community stakeholders and potential leaders who can be involved in projects; (2) to identify the most relevant capacity-enhancement project based on local assets, needs, and circumstances; (3) to provide social workers with an opportunity to gain a better understanding of the community, its history, previous successes, demographic changes, and hopes for the present and future; and (4) to lay the necessary foundation (analytical and interactional) for the ultimate development of a project.

Key Practice Concepts

The assessment phase provides practitioners with an immense body of theory to draw upon in helping to shape interventions. The critical nature of this phase involves theoretical considerations and political skills for a multiplicity of assessment goals to be achieved (Delgado, 1996b; Kretzmann & McKnight, 1996a, 1996b). Thus, the practitioner must systematically balance a number of considerations in the planning and implementation of an assessment that will provide requisite data for decision making.

The concept of community markers incorporates key theoretical material that social workers have been exposed to during their academic experiences. Much work has been done on identifying strength and resilience factors in individuals and families, and social workers are much more accustomed to reading literature on this topic (Fraser, 1997; Fraser & Galinsky, 1997; Nash & Fraser, 1997; Saleebey, 1992a, 1992b, 1996).

Community markers, in turn, are predicated upon community assets and represent community "artifacts" that must be properly identified and understood during the assessment phase. These assets, of course, can vary according to the ethnic and racial composition of the community and local circumstances. Consequently, there is no hard and fast rule concerning their presence. However, when present, they provide social workers with a starting point from which to learn more about the conditions and individuals who were involved in their creation.

In communities with a rich and long tradition of undertaking community capacity-enhancement projects, such as murals (Weber, 1998), the presence of these projects will make the assessment process easier to accomplish and set the stage for an intervention project of a similar kind. In communities in which there are no murals, gardens, playgrounds, or sculptures, however, the assessment process then must focus on identifying public spaces where these projects can be created to maximize their intervention value. Thus, abandoned lots, lots attached to agencies, abandoned buildings, and parks and playgrounds that are not usable must be identified and their dimensions and locations noted, so they can be mapped for the purposes of analysis and planning. Any information that can be obtained about the owners of the properties will be useful in the later stages. However, it may be easier to learn about the owners when the property is owned by a governmental agency than when it is privately owned.

Key Practice Challenges

Assessment is never an easy process, any form of assessment presents numerous challenges. However, the challenges related to assessment from a community capacity-enhancement perspective bring a different dimension to the practice arena. These challenges must be viewed from two perspectives: when a marker is present and when no marker is present.

When a marker is present, the practitioner must gather as much information as possible concerning its presence. This process can be labor intensive and require detection and astute analytical skills. When a marker is not present, the practitioner must locate and identify strategic sites for a project and take into consideration accessibility factors, such as geographic location and psychological and cultural factors (comfort level with the site and the possibility of cultural dimensions to a capacity-enhancement project). The consideration of cultural factors, for example, requires the practitioner to know as much as possible about the cultural backgrounds of the residents. In communities where there are many different ethnic-racial groups, the acquisition of this knowledge can prove formidable.

Practitioners face the additional challenge of specifically looking at space from an assets perspective. A building that has been abandoned, has broken windows, and is just waiting to crumble may be a tremendous asset. However, practitioners may not even think of it as a potential asset because they are not capable of thinking about it in that manner. The shift in paradigms is never easy, theoretically or practically.

Case Illustrations

Five cases representing four cities, three states (Illinois, Massachusetts, and New York), and one foreign country (Canada) were selected to illustrate several key elements of assessment approaches. These cases address a multitude of situations and interventions and provide the reader with a variety of possibilities for use in their own practice. Community capacity enhancement, as operationalized in this book, can take many different forms, allowing for flexibility in local circumstances, resources, the practitioner's knowledge and skills, and organizational goals.

The first case illustration, originally reported by Delgado and Barton (1998) and substantially expanded here, highlights how murals can provide important, but often overlooked, information on a community. The site of the case is Holyoke, Massachusetts, a city with a population of approximately 44,000, located about 100 miles west of Boston. The Latino community numbers approximately 12,700 (28.9 percent of the total population), 93.5 percent of whom are Puerto Ricans (Gaston Institute, 1992b, 1994).

The case could be entitled by the local press "En Busca de Unidad [In Search of Unity]: Hard Lessons Learned by Holyoke Latino Youths." Although it focused on Latino youths, it also involved numerous adult stakeholders and just "ordinary" residents:

> In the spring of 1996, a group of twenty Puerto Rican youths aged 9–17 were hired to paint a mural on a wall of a centrally located building within the Puerto Rican community. This group of youngsters was hired by a local Latino community-based organization called Arco Iris (the Rainbow). Although the building had been abandoned by its owner, the group sought and received permission to paint a mural. The mural was significant because it also functioned as a backdrop to a well-established community garden. The youngsters spent a considerable amount of time researching the subject of the mural in the library and speaking with community residents.

The research aspect of murals serves not only to gather information on a subject that may not be readily available in a library, but to engage the community in the project. Furthermore, this process helps youths develop skills that can be applied in other aspects of their lives.

> The mural's subject focused on identity and was not unusual for a Puerto Rican community in the United States. The mural portrayed two flags (of Puerto Rico and the United States) as a representation of the youths living in two communities at once. Shortly after the mural was painted and dedicated, a controversy erupted after several Holyoke veterans voiced their discontent to a city councilor, who had a less-than-stellar reputation regarding the Puerto Rican community. The mural depicted the Puerto Rican flag on top with the United States flag just below it and upside down. The councilwoman and veterans threatened to paint over the mural if the mural was not corrected to have the United States flag on top and right side up. After much debate that involved large sectors of Holyoke and almost the entire Puerto Rican community, the youths decided to paint over the U.S. flag by extending the Puerto Rican flag. In essence, they believed that such a move was a compromise for all parties.

The themes represented in the Holyoke mural are not unusual in communities of color. In the Latino community, these themes are manifested in a variety of ways, depending on the region of the country and the country of origin of the Latinos painting the mural.

> The primary goal of the mural was to highlight how the youth's lives are caught between two different worlds in this society, with the flags symbolizing these extreme contexts. The controversy that ensued brought to the general public how the issues that Puerto Rican youths were facing—namely, questioning of their identity, alienation, and oppression—were still affecting their lives, even when they were trying to be constructive in expressing these sentiments. The mural project, however, accomplished much more

by bringing the Puerto Rican community together to ward off the councilor and veterans and strengthened the voice of the youths and the community in the process. If a painting speaks a thousand words, then the Holyoke mural spoke volumes.

The assessment of the Holyoke mural brought to the forefront areas of tension between one Latino group and city government and focused on certain members of the city government and the perceptions of the community concerning their racial biases. As with any assessment, practitioners should be able to identify the key stakeholders, organizations, history of past issues, and potential future projects. In the Holyoke case, the ramifications of the incident resulted in classroom discussions and assignments related to the status of Puerto Ricans in the United States, the importance of identity for youths of color, the need for dialogue within and between groups, and the importance of the community coming together.

The second case illustration was chosen because it, too, transpired in Holyoke, Massachusetts; involved youths in a different type of public-art project (banners); and was sponsored by the same community-based organization that sponsored the mural (Breitbart, 1998; Coleman, 1994a). The assessment undertaken by the youths in this project typifies how it can influence other types of community capacity-enhancement projects.

In the summer of 1990, a group of approximately thirty primarily Latino youths (aged 11 to 15) undertook a public-arts project to achieve three goals (Breitbart, 1998): (1) encourage youth participants to express their feelings (positive as well as negative) about their neighborhood and the city of Holyoke; (2) assess their environment critically; and (3) enhance their environment through the production of public art—in this case, a series of street banners.

The assessment process consisted of several stages, each stage requiring the participants to exercise different talents and cognitive functions:

The youths were charged with drawing their neighborhood to include what interested and moved them. There were restrictions concerning this dimension. Initial drawings and individual commentaries reflected a variety of important themes for the youths. Social settings, tenements, the importance of residents having space where they could congregate and play music, and improvements in local housing were repeated themes. After this "official" initial entry into the neighborhood, a systematic assessment process was implemented.

The assessment phase utilized a variety of techniques according to Breitbart (1998, pp. 317–318):

Neighbourhood walks, planned by the youth followed. While on these walks, teens photographed lots of desirable cars and took innumerable pictures of themselves. Familiar buildings and the homes of friends and family members were also popular targets in the viewfinder. Gradually, however, the angle widened to encompass tenements in disrepair, parks in various states of decay and a whole landscape of only potential delight. As we walked past many a broken fixture, the teens were quick to say that "somebody should fix that up.". . . Young people had no shortage of ideas about improving their environment and were also quick to comment on what they liked."

The assessment was not expected to be straightforward, as evidenced by the youths' inclination to photograph themselves and other aspects of the community. Nevertheless, this step led to an important discovery and determination, as Breitbart (1998, p. 318) noted:

Teens expressed a desire, however, to move beyond a documentary of the problems and causes to ways of addressing the symptoms and expressing their feelings, and hopes for change. These latter themes include a desire for water as a source of beauty and recreation (e.g., such activities as paddle boating, swimming and fishing); having "more fun things to do" in the city as a whole including the opportunity to enjoy their families' needs and provide them with increased privacy and control; the importance of warm and friendly people in the neighbourhood and how valued they were; and finally, and perhaps most importantly, the desire to introduce peace, order and tranquillity into their own lives. To give visual expression to these themes and draw public attention to the needs and desire of Holyoke youth, large street banners were produced.

The use of street banners as an intervention is addressed in Chapter 11 and illustrates the multiple gains for the participants and the community that can result from a public-art project that seeks to enhance the community's capacity in the process.

The use of a systematic assessment approach and mapping is well described in the third case example, of an initiative by Harlem Hospital in New York City to create a community playground (see Chapter 11 for a detailed description of the creation of the playground). As Hynes (1995, p. 14) reported:

Many Harlem children are confined to their apartments or play on the streets nearby, which explains the many injuries caused by falls and car accidents. The parks and playgrounds where the children should have been able to play contained multiple hazards from broken equipment and metal spikes to rats and drug dealers. To demonstrate the link between the neglect of parks and rising rates of traumatic injury . . . [two lifelong residents of Harlem were hired] to walk through, photograph, and document 120 outdoor play areas operated by the city's public school system, the public housing authority, and the parks department. [The field researchers] provided firsthand accounts of the contents and condition of Harlem's parks and playgrounds; they were littered with syringes and needles, condoms, rat holes, garbage, mattresses, tables and chairs, old cars, broken concrete, broken metal play equipment, broken glass, broken sewer grates, and non-functioning lights. . . . The two women kept a separate notebook for each play site, which included photographs, descriptions, and documentation, as well as the number of children who had been injured on the playground within the past few months according to records from the Harlem Hospital Emergency Room, outpatient clinics, and school health files. They also recorded their own recommendations for removing the hazards and replacing equipment and play surfaces to make the playgrounds safe for children. [They also] identified which organization was responsible for each park and play site.

The multifaceted nature of the Harlem assessment is a fine example of many of the methods addressed Chapter 4, including the use of patients' records. This multifaceted approach rested squarely on a foundation that was based on field-based research and documentation and could be considered labor intensive. Nevertheless, the nature and detail of the information gathered proved extremely beneficial in gaining the media's attention, mobilizing political support for the key stakeholders, and informing and engaging the community in the process.

The fourth case example, of Victoria Hills in Kitchener, Canada, provides an international perspective and stresses the importance of assessing the role and impact of vacant lots on a community. As McKay (1998, p. 1) reported:

Criminals consciously scan the environment for criminal opportunities. A public place that lacks significant ownership interest is often perceived by prostitutes, drug dealers, and others as an environment in which their activities will be tolerated and supported. These and other under-utilized and empty spaces are readily recognized and exploited by criminals. Often referred to by environmental criminologists as "good" (for the criminal) environmental cues, they draw the offender's attention with their apparent lack of activity, ownership, or care. Equally important is the fear empty spaces generate in the average resident or normal user. . . . Vacant lands can be exceptionally problematic given that many absentee landlords pay little attention to them.

The Victoria Hills community is an excellent example of how the identification and assessment of vacant lots represents an important step in setting the foundation for a capacity-enhancement project, in this case, a community garden (see Chapter 11).

The fifth case example, of a Chicago mural project, brings a different dimension to the assessment process by focusing on the presence or absence of graffiti.

The project was a collective effort by lead artists and apprentice artists (14–19) to paint a 2,500 square foot mural on the front side of the Fellowship House building. . . . The final product is a vibrant mural which de-

Figure 8.1. "For Our Brothers and Sisters Who Died Too Soon." Lead Artist: Corrine Peterson. Assisted by Apache Wakefield and Ten-Member Youth Team. Chicago Public Art Group, Gallery 37, and Bethel New Life.

picts the many different kinds of cultures in our neighborhood. It serves as a positive symbol of the benefits of understanding and appreciating one's own ethnic identity as well as another's. . . . Fellowship House sits in the middle of a neighborhood which is covered by graffiti. Since the mural has been completed, no graffiti has been painted onto the Fellowship House building. It is as if there is an unspoken word that Fellowship House is off limits—a respect not easily given by gangs. We take that as a message from the gang members that even they understand and respect what the mural is all about (Gallery 37, 1997b, p. 2).

The ninety-seven-foot clay relief mural was created on a wall of a former hospital that was being converted into a senior housing development. The artists sculptured positive images into the tiles and the names of close friends and family members into the "door frame" tiles ("1997 Year in Review," 1998). The importance of the mural's subject, combined with the degree of community involvement, made this capacity-enhancement project community owned. The presence or absence of graffiti on a mural can be an important indicator of how a community views an organization or mural. The message the mural depicts becomes an important indicator of what a community values and must be taken into account in an assessment process.

Key Practice Skills

The presence of murals, gardens, playgrounds, and sculptures in a community does not ensure that the community did, in fact, play a critical and supporting role in their creation. There may be instances in which the project was sponsored by and built by outside authorities, thereby making these projects an antithesis of community capacity enhancement. The only "community" aspect of such projects is their location in the community. Thus, the presence of a mural or other project, cannot be accepted at face value as representing a community capacity-enhancement project.

Breitbart's (1998, p. 306) eloquent plea for adults to take stock of their environment and the contributions of youths to a community's well-being applies to any age group and the role of community capacity-enhancement projects: "One of the clearest demarcations of power, wealth and influence in the urban landscape has always been the ability to invest one's living space with meaning—to literally occupy, define and decorate one's surroundings. . . . Taken together, there are numerous forms of cultural expression and politics that are thought to provide a means for youth to establish their unique identities in an urban setting while also drawing attention to, and, at times, resisting publicly assigned meanings to their lives."

Assessment, as a result, requires that the practitioner play the role of historian and detective in trying to uncover the circumstances behind a project. Furthermore, although the community may have used a project as a means of enhancing its capacity at a certain point in time, much has transpired since then, and the project is no longer maintained. In such circumstances, the practitioner also plays the role of historian or detective in trying to gain a better understanding of the circumstances that led to the creation of the project and its lack of upkeep. Members of the original effort may still be around and can be interviewed.

Thus, one of the greatest challenges that practitioners face during the assessment phase is the labor-intensive aspects of it. Rarely will a practitioner be able to pick up a local newspaper and obtain all the pertinent details related to a project. This type of information requires the social worker actively to trace all the key players in the initial effort and interview them before deriving conclusions.

Conclusion

The assessment conducted as part of a community capacity-enhancement initiative can take various forms. However, it must be undertaken to maximize available resources and provide a vision of where a community wishes to go as a result of an intervention.

There is sufficient flexibility in how an assessment is conducted to allow practitioners and communities to take into consideration local circumstances. Assessment does not have to be an expensive or highly complicated process. When communities are actively involved in the process, skill enhancement results for the betterment of the individuals involved and, ultimately, their communities. The skill-enhancement dimension represents a dramatic departure from conventional assessments that focus primarily on gathering data and pay minimal attention to enhancing the residents' skills.

9

Application of the Framework to Practice: Mapping

Practitioners have a tremendous need to develop and utilize intervention tools that can serve to involve and unite communities, as well as assist in the analytical aspects of planned change. Mapping is such a tool. With mapping, practitioners have a great deal of flexibility in any given situation because they are able to gather a range of complex information that is not readily available from conventional sources, such as resource directories.

Mapping can be used to enhance a community's capacities, which will prove to be an essential element of any form of intervention targeting a community. Practitioners, in turn, can tailor the kind of information they need to gather and to do so with a minimal amount of effort.

Description of the Phase

The mapping phase of community capacity enhancement assists the practitioner in selecting a site and a project. The phase generally consists of two stages. The first stage provides the practitioner with information about the availability of open space for a project—its location, size, and availability. This information, in turn, is mapped on a community map.

The second stage gives the practitioner a detailed understanding of what projects have been tried in the past, if any, and their location; where the community wants a project; and, depending on the space that is available (perceived versus actual), what kind of project (size and complexity) can be undertaken.

One prominent example of community mapping (Boyle Heights, Los Angeles) conceptualized the mapping process as consisting of six steps: (1) a clear definition of the community or area being mapped—the explication of geographic boundaries so as not to miss areas and to determine the field researchers' work load, (2) the development of a process for selecting and wording key questions to be answered during the mapping process, (3) the development of a standardized method for recording information that will be used in mapping (photographs, videotapes, audiotapes of descriptions and the like), (4) the mapping process, (5), the analysis, and (6) the presentation of results and recommendations to the community and key stakeholders.

Goals

The primary goal of mapping is simple: to analyze a community and the role, or potential role, that community capacity-enhancement projects can play. As a result, mapping can best be described as an analytical technique. There is no one way of undertaking mapping.

The goals of intervention will dictate how mapping transpires. However, the following six goals will be present in any form of mapping: (1) to provide an opportunity for community residents to participate in the process, (2) to identify new insights that will lead to changes in the community, (3) to reenergize the community through the experience of mapping, (4) to provide the community with directions for how to maximize their indigenous resources, (5) to make the experience in undertaking one form of mapping transferable to the initiation of other types of maps in the future, and (6) to make the skills and knowledge that the participants gain from the experience transferable to other aspects of their lives.

Key Practice Concepts

The foundation of mapping can be traced to many different sources. Within the field of social work, however, the primary, and most significant influence, is probably the studies conducted in the area of social support and social networks during the 1970s and 1980s (Baker, 1977; Collins & Pancoast, 1976; Gottlieb, 1981, 1983, 1988; Maguire, 1991; Whittaker & Garbarino, 1983). The research pioneered during that period established the foundation for mapping during the 1990s.

However, as conceptualized in this book, mapping has added a different dimension to the work of the previous decades. Earlier research focused on individuals and their social support systems and networks. Capacity enhancement brings in the dimension of structures. These structures must be examined within the context in which they appear and are not tied to any particular individual or family.

Key Practice Challenges

Mapping, like every other phase of the framework, is not without its challenges. The key challenge is the need to be specific about the extent of details that will be represented on the maps. It is essential for practitioners, and the residents who work with them not to attempt to convey a tremendous amount of information on the maps because doing so may overwhelm not only the individuals who are doing the actual mapping, but the audiences the maps are intended to influence.

As was noted earlier, it is not unusual to have multiple maps, each representing an important dimension or type of data. For example, it is possible to develop two maps related to murals—one showing the location of current murals and the other indicating possible sites for murals. The same approach can apply to gardens, playgrounds, and sculptures. With sufficient funding, two sets of transparencies can be developed—the first utilizing four, with each representing one type of project, such as murals, and the second representing potential sites for projects.

Mapping can be made much more "sophisticated" by devising codes for various types of gardens, murals, playgrounds, or sculptures placing the symbol for a type of project on the map with a corresponding code to indicate the characteristics of the project, such as size of a mural, the themes represented, and the importance of the location. In short, mapping provides sufficient flexibility to allow a community to dictate how complex it needs to be to accomplish its goals.

Case Illustrations

Unlike the other phases of the framework, in which multiple cases were used to illustrate important principles, techniques, and issues, this chapter presents only one case illustration. The author was able to find only one case involving the mapping of a community as conceptualized in this book— meaning that it addressed not just institutional or residents' assets, but murals, gardens, playgrounds, and sculptures.

The practice of mapping has not enjoyed widespread appeal or use in the field. Nevertheless, this case example does a wonderful job of illustrating how mapping, both as a technique and an analytical tool, has tremendous potential for community capacity enhancement. It also illustrates the numerous challenges that practitioners face in trying to meet the needs of all the key stakeholders.

The case example, of Boyle Heights, Los Angeles, represents the collaborative work of four organizations (the Getty Research Institute for the History of Art and Humanities, the Los Angeles Public Library, Roosevelt High School, and California State Polytechnic University). Boyle Heights is located east of downtown Los Angeles. The community is predominantly Latino, with Mexican Americans the largest subgroup.

The Boyle Heights case example incorporates a multitude of dimensions, including key nontraditional settings, such as churches; community-decided key institutions, such as the social security office, police station, and the National Hispanic Vietnam Memorial (which has not yet opened); playgrounds; parks; and murals. The mapping project resulted not only in a "map" of the community, but in a mural depicting the location of these "markers" (*Community Mapping*, 1996).

However, once the artist created the map, he was unsuccessful in getting the youths in the community to accept the final product. Nevertheless, this case example illustrates both the potential and challenges associated with undertaking a community capacity-enhancement project. This mapping project started with a premise that would resonate with any social worker undertaking community-based practice:

> The starting point for this endeavor is the knowledge that the perspective of the city as viewed from the streets of city neighborhoods is an often undervalued yet very important part of a complete understanding of the urban fabric. Local narratives—histories, contemporary impressions, visions of the future—reflect the neighborhoods that are not visible to the outsider. These unwritten stories, however, serve to bring neighborhoods and [the] city at large together as similar experiences are shared and validated. Using a youth's vision of the neighborhood as a starting place, this project affirms the street-level perspective on life, family, and community. (*Community Mapping*, 1996, p. 2)

Mapping is not possible or advisable unless the participants are adequately prepared for the actual experience through some form of in-service training. The Boyle Heights project did just that by offering the participants, in this case high school students, a four-part workshop (*Community Mapping*, 1996, p. 3):

> (1) Interweaving histories—participants were exposed to commentaries and historical lectures on the community from a variety of ethnic and racial perspectives; (2) Mapping workshop—the first part required students to walk through the community and discuss key landmarks and other important aspects of life in the community. In the afternoon, they came back together and shared their impressions and transferred them onto a "mental map"; (3) Artists workshop—students worked with a local muralist and poet in their effort to create an artistic rendition (collective and individual poems), and a mural representative of Boyle Heights; and (4) students created a web site incorporating their maps, poetry, and art projects, along with their personal statements and observations.

The Boyle Heights mapping project resulted in the creation of a mural of the community that highlighted the key institutions and sites within various quadrants of the community. The map was much more than a map of key streets and organizations. It was also a mural that sought to capture the community's history and pride and hoped to serve as a force for unifying the residents through a collective vision of their neighborhood.

However, as was already noted, the mural was never placed in a prominent place in the community. The artist who was responsible for putting together the themes raised by the youths had a great deal of difficulty pleasing the youths. The youths took great issue with the manner in which the mural took shape. As the result, the mural currently hangs in one of the classrooms of Roosevelt High School.

Key Practice Skills

As was noted in previous chapters, the importance of mapping and the ease with which it can be practiced make this phase both interesting and fun for the practitioner. The Boyle Heights mapping project resulted in a number of lessons for practitioners who may want to use this technique in their interventions. The main lesson is that participation and support are clearly of great importance if maximum benefits are to be achieved for the participants, community, and funding agencies.

The creation of a vehicle, in this case a mapping project, for creating and channeling residents' visions is both possible and necessary for any form of empowerment to occur. Collaborations, too, are essential elements in the creation of a map with meaning for a community. The mapping experience, when placed within a collaborative context, results in networking that will prove useful to a community after a project is completed. Community institutions, such as libraries and schools, also benefit from the experience. Consequently, a properly executed map results in a "win-win," situation for all parties, but more notably for the community.

The analytical aspects of mapping, in turn, give the participants an opportunity to expand their cognitive abilities in pursuit of common goals for the community. These skills, however, can easily find outlets in other pursuits, individual or community focused. Developing an appreciation of a community's assets and finding a vehicle to showcase them to the outside world are powerful achievements for a community, particularly those who live in the constant shadow of negative media attention.

One of the key practice challenges is to create opportunities for a community to highlight their strengths to the outside world. Strategic involvement of the visual and print media in presenting the results of a mapping project can play an important role in creating the necessary political support for an intervention project, such as the ones recommended in this book, although many other possibilities exist. Furthermore, support for an intervention in the community can also be achieved by bringing together groups that would normally not work together.

Conclusion

The potential of mapping within community social work has not been fully explored or exploited. Mapping is sufficiently important for it to be both a means to an end and an end in itself. It can serve as an empowerment tool and analytical approach to obtain a better understanding of a community, particularly a community that has historically been viewed from a deficit perspective.

Mapping is a sufficiently flexible tool to accommodate numerous community-focused goals, ranging from gaining widespread community participation to serving as a public relations tool to communicate with the outside world. It takes on even greater importance when it is used from an assets perspective.

10

Application of the Framework to Practice: Engagement

The importance of gaining the cooperation and investment of the parties who will ultimately benefit from an intervention should never be minimized. The principles that guide practitioners in this area have a long and distinguished history in the social work profession. Community participation forms the cornerstone of capacity enhancement and thus warrants extraspecial attention and scrutiny. This chapter examines the role this phase plays within a community-intervention framework.

Description of the Phase

As was noted in Chapter 4, engagement is sufficiently important both to warrant its own phase and to play an integral role throughout all phases of an intervention. Engagement refers to the sociopolitical process of developing relationships, eliciting commitments from community residents, and helping to ensure a harmonious working agreement between all significant parties.

The engagement phase, however, must be conceptualized as starting with the assessment phase to ensure that necessary information is gathered and contacts are made; thus, relationship building commences way before the actual engagement phase "officially" starts. The engagement phase further reinforces the work that was accomplished earlier and helps the practitioner focus on the importance of the task at hand—namely, to get the community committed to the project and work out an understanding between all parties. Thus, the process of engagement is critical to the ultimate success of any community capacity-enhancement effort. It takes on added significance when it involves population groups that have historically been ignored in setting agendas for change.

Goals

The goals of the engagement phase are simple, but highly labor intensive: (1) to establish a working relationship based on mutual trust and respect, (2) to bring together all significant groups to achieve a common purpose, and (3) to obtain the community's commitment to undertake a project. These three goals are interrelated and will set the foundation for a project and its eventual success.

Key Practice Concepts

The foundation of engagement within a community practice framework requires that the residents and practitioner both respect and trust each other. In the field of community social work, the interactional aspects of intervention clearly stand out (Googins et al., 1983; Hardcastle et al., 1997). Community capacity enhancement relies heavily on mutual trust and respect, concepts that are certainly not alien to social workers, regardless of their method of practice.

However, capacity-enhancement practice adds a slightly different dimension by emphasizing the skills and abilities of community residents. This emphasis, in turn, requires the practitioner to develop the necessary skills and patience to help residents identify their abilities (Kretzmann & Mc-Knight, 1993, 1996a). On the surface, this may appear to be an easy goal for a practitioner, thus facilitating the engagement process. In actuality, however, engagement is not possible unless the residents truly believe they have capacities.

Many residents of undervalued groups have historically been told that they do not have abilities and that the knowledge that they do possess is of little value in this society. Consequently, a process that actively seeks to engage them in the design of interventions, telling their stories, and seeking change rests on restoring their beliefs that they are, in fact, capable. This process is labor intensive but critical to the engagement process and phase.

Key Practice Challenges

As was already indicated, engagement as an activity is labor intensive, particularly when it involves working with community residents who deeply distrust social workers—many times for good reasons. Thus, there is no shortcut to achieving all the goals associated with engagement. If a social worker does not have the time or inclination to invest time and energy in engagement, the projects that result from the intervention may be of limited or no success. Consequently, one of the greatest challenges is to find the will and time to engage the residents.

In communities that consist of groups from disparate backgrounds (culture, language, and circumstances pertaining to how they entered the country), practitioners will have the challenge of how to develop communication bridges between them and all the groups. They may have to address potential distrust among the various groups as well.

Case Illustrations

Six case studies were selected to illustrate the process of engagement. These cases reflect a variety of approaches, ranging from those that are not labor intensive, based on one-to-one engagement of neighbors, to more "systematic" systematic efforts initiated by providers. These cases took place in New Orleans; Chicago (two cases); Minneapolis, Minnesota; Los Angeles; and San Diego, California. The Minneapolis, New Orleans, Los Angeles, and San Diego cases are also addressed in Chapter 11.

The first case example, of the creation of a community garden in New Orleans, was simple in approach, but relied on many key factors that are often overlooked—namely, the importance of a resident taking control over her environment and in so doing, setting an example for others.

> When Edith moved to Lafitte [a New Orleans housing development] from Baton Rouge in 1980, she found that in the project, cleanliness was not next to godliness, it was next to impossible. Few residents seemed to take pride in the property surrounding their low-income units, she says. And Edith understood why. As public housing tenants, they felt no sense of ownership in their apartments or small yards and thus no urge to beautify them. The government's inability to maintain the area added to this sense of disenfranchisement. One sad result of this neighborhood indifference was that criminals felt right at home. The unkept lawns, sidewalks, and streets provided fertile territory for conducting gang business. (Fifer & Fifer, 1994, pp. 46–47)

These conditions prompted Edith to start a garden of her own as an effort to beautify her area. Two neighbors, inspired by Edith's garden, decided to plant gardens of their own. After several years of being productive in growing flowers and shrubs, they decided to expand their gardening project to involve other neighbors. Their "pitch," so to speak, went as follows:

> "We needed to get across that it's important to keep things up where you live, whether it's in the projects or someplace else." . . . Neighbors were recruited with a sales pitch as soft as rose petals. "I know you're renting," Edith would say. "But nothing's impossible. All you have to do is make up your mind to try to change things." As proof she could point to the three mini-Edens on the block. Soon club membership totaled one dozen—all women, as it happened—and Galvez Street took on a very different look." (Fiffer & Fiffer, 1994, p. 48)

The process of engagement used by Edith and her neighbors was slow, methodological, and clearly based on the importance of being examples for their neighbors. The project grew to involve twelve homes and thus was not large by many standards. However, this initiative (the Lafitte Garden and Beautification Club), as it is noted in Chapter 11, resulted in many gains for the community that went beyond beautification.

The painting of a mural is virtually impossible without a community being involved in all facets of the project, including the actual painting itself. The concept of town meeting has been applied to the interchange that takes place during the painting phase and highlights the important role a community places on open dialogue. This engagement of community residents is greatly facilitated when the artist who leads the painting actively welcomes interaction and comments and is willing to modify the design so the mural better reflects the community in which it is located. The second case example, the mural of Gallery Gill Park: Friends of the Park (see Photograph 10.1) in Chicago, reflects many themes of matriarchy and the important role women play in the neighborhood.

Lakes's (1996, pp. 79–80) vivid description of the dialog between the artist and community residents brings to the foreground the dynamic nature of this form of community capacity-enhancement project:

> At the site of one mural in the Uptown neighborhood on Chicago's near-Northside, artist Turbado Marabou recounted these aspects of a "town meeting" during the two weeks it took his crew of six local teens and one artist's assistant to complete their wall project, titled "Living Off the Waters of Creation." Young kids came by and asked to paint (they were given

Figure 10.1. "Matriarchy for a New Millennium." Gallery Gill Park: Friends of the Park 1997 Neighborhood Program. Lead Artists: Bea Santiago Muñoz and Tim Potlock with Youth Team. Chicago Public Art Group, Gallery 37, and the Gill Park Council.

a very small brush). People from nearby apartment buildings look out their windows periodically to view the progress. An orange-robed Hindu swami who lived nearby was a colorful pedestrian, and his likeness was incorporated into the mural design. The prostitutes, alcoholics, and drug dealers who frequented that street corner where the mural was placed moved to the opposite side of the street during its execution. A spray-artist stopped by to assess the quality of workmanship, and Turbado let him "hang with the situation." An older street artist who frequented the worksite was named in the mural's credit box out of respect for his seniority among graffiti writers. Numerous people came by to speak to Turbado and ask questions of him and his helpers, monitoring the situation as it progressed, perhaps claiming they didn't understand the meaning of the mural, or simply thanking the artist for helping to beautify the community. Mr. Imagination (a.k.a. Gregory Warmack), a nationally known self-taught Chicago artist, was on the street viewing the completed murals as well.

Lakes's description illustrates how a mural takes on the personality and themes of the community and provides multiple avenues for getting the community involved. It also stands as a testament to the important role an artist can and should play in creating a mural.

The third case example, also from Chicago, illustrates another way of engaging a community during the mural painting process:

Photographs were used of people who walked by Fellowship House so that the faces on the mural are actual people who live, work and play in our neighborhood. These photographs were used to paint larger scale drawings on the front of the building. (Gallery 37, 1997b, p. 2)

The fourth case example, of the Garden Angels in Los Angeles (see Chapter 11 for a more detailed description of the project), shows how the process of engagement can be carried out in a one-to-one manner with great results. The garden, as illustrated in photograph 10.2, is so impressive in its size and diversity of vegetation that it is difficult to believe that it is located in a major urban area.

The garden was made possible through creative fundraising from the private sector; the community was reluctant to apply for governmental funds because of the amount of paperwork involved and the fear that the conditions imposed by the funders would comprise the project. However, involvement of the residents was critical to the entire project. As (Fiffer and Fiffer (1994, p. 111) stated:

Having achieved support from the public and private sectors . . . the urban garden was taking shape. One ingredient was still missing, however: the urban gardeners. The target group included those residing in the south central, south, and Pico-Union neighborhoods, a largely African American and Latino population. The food bank designed leaflets in English and Spanish, which the loyal foot soldiers of the Conservation Corps distributed

Figure 10.2. "Garden Angel." The Los Angeles Regional Foodbank Urban Garden. Doris Bloch, Executive Director.

throughout the neighborhood. Special outreach was made to local block clubs, high schools, and community organizations. One might think that the offer of seeds, supplies, and the fruit of the harvest would result in a land rush, but says Doris [founder of the community garden], "The response was lukewarm. Why? The people thought we were trying to sell them something. They couldn't believe everything was free and they could keep or sell everything they grew. Some thought that land here was 'only for Americans.' I had to keep stressing that the land belonged to them for as long as the city would let us use it."

Although much effort was devoted to engaging the community during this phase, success was limited and reflects the need to conceptualize engagement over an extended period as Bloch (1998, p. 1) noted:

[I] decided to dedicate the garden to the community even though not many had signed up [the ceremony occurred during the second day of the Rodney King verdict] . . . . Many families began asking for plots after that dedication ceremony.

The residents' different ethnic backgrounds and documented status influenced their perspectives on the garden. Outreach, which included contacts with individual residents in their native languages, played an important role in the engagement process and continued even after the garden was dedicated.

The fifth case example, of Chicano Park (San Diego), involved the engagement of what one community organizer called "hard dudes" in the painting of murals. It shows that with the "right" approach, even individuals with "hard-to-reach" labels can be actively engaged in various kinds of community work. As Fisher (1998, p. 12) reported:

> On still another level, the painters of the mural, Victor Ochoa and Raul Jaquez, recruited a number of what Ochoa called the "hard dudes" who hung around the park to assist in the mural painting project. Ochoa had been working with these "hard dudes" and was successful in organizing them into a collective called the Barrio Renovation Team, whose goal was to repair and repaint houses of the community's elderly and impoverished residents. With city funding, the team increased its numbers and continued its work in Barrio Logan and other poor sections of San Diego.

The involvement of hard dudes was essential to the mural artist because he stressed the importance of community involvement, ownership of the mural, and the need make sure that the mural would not be "tagged" after it was painted (graffiti written on it). The mural artist developed a unique way of engaging the hard dudes:

> The reputation of the artist preceded his entry into the community. This positive reputation, in turn, facilitated his entry. The artist stressed the importance of being able to speak the language of the hard dudes—their vocabulary and themes in addition to Spanish. He developed an informational slide show that was shown to the residents and talked about why murals were important to a community. The practice of "Chicano democratic dynamics" was an important dimension of the engagement process. It provided an opportunity for and encouraged the community to ask questions and provide input into the mural-painting process. In essence, the mural was the creation of the community.

Key Practice Skills

Flexibility in determining how engagement is operationalized is a key element in community capacity-enhancement projects. Time must be devoted to this phase, since engaging individuals is, without doubt, a time-consuming activity. This engagement, in turn, may necessitate that contact is made in a variety of community settings, including the homes of residents. However, as is shown in Figure 10.3, of the opening of the Coxsackie Playground, the joys and benefits of involving residents can rarely be captured by words.

The fifth case example, of a community-build playground in Coxsackie, New York (near Buffalo), highlights the need for the leaders of a project to be from the community and the importance of involving children:

> The playground idea originated from the desire of a local parent to deal with numerous concerns about the quality of life, most notably the lack of connectedness, in the community. This motivation, combined with the de-

Figure 10.3. "Coxsackie Playground Grand Opening." Coxsackie, New York. Photo credit: Bruce Whiting.

sire of one of the playground's leaders to replicate the experiences associated with community connectedness in his birthplace in Massachusetts, led to the creation of the community playground. Bruce Witting convinced another colleague (a fellow member of the Rotary Club) to colead the effort. Their key positions in the community, combined with their persuasive powers, facilitated the engagement of the other residents.

The process of engaging elementary-age children is also well illustrated in the Coxsackie playground case (Coxsackie Community Playground, 1998; Limer, 1998 Vernol, 1997). The engagement process consisted of a two-pronged approach during the design stage of the project: classroom participation and the establishment of a steering committee. Classroom participation was labor intensive for one day. As Vernol (1997, pp. 1A, 9A) reported:

> The Committee also enlisted the help of students at Coxsackie Elementary who spent the morning providing Hayes [the architect] with what they would like to see as part of the playground. Hayes began by drawing an aerial view of the playground design incorporating the ideas the children gave her. [The architect spent fifteen minutes with each class to gather the children's ideas.] Later in the day, representatives from each class gathered in the library to help Hayes design some of the individual items to be included in the playground design. These items included a pirate ship, a castle, a treehouse, and a haunted house. The students divided into groups to draw the items as they saw them in their minds and the drawings were then given to Hayes who went back to the drawing board to work on the final design . . . . Although some of the ideas like virtual reality, water slides, an arcade and a bungee cord didn't make it into the final drawing, Hayes said that most of the ideas were used.

That evening, the plans were unveiled at a public meeting at which over two hundred adults and children were present. There are many advantages to making the presentation quickly. However, reinforcing the children's hard work and initiating a big event to start the process clearly stand out.

The creation of a children's committee also served as a valuable engagement mechanism:

> To encourage enthusiasm and involvement, each classroom in the Coxsackie Elementary School has at least one child who serves on the Children's Committee. These children have been hard at work over the past year keeping their fellow classmates informed about the progress of the playground. They have also been busy writing and coloring individual thank you notes for playground donors. (Coxsackie Community Playground, 1998, p. 2)

As this case example illustrates, engagement of the community must never be restricted to any one group, regardless of age or any other characteristic. Children can and must play significant roles in projects directed toward them. The development of a playground is an excellent mechanism for enlisting the support of children and enhancing their capacities in the process. It must not be forgotten that children are destined to play influential roles in the future of their communities, and there is no better way to help them do so than to involve them in building their communities.

South Minneapolis was the setting of the sixth case illustration, which involved a park, a mural, and a sculpture. This community has been the setting for numerous capacity-enhancement projects, such as murals. The mural entitled "We Claim Our Lives," for example (see Photograph 10.4) gave youths an opportunity to express how they see their community and their future within it. Simply, meaningful involvement equates with engagement.

Figure 10.4. "We Claim Ourselves." Painted by the Youth Team of the Neighborhood Safe Art Project. Marilyn Lindstrom, Executive Director.

These community capacity-enhancement projects, however, could not have been possible without residents playing a leadership role. They were undertaken by an organization, Neighborhood Safe Art Spot, established by a community resident (Marilyn Linstrom), who initiated the projects in collaboration with a neighborhood youth.

> Marilyn Linstrom is a muralist by profession and has studied and painted murals internationally and nationally. She lived in a community near the Phillips neighborhood. The Phillips neighborhood is primarily low income, highly diverse ethnically and racially (it has the highest concentration of Native Americans living in an urban area in the United States), and has an image as an "unsafe" area in Minneapolis. In her capacity as cochair of a block club, Ms. Linstrom attended a community crime prevention presentation during which the speaker challenged the participants to get involved and to use their creative talents to help the community. Ms. Linstrom, although a muralist, had never painted at the local community level, and she decided to do so. She enlisted the help of a teenager who was her next-door neighbor. This teenager knew the community well and agreed to help.

The combination of two residents working together, with one of whom is of color and an adolescent, made the process of engaging other youths much easier. Furthermore, it demonstrates the power that residents command in the engagement phase and the importance of working with them in capacity enhancement.

Conclusion

Engagement, as highlighted in this chapter, serves many important roles in a community capacity-enhancement initiative. This phase, however, can prove to be extremely labor intensive, and its duration can be highly unpredictable. Nevertheless, practitioners must be prepared to take as long as necessary if they hope to have their projects succeed.

Most practitioners are aware that relationships based on mutual trust and respect take time to develop. However, sometimes because of funding pressures, they invariably tend to rush an intervention by getting a community to "sign off" quickly without having done the necessary preparatory work of getting their input. Such efforts at engagement are superficial and may foster resentment among community residents.

11

Application of the Framework to Practice: Intervention

It may seem like a lifetime before a practitioner gets to design and implement an intervention. If she or he has invested the necessary time and energy in the previous phases of the framework, then the intervention phase will prove relatively easy to carry out. Since this phase is probably the most concrete of all the phases, it is the easiest for the community to visualize.

Nevertheless, this phase is not without its share of challenges to go with the rewards. Depending on the project, it may take years before a community can realize the benefits of its hard work. Practitioners must be clear that intervention is much more than a finished product; it must also seek to enhance residents' skills in the process.

Description of the Phase

The intervention phase is often categorized as the "bottom line" for most social agencies. It represents the ultimate benefits of much hard work and preparation, as evidenced during the initial three phases. Funders are generally interested only in what actually transpired, rather than the circumstances leading to the intervention. Consequently, it is not unusual for practitioners to emphasize this phase over all the others. Nevertheless, this phase is not possible without serious considerations and efforts in all the previous phases.

The nature of intervention (goals, type of project, target group, complexity, extent of resource allocation, and time) is greatly dependent on local circumstances. Practitioners, as a result, must always be prepared to modify the intervention to take into account local issues and priorities.

Goals

Although the specific goals of any community capacity-enhancement intervention will vary from community to community, these types of projects must address at least four central goals: (1) to make physical changes in the environment; (2) to enhance the experiences and qualifications of the participants; (3) to result in collaborations that have the potential for involving sectors not normally involved in partnerships with each other; and (4) to serve as a foundation for future and, it is hoped, more ambitious community capacity-enhancement initiatives. In essence, community capacity-enhancement initiatives must clearly stress both current and future gains for a community, in addition to the achievement of physical changes in the immediate environment.

If a community's capacities are to be enhanced, interventions must stress community ownership and participation throughout all aspects according to Jason (1997, pp. 89–90),

> Community input, community ownership, and community effort are all required if an intervention is to have long-term success. Too many communities have been purely subjects of intervention, rather than their co-creators. Too often the positive effects of these interventions have faded with the withdrawal of professional attention. A truly effective intervention creates a self-sustaining initiative that will nurture community health and progress long after the intervention is complete.

Key Practice Concepts

The process of working together to assist oneself and others creates or enhances a sense of purpose and community for residents. Thus, community capacity-enhancement interventions must foster this cooperation and exchange. They are not possible without the use of a variety of practice concepts: (1) cultural competence, (2) collaboration, (3) participation, (4) empowerment, (5) being community based, (6) open spaces.

These key concepts ground the practitioner in a practice stance that not only encourages the participation of community residents, but insists upon it. For participation to be meaningful, it must take into account local circumstances and be based on the residents' experiences with previous efforts. In short, practitioners must be aware of historical events and the backgrounds of the residents to determine what "participation" means to them and how to maximize it.

Key Practice Challenges

A primary challenge that practitioners face is how to translate a well-laid-out plan into reality. As a result, implementation will no doubt require considerable flexibility by all the parties involved and necessitate minor, or even major, modifications, to bring a community capacity-enhancement project to life. Although a proper assessment should minimize any major surprises for community practitioners, changes in the project are inevitable.

The development of collaborations, although a much talked-about goal and desired in the field of practice, is never an easy task for any practitioner, regardless of his or her experience. This goal, in turn, presents a series of challenges when collaboration is sought between entities that have not worked together in the past. The practitioner, to be successful, must learn a new language and mindset (that of the organization he or she hopes to involve), in addition to confronting a whole set of stereotypes about social workers. Consequently, collaboration, although highly important in community capacity-enhancement work, takes on new meaning in this form of work.

Case Illustrations

This chapter examines a variety of community capacity-enhancement interventions in nine cities (Atlanta, Craige, Chicago, Holyoke, Minneapolis, New Orleans, New York, Philadelphia, and San Diego), ten states (Alaska, California, Georgia, Illinois, Louisiana, Massachusetts, Minnesota, New York, Pennsylvania, and Wisconsin), and two foreign countries (Canada and Israel) that involved murals, gardens, playgrounds, and sculptures. The initiatives addressed in this chapter highlight the potential for various types of interventions.

As was noted in the introduction to Section 3, the case example of San Diego's Chicano Park receives a disproportionate amount of detail and attention in this chapter. In addition, every effort was made to highlight cases in which a community initiated more than one type of capacity-enhancement project as a means of illustrating how the potential of these projects is enhanced when there are multiple projects.

Murals and Other Public Art

The assessment of murals must be able to capture important information from a variety of perspectives, as noted in Chapter 6. At a minimum, practitioners must take into consideration the location of and the themes addressed in a mural. As was already noted, a mural does not have to involve many residents, although ideally it should. However, the themes addressed in the mural provide a window into the major concerns, fears, and hopes of a community. The following case, based in New York City, is an example of how violence is perceived and its impact on a community:

> Respect is why the mural is there in the first place [East New York]. It shows a white jeep breaking through the brick, with an inscription reading MEMORIES OF DIAMON-D, a friend's brother who was shot dead during a Christmas week holdup inside the bodega [grocery store]. Taken away by someone with no respect for life, Diamon-D lives on in this grim patch of

Brooklyn thanks to the respect of his friends. Above the mural, a billboard for the latest Friday the 13th movie screams out JASON GOES TO HELL in fiery letters, as if the make-believe mayhem could ever compete with the neighborhood's commonplace horror. Along Brooklyn's bloodiest blocks—last year there was the equivalent of a murder every third day—death doesn't wear a grotesque hockey mask when it comes calling. It looks just like you and takes you out on the corner, in your hallway, or inside your car—anywhere, everywhere. A friend once called Angel the Grim Reaper of the block, a title that makes him visibly uncomfortable. . . . Over the past few years, Angel has painted 10 of these memorial walls, curbside shrines to lives that ended before they ever really began. Little Jimmy, hit in the head by a stray bullet. Magaly, killed by mistake during a fight over a traffic light. Frankie, shot dead in a hassle over drugs. Antonio, killed in a car crash coming home from a party. "I pick up where the cops leave off," Angel says. "I kind of got used to it. What's depressing sometimes is all the stories I hear about how good they were and never started trouble. What gets me angry is when I put up the dates and realize how young they were." (Gonzalez, 1994, p. 67)

Memorial murals often represent one of the few ways that the families and friends of victims can publicly acknowledge their existence and virtues. As Gonzalez (1994, pp. 67–68) noted:

In a city where violence in black and Latino neighborhoods has become so numbing and so routine, these stories seldom rate a mention on the evening news. Instead, names and faces peer down from memorial walls on buildings, handball courts, and school yards in silent testimony that those who once lived are still loved. But the walls, sometimes playful in spirit and other times dripping with menace, are also a visual chronicler of each beleaguered neighborhood's history. Played out block by block, the results of bad luck, bad health, or just plain badness are etched onto brick and concrete, looming as a cautionary backdrop for those who survive another day, an uneasy reminder of how chaotic city life has become. In an age when guns and anger are abundant and opportunities are not, mothers pushing strollers, the elderly trudging home, or teenagers hanging out all know with a glance that in the urban drama, death is the ultimate scene-stealer. . . . The memorial walls are the latest outburst and refinement of ghetto art springing up in Brooklyn, the Bronx, and beyond.

Although murals address many different themes, the scenes depicting the early deaths of neighborhood residents, particularly youths, boldly bring to the foreground the importance of any form of assessment noting the prevalence and the reasons for the deaths. Memorial murals, just like other murals illustrate historical themes and themes of social and economic justice, have a place in community capacity-enhancement initiatives.

There may be situations in what a mural was painted on a wall that already had a mural that was in bad condition as a result of poor upkeep. The following example involving the painting over of a women's rights mural in Chicago shows how this can be done in an affirming and respectful manner.

> The wall that we were preparing to paint had an 18 year old women's rights mural badly peeling and fading on it. We realized early on in the process of discussion that we wanted to preserve the idea of women's rights as a central theme in the new mural. During discussions with the students we brought up the issue of gender and gender differences, and this provoked very lively discussions. We realized that as a largely male group [eleven of the thirteen members], the issue of women's rights affected them through their relationship to their mothers. We talked about single motherhood and its challenges, but also about single mothers as strong, feminist women."
> (Gallery 37, 1996, p. 1)

Further discussions of other themes that had to be incorporated into the mural uncovered many major community issues. The mural's content, as a result, provided a picture of what the youths thought were the community's major concerns.

> During one of the first discussions with the students we asked how they would describe their community to someone who had never been there. The drawings that the students produced were of images of people moving out, evictions, building demolitions (a building where one of the students lived was torn down to become a parking lot for new condominiums), and of the new residents moving in oblivious to their surroundings. We decided to include some of these images as well as images that related metaphorically to the process of gentrification and displacement. We agreed that an image that represented collaboration would be included in the mural as well as the students experiences. (Gallery 37, 1996, p. 1)

After much discussion, the mural incorporated images of women carrying multiple roles as providers, nurtures, leaders, and so forth in addition to themes regarding gentrification. The mural-painting process stimulated discussion about oppression based on gender, class, and ethnicity. Murals, as highlighted throughout this book, are excellent mechanisms for increasing consciousness among participants.

The Holyoke, Massachusetts, street banners project, described in Chapter 8, consisted of a series of banners designed by youths and placed on telephone polls throughout the neighborhood (Breitbart, 1998). Community capacity-enhancement projects must address multiple goals. However, a primary goal is to focus on individuals. As Breitbart (1998, p. 323) indicated:

> "Banners for the Street" also involved a personal exploration by young people of their feelings and emotions. Though no lasting improvements were made to the built environment of South Holyoke, this project . . . underscore[s] how important even the temporary personalising of small spaces or the creation of symbolic new spaces can be for young people who live daily

amidst stress and who, perhaps more than adults, notice and suffer the effects of the absence of colour and items of interest in their environments.

Intervention not only provided the Holyoke youths with new skills and an opportunity to express their sentiments, it resulted in environmental change.

The public art and other forms of environmental intervention that resulted thus represent forms of direct action. They can provide urban youth, at least temporarily, with a means of escape, a voice in community affairs, and the reality or vision of a more pleasurable living environment. (Breitbart, 1998, p. 324)

The methods used to assess the community can also be conceptualized as enhancing participants' skills that can be used in other types of projects, while helping the participants develop new, highly critical perspectives of their community. As Breitbart (1998, pp. 331–322) reported:

The research, writing, discussion and photography work that often accompanies the art and design projects also reminds youth of the specificity of their neighbourhoods and their unique, though often intersecting, lives. Though it is common for the media to lump all low-income communities together and present them as homogeneous and problematic, the exploratory techniques employed . . . emphasized the richness and complexity of local life.

The Banners for the Street project was a form of direct, nonconfrontational action that was designed and implemented by youths. The youths sought and obtained permission to display the banners. Furthermore, public art gave them a voice in community affairs, provided adults (Latino and non-Latino alike) with a positive perspective on the youths, and brightened their environment through the use of an art form that is not expensive and within the capacities of other youths. In essence, this type of public-arts project illustrates that personal growth and change can be achieved in the process of creating environmental change.

The case study of Chicano Park in Barrio Logan in San Diego, California, represents a dimension that is rarely talked about in the professional literature, but illustrates how art, in this case a series of murals, and a park can be used as an organizing and community capacity-enhancement method. Chicano Park symbolizes the prominence, persistence, and potential of parks, murals, sculptures, and gardens to provide undervalued communities with a voice and a method for galvanizing and empowering the communities. Although the Chicano Park example can easily fit into the other types of projects addressed in this book, its fame is, arguably, due to the role that murals have played in the community; therefore, the case example is addressed in this chapter. The murals depicted in the following Figures 11.1 and 11.2 provide but a brief glimpse of the artistic talents of the residents.

Figure 11.1. "Mexico's History." Chicano Park, San Diego. Painted by Victor Ochoa and Sweetwater High MECHA.

A brief history of Chicano Park (Barrio Logan) is needed to place the role of capacity enhancement within a context (Fisher 1998). Barrio Logan is located seventeen miles from the United States–Mexican border. Since the early 1900s, it has consisted primarily of working-class Mexicans. Logan Heights has traditionally been a self-contained community, with a wide range of local-based businesses, houses of worship (primarily Catholic), and schools. In the 1950s, as a result of zoning changes, the community changed from residential to mixed use. Because of this change numerous businesses, such as junkyards, wrecking operations, and other light industrial plants, moved in. The consequences, most notably the dislocation of families and the change in environment, dramatically altered the composition of the community—a decrease from 20,000 residents in the 1940s to 5,000 in 1979. The description of the neighborhood by one of the residents (quoted in

Figure 11.2. "Cuatlicue diosa de la tierra: Goddess of Mother Earth." Chicano Park, San Diego. Lead Artist: Susan Yamagata.

Ochoa, 1997c, p. 266) places the importance of murals within a sociopolitical context:

> The Logan heights neighborhood was always real central to San Diego. It was flourishing, gaining a lot of strength locally. We had markets, doctors' offices and movie houses—all the stuff that made a community. The white power structure felt bothered by Logan Heights because it was gaining political strength and responsibility as a community, so they put a lot of effort into trying to destroy that. They designed Interstate 5 (mid-1960s) to split the residential area from the commercial area, cutting it off. It was a death blow to the community. Six thousand families had to move.

The building of the Coronado Bridge in the late 1960s further affected the community. A series of other intrusions occurred, culminating in the state's decision to build a highway patrol station and parking lot in the community after the residents were promised a park. The decision to build a patrol station was the catalyst for the community. On April 22, 1970, the community "took" the land and started its own park by planting flowers and trees:

> Since at least 1967, many residents in Barrio Logan had believed that they would be given some land for a park. On April 22, 1970, the formal struggle for a park in Barrio Logan began when Jose Gomez, a long-time resident of the neighborhood, and students, families and children occupied the land under the approach ramps of the San Diego–Coronado Bay Bridge, after they learned that a California Highway Patrol station would be built there. Between 250 and 500 people representing a wide cross-section of the community disrupted grading work that was already in progress. They occupied the site for twelve days and demanded that a park be created immediately. To emphasize their point, the occupiers began the work of creating a park by using shovels, pickaxes, hoes, and rakes to prepare the ground for the planting of grass, shrubs and flowers. (Fisher, 1998, p. 9)

The community considered the establishment of a California highway patrol station a particularly offensive act, according to Fisher (1998, p. 9):

> The establishment of a CHP station under the new bridge was viewed as an affront to Barrio Logan, a community that already had many grievances against local police actions. Further, the CHP station was of an impressive size, proposing to employ some 195 uniformed personnel and 15 civilian employees and provide parking spaces for 115 cars. "Our neighborhood had already been invaded by the junkyard, the factories and bridge had even been built through the barrio," Gomez declared. "Some of us decided that it was time to put a stop to the destruction and begin to make this place livable."

The community formed the Chicano Park Steering Committee to negotiate with the city and was successful in acquiring 4.5 acres for a park. The creation of the park proved to be an important step for the Barrio Logan community. As Fisher (1998), p. 10) noted:

> The creation of "the park" was a major defining moment in the history of the Barrio Logan community. . . . "It was the first time in a long time that the community had come back together." Victor Ochoa, mural coordinator in Chicano Park from 1974 to 1979, recalled: "What I still remember is that there were bulldozers out there. And women and children made human chains around the bulldozers to flatten it out, and they started planting napales and magueys and flowers. And there was a telephone pole there, where the Chicano flag was raised: "We can't think of Chicanos in San Diego without thinking of Chicano Park. It is the main evidence, the open book of our culture, energy and determination as a people. One of the main proofs of our existence."

One of the original organizers (quoted in Fisher, 1998, p. 19) commenting eloquently on the importance of the park:

"There was an energy that's hard to describe when you see your people struggling for something its very inspiring. We have to show our youth the value of what we did. The park was brought about by sacrifice and demonstrates what a community can do when they stick together and make it happen."

The creation of the park, including its gardens and playgrounds, inspired the community to undertake further capacity-enhancement initiatives, in which artwork took center stage. It was not until 1973 that the painting of murals on the bridge's support (pillars) commenced.

There was an ambiance about the park, however, that made it unlike any other park in San Diego or California. Notably, it was sited directly under a busy toll bridge and its six approach ramps that in 1971 alone carried more than 8 million vehicles. Music and merrymaking in the park competed with the deafening rattle of trucks and cars moving across the superstructure's floor high above park revelers. The support columns of the bridge occupied hefty portions of the park's space and gave the surreal illusion of a compacted concrete forest that contradicted the notion of an urban park being an area of open space. Shadows predominated, inspiring at once and wariness." (Fisher, 1998, p. 11)

The transformation of Chicano Park required an additional stage—namely, the use of art both to beautify and enhance the community's capacity. Murals and, to a lesser extent, sculptures have served to transform Chicano Park. The murals have been painted there every since by numerous local and invited artists and cover a variety of community-related themes, particularly those related to social and economic justice. As one participant (quoted in Ochoa, 1997c, p. 267) explained:

We didn't actually start painting anything in Chicano Park until March 1973. We've been painting murals since then on different Chicano issues, such as the farmworkers, our indigenous art history, bilingual education, immigration, police brutality, the downfall of Allende in Chile, role models of history, boycotts of Coors, Gallo and lettuce, and things going on in Latin America that we feel close to. Cuba influenced us quite a bit.

The use of pillars as backgrounds for murals was not only feasible (because the pillars had a smooth surface), but served an important symbolic function—the actual structure that disrupted the community was also going to bring the community together in search of a voice to articulate issues of social justice. These pillars, in turn, were to be transformed by murals into an "endless canvas" by leading muralists from within and outside Chicano

Park; hence, the pillars were a venue for bringing these artists together. As Ochoa, 1997b, p. 210) stated:

> One of the leading spirits of Chicano Park since its inception was Salvador Robert "Queso" Torres. . . . Beyond the question of muralized pillars, Torres has had a longstanding interest in the park as an environmental project involving its extension into the water under the bridge. . . . Pillars were painted by local and invited artists: groups came from Santa Ana, Los Angeles . . . , and Sacramento. . . . To the local artists over the years were added . . . many others. . . . Many murals were painted with the assistance of community activists and students.

The Chicano Park murals also provided the community with an opportunity to pay homage to one of the original leaders who had recently passed away:

> Laura Rodriquez (1909–1994) was the grandmother of Chicano Park, because, when we took over in 1970, she was there in front leading the takeover. I think she was a housewife, maybe a widow. She knew that we were going to be safe because the Elders were with us students and community people. After we took over the park, she would bring us food, tamales. She went on to found the Chicano Free Clinic. I did a poster of her for the 25th anniversary of Chicano Park (in April 1995). And from the poster, we made the mural as a community—all the organizations. (Torero, 1997, p. 268)

The mural, painted by two artists (Mario Torero and Carmen Kalo), depicted the following images (see Photo 11.2):

> Laura Rodriguez's brownish face, shown in the center of the mural, rests in the palms of two brownish-painted, large hands. Directly beneath her face and the arms, there is a picture of an Aztec Indian in full ceremonial attire, each hand holding a snake. Laura Rodriguez's name is painted on one of the palms with the dates 1909–1994.

Philadelphia's Peace Wall (see Figure 11.3) represents a community's response to racial incidents and tensions in one of its neighborhoods (Grays Ferry) in 1977. As Kaufman (1998, p. 24) reported:

> After last year's angry racial standoff in Gray's Ferry, Golden came up with the idea of painting a large, racially healing mural in the community. Her standard approach is to talk with the people who live nearby the proposed mural to find out what they had in mind. This time the neighbors, both black and white, kept talking about hands—not balled in a fist, but joined together, united in peace. And so the finished work is a joining of hands. There are 11 of them, the oversize hands and forearms of Grays Ferry folk, open hands of many skin colors unafraid to touch each other.

Figure 11.3. "The Peace Wall." Painted by Jane Golden and Peter Pagast, Philadelphia Mural Project. Photo credit: Jack Ramsdale.

The tracing of the images took three nights to complete, and the actual painting was completed just before Christmas 1997 (Naedele, 1998). The mural, striking in content and size (25 feet high by 45 feet wide), is located across the street from a community playground and ballfield. Much went into the design, execution, and painting of a mural of this size. As Kaufman (1998, p. 24) indicated:

> When the mural was dedicated in January, Lillian Ray, a long-time community activist, exclaimed: "If you stand and look at it for a while, you can feel the love come off the wall." To create the mural, Golden's husband . . . climbed a ladder and asked people to stand in circles beneath him while he photographed their extended arms. After Golden had come up with the design, she said "we went out after dark in the middle of October, projected the image onto the wall, and began to paint it."

Murals do not have to be exclusively a neighborhood phenomenon. In New York City, there is an active campaign to introduce artwork into the subway system. Passengers, in select stations, have the opportunity to view a work of art in media, such as glass, steel, mosaic, and murals; each station's themes reflect the history and character of the neighborhood in which the station is located. According to Dunlap (1998, p. B37)

> Artwork was integral to the design of the subway system in the early 1900's, and much of the original ceramic and mosaic ornament remains. But in

1985, the Metropolitan Transportation Authority set up the Arts for Transit program, to bring new works into the system, and it recently added some of its most stunning. . . . "All the works we do have to relate to the community: the community of riders and the community above. . . . "The Arts for Transit program adds a quality of life to the station environment that touches all of our customers."

The murals of Chicano Park have served as vehicles for the community to tell its stories to the outside world and could not have been possible without community support.

The development of Chicano Park and its murals is an ongoing process ("a work in progress . . . "). Moreover, the murals serve as a reminder to people in the community that they can change their environment. . . ." The community needs the murals to speak up on certain issues" . . . "murals are illustrated sentiments" designed to overcome the limitations of physical conditions and non-literacy. Since 1973, the murals have become the icons they depict. Their maintenance involves the city, the people of the barrio and especially the artists who are continuing their work on the pillars of the bridge. The murals that adorn the columns of the San Diego–Coronado Bay Bridge have received widespread recognition by scholars and city officials and have become a tourist stopping point in San Diego. (Fisher, 1998, p. 13)

Thus, the importance of public art makes it a popular vehicle for addressing community needs. The Arts for Transit program in New York City relies on the work of established artists, but community input is sought and valued in determining the themes of the artwork. Although not as powerful as community capacity enhancement as conceptualized in this book, this program, nevertheless, highlights the role that art can play in a community's life.

An international perspective on murals and the role that they can play in revealing neighborhood tensions, is well represented in the case of Jerusalem. The goals of the mural were noble and inspirational, as Bronner (1998, p. A10) noted:

It was a noble plan: Three peace-loving artists from conflicting backgrounds—an Israeli Jew, an Israeli Arab and a Palestinian—would produce a mural depicting a future without fear, a symbolic guide to trying to live together in this disputed land. But the process proved far more tortured than any of them imagined, a microcosm of mistrust and betrayal that mirrored the hostilities they had set out to overcome.

However, the painting of the mural, although commendable, cannot be separated from the context in which it is painted. The community, or in this case, the three groups representative of their communities, could not escape the tensions among the three groups. As Bronner (1998, p. A10) reported:

The Jewish artist, with approval of the others, had painted in an ethereal angelic figure to represent his people. But after the mural was unveiled, the

Palestinian stunned his Jewish colleague by describing the figure to the audience as a devil that only looked like an angel, "like the Israelis themselves." The Jewish artist felt betrayed. The Palestinian, for his part, was furious at what he saw as an attempt to make Jews the heroes of the story. On a personal level, in private, the men forged a bond, made each other laugh and shared a deep mutual respect. And the artists' determination to pursue further work together provides reason for hope. But burdened by history and communal expectations, their mural became a battleground of symbols.

Many lessons were learned from this experience that will no doubt influence future collaborative projects of this type.

Looking back, the artists have concluded that despite the tension, there was still a remarkable peace to the enterprise. They have just secured Norwegian grant to document the making of the mural and plan to collaborate next on a huge mosaic of children's images to be placed, they hope, on a future Israeli-Palestinian border. "This was a stage that you have to go through. . . . There is hatred and stigma on all sides, but that is the only hope of getting beyond them. It's going to have to happen for everyone here. There is no other choice." (Bronner, 1998, p. A10)

Consequently, the goal of fostering dialogue between different groups in the community is never easy. However, the use of a mural as a mechanism for achieving this goal is not unique to the Jerusalem example. The painting of a mural cannot be divorced from the reality of life in a community. Nevertheless, it can serve as a capacity-enhancement project that can foster the development of relationships.

The example of finding alternatives to graffiti draws attention to the role that community capacity enhancement can play in this arena. There is probably no art form that is more closely associated with urban areas than graffiti. Graffiti painting is often considered a blight on a community and is the result of adolescents and young adults searching for recognition. The lack of positive alternatives for these artists has been cited as one of the primary reasons for an outbreak of graffiti, or what is commonly referred to as "graffiti wars."

The removal of graffiti has been estimated to cost governments more than $7 billion dollars a year. The following breakdown of the costs of several major urban areas highlights this point: Los Angeles school system, $10 million; New York City Transit Authority, $10 million; Seattle, $2 million; City of San Jose, $1.2 million; Philadelphia school system, $1.2 million; Phoenix, $750,000 (Boyle, 1998). The cost of removal, combined with the constant struggle to apprehend and punish the perpetrators, has resulted in clashes among authorities, artists, and communities.

The development of projects to identify and involve artists has started to gain national attention because these initiatives cost a lot less than the removal of graffiti. The following case example, based in New York City, was selected because it involved many of the elements found in the more progressive approaches and entailed a resident development of the project (Phun Phactory). The example also illustrates many of the elements associated with community capacity enhancement. As Boyle (1988, pp. 50–51) reported:

> "Some of them stop tagging, some of them don't," says DeLillo as he sits in a graffiti-adorned minibus that serves as the Phactory's official vehicle. "This isn't a criminal justice program. It's an art program." Ironically, DeLillo began his activism by trying to wipe out that art. Recovering from back surgery in 1992, he got a good look at the aesthetic condition of his neighborhood. He didn't like it, and launched Graffiti Terminators—a group of community residents and work-release inmates who set out to buff [clean off or paint over graffiti]. To his surprise, DeLillo admired some of the artwork he saw. So he went looking for a place where graffiti artists could work legally. "They're good kids. They just have nothing to do," he says. "Why can't we give these kids an outlet?" Jerry Wolkoff let DeLillo invite artists to paint the outside walls of his Long Island City [Queens, New York] warehouse. Several neighborhood business owners volunteer their walls also. "You'd probably have regular graffiti" anyway, says Stu Ehrenberg, who runs a Phactory-decorated auto repair shop. This way, he says, "you really have some beautiful artwork. It helps to improve the whole environment of the neighborhood."

The Phun Phactory project is attractive to local graffiti artists because of its philosophy and its willingness to allow works of art to stay a considered period. As Boyle (1998, p. 51) noted:

> DeLillo is an in-your-face New Yorker. Among his written rules: "Pat is in charge." No gang art. No tagging in the surrounding neighborhood, or "your piece gets buffed!" Artists must show designs on paper before beginning a work. They get a permit for a section of the wall. Works usually stay up for about three months. The relatively lengthy lifespan of the artwork is a major plus to doing a piece here rather than on a school wall. Another plus, says a veteran writer named "Dono," is camaraderie, and learning from other writers.

Initiatives, such as the one typified by Phun Phactory, can address multiple goals in an urban community. In addition to beautifying areas that are considered unattractive, they also provide avenues for young artists to engage in their art without breaking the law. Communities, in turn, experience a dramatic drop in graffiti, and the negative measure that such artworks convey to the external work, considerably decreases.

The mural projects used to illustrate practice strategies, principles, and methods, provide the reader with a variety of examples of how public-art projects, such as murals, can play a role in helping marginalized communities both obtain a voice, and serve as a vehicle for enhancing capacity.

Community Gardens

Community gardens make excellent community capacity-enhancement projects by providing social workers and other helping professionals with a vehicle for involving residents in shaping and changing the landscape of their community (Hinkle, 1997). These projects, as was noted earlier, not only change their environments but generate much-needed food for the residents.

The following two case illustrations of community gardening projects in Madison, Wisconsin, and Atlanta, Georgia, present a view of the multiplicity of goals that can be achieved by using community gardens as community capacity-enhancement interventions. Both projects utilized broad-based coalitions of groups in addressing their primary objectives. The Madison example focuses on the acquisition of land (the most critical element of community gardening) and the generation of revenue-generating activities (Holmes, 1997).

The Atlanta example, highlights how a partnership among various organizations can teach gardening skills to public housing residents, cut the cost of food, and encourage community residents' participation in other dimensions of their lives (Puckett, 1995).

> The Madison project consisted of a collaboration among neighborhood groups, residents, and state officials (the Troy Gardens Coalition). This coalition was extremely successful in preventing the state from selling to developers 35 acres of garden and green space. Approximately 15 acres of this land has been devoted to gardens (1,523 plots in 18 community gardens), cultivated by approximately 1,100 families, many of whom were low income and newcomers. The coalition has taken the additional step of planning to build affordable housing as an income-generating activity. These funds will be used to help purchase the land, which was leased to the coalition by the state, over an extended period. The coalition was successful in stemming the trend of outside developers building in the community.

The Atlanta Project example brought together the community; the Atlanta Urban Gardening Program, an organization focused on teaching gardening skills to public housing residents; and Hands on Atlanta, an organization that recruited and placed volunteers in programs.

> The partnership was called the Urban Garden Alliance and facilitated the expansion of ten public housing projects. The gardening project emphasized teaching youths and adults about gardening and, in so doing, helped the residents cut their food budgets, increased nutritional intake, and served as a vehicle for involving residents in their housing developments. In addition to beautifying the community, the gardens used space that had attracted criminal activity.

Community gardens provide a wide range of flexibility concerning their size, goals, and potential impact on a community. The example of the Lafitte

Garden and Beautification Club in New Orleans, discussed in Chapter 8, is a case in point. Although the club never grew larger than twelve members, its influence far exceeded what could reasonably be expected by that number. As Fiffer and Fiffer (1994, pp. 48–49) indicated:

> Tending their gardens, club members tended to see more of what was happening on the streets than their neighbors. Aware that the projects were a ripe place for crime, Edith frequently flagged down police cars, introduce herself, and expressed concerns about the drug dealing and other illicit activity. Eventually she and other club members sought to beautify the neighborhood not only by adding gardens but by subtracting criminals. They formed a Neighborhood Watch group, which meets regularly with the police and monitors and reports serious behavior in the area. Such behavior has decreased significantly in recent years. . . . "They may be criminals, but they still respect us for what we're doing in keeping up the neighborhood." . . . In recent years the club has expanded its efforts to make life more beautiful for those in the projects by playing Santa to needy children and providing food baskets to senior citizens.

The case of a community garden in the Roxbury section of Boston illustrates the importance of having youths develop a greater awareness of social problems and how best to address them through the use of gardening:

> If growing awareness in children is one way to tackle racism, hunger, and other big problems, The Food Project, of Boston, is sowing seeds in fertile ground. For the past seven years, the program has taken on fifty kids every summer, paid them $100 a week, and put them to work growing vegetables, which they then sell at farmers' markets, donate to food pantries, and serve at homeless shelters. Their labor provides food for the hungry, reclaims barren land, and creates green oases in city neighborhoods. It also brings together a diverse array of teenagers of both sexes, and various racial and class backgrounds, who have one desire in common: to learn how to work the land. (Ridout, 1998, p. 75)

Although the Food Project emphasizes growing food, harvesting approximately 40,000 pounds each year (beans, beets, broccoli, cabbage, cauliflower, peppers, potatoes, squash, and tomatoes), and serving meals to the hungry, it still seeks to enhance the capacities of youths in the process. As Ridout (1988, p. 75) noted:

> The Food Project is, at heart, a youth development program. It emphasizes the skills that young people need to build community by encouraging services, team work, and responsibility, while integrating lessons on the environment, sustainable agriculture, poverty, and bridging gaps between people. All this takes place within the framework of farming the land.

The Food Project's goals are not different from those of many other organizations except that the project uses gardening as the primary mechanism for achieving the goals

The Food Project's underlying principles, structure, and goals all focus on creating deep and lasting change, both personal and societal, through creating an integrated system for growing and distributing food in metropolitan Boston. "A vision without a task is but a dream. A task without a vision is only drudgery, but a task with a vision can change the world." We believe this and invite youth to work side by side with staff in realizing our dream. Young people hunger for challenges, not just programs. They want to believe that they can make a difference. (The Food Project, 1997, p. 1)

Youths are selected for the project through a highly competitive process (approximately 14 to 16 out of 150 are chosen) that results in a diverse group representing a variety of backgrounds. As Ridout (1998, p. 75) reported:

The workers are carefully chosen . . . to represent the various populations in both urban and suburban communities of Boston. The balance, however, is purposely skewed: fifty-five to sixty percent of the kids come from the city, while forty to forty-five percent come from the whiter, more affluent suburbs. The point is to put minorities in the majority, because in most situations the dynamics are reversed.

The deployment of the youths increases their knowledge of gardening, but also seeks to break down stereotypes and misperceptions:

Once accepted, the kids get divided into four groups of twelve each, including two older teenagers who serve as crew leaders, and travel between the Food Project's two farms. One is a large field in suburban Lincoln, where they grow most of the food, and learn about plant cycles, insect control, and blisters. The other is an urban garden in Roxbury, one of the city's poorest neighborhoods, where they work with community members to create fertile and flowered grounds. As they dig and sow and weed, these kids learn to communicate, cooperate, and problem-solve; by harvest time, they have formed a community. Before, they had never worked outdoors in sweltering sun; they knew nothing of growing things. They had also defined each other by stereotype, and approached each other with suspicion and anger. By summer's end, they have developed friendships, respect, and a commitment to working together. (Ridout, 1998, p. 75)

The work schedules have been thoughtfully constructed to enhance the youths' capacities and understanding and illustrate how carrying out an activity can also mean thinking as well:

Thinking and learning are built right into the day's work. Each week of the summer is structured around a theme—such as hope, goals, courage—and each day, the entire group gathers under the lunch tent to discuss it, listen to guest speakers, and participate in activities that explore the theme. In an exercise that promotes trust and responsibility, each person must risk standing at the end of a picnic table and falling backwards into the arms of the other eleven crew members. The laughter, encouragement, and reliable catching bring the teenagers together. One girl admits she was scared, then surprised when she was caught. "It was great when I realized my friends would support me—I felt like a part of a community." (Ridout, 1998, p. 75)

The following typical work schedule stresses the development of a wide range of skills:

> The youths spend four days a week on the farm engaged in tilling, planting, composing, weeding, and harvesting their crops. They then spend one day a week in Boston at one of the city's shelters preparing the food they have grown. Participants . . . are bound by a workers' contract at the rural and urban sites, on field trips, and on public transportation that identifies inappropriate workplace conduct. A range of offenses can result in warnings, several day's lost wages, or termination for infractions such as absence, tardiness, smoking, littering, vandalism, fighting, drinking, drug dealing, stealing and weapons possession. The teens are placed into manageable crews, led by an older youth leader, and engage in a variety of manual labor activities related to the production functions of a working farm. (Lakes, 1996, p. 50)

The Food Project worked out agreements with Boston-based families (shareholders) to purchase the produce:

> The Food Project sold shares in the harvest . . . and delivered the organically-grown produce weekly to residents. . . . Over eight thousand pounds of fresh vegetables were delivered, washed, weighed, and boxed by . . . youth workers for two-dozen shareholders that season [1993]. Accompanying each grocery bag of produce was a weekly bulletin prepared by the Food Project crews that reported the latest news from Drumlin Farm, listed various recipes, and profiled youth workers, staff, and community participants. Shareholders were invited to the Farm to visit or work in the fields along with the teens on Fridays during the summer months. In fact, Friday was community lunch day at the Food Project; workers, staff, volunteers, guests, and shareholders joined together under a tent to taste a diversity of culinary treats, and each crew was responsible for choosing recipes and gathering fresh produce in the preparation of these dishes. (Lakes, 1996, p. 52)

The example of the Food Project case identifies the variety of goals that can be achieved through a gardening intervention (Floyd, 1997; Gale, 1996; Levinson, 1997). The enhancement of capacities, in this case of youths, is possible at multiple levels, and families and communities also benefit.

The use of a community garden as a vehicle for the generation of food to be distributed takes on added relevance when the parcel of land is sufficiently large to generate large quantities of food, in addition to using vacant land that has historically been a source of community problems. The case example of the Garden Angels in Los Angeles ties a community garden into a foodbank for the community and is based upon many of the community capacity-enhancement principles outlined in this book. As Fiffer and Fiffer (1994, pp. 108–109) reported:

> Doris, who had conceived the idea of transforming the vacant lot across from the food bank headquarters on East 41st, saw the garden as a symbol of post-riot hope. It would provide residents of ravaged south central Los Angeles and adjacent neighborhoods with a means of growing some of their own food, afford participants the opportunity to learn marketable job skills and become more self-sufficient, and give residents a greater sense of pride in their community. Success, Doris hoped, would lead to the growth of other gardens in neighborhoods across the city.

The community capacity-enhancement goals are well articulated in the philosophy of the garden's founder. The success of the gardens far exceeded her wishes:

> Today scores of Angelenos of different ethnic groups can be found tending their corn, tomatoes, melons, and numerous other vegetables and fruits in the 160 plot [seven and one-half acre] urban garden. Some of what they harvest will be sold at market, but most will be taken home to feed their families. . . . Until it initiated the urban garden, the foodbank, founded in 1973, was solely in the food distribution business. (Fiffer & Fiffer, 1994, p. 109)

The garden is divided into plots of land up to 45 by 55 feet for 115 families, with plans to expand the garden since there are 175 people on the waiting list for plots (Feldman, 1993; Simonds, 1993; Watson, 1993). The Los Angeles-based community garden also facilitates interethnic relations in a community that is rapidly changing in composition from African American to Latino. As Fiffer and Fiffer (1994, pp. 111–112) noted:

> Urban gardeners make strange bedfellows. Doris marvels at the ethnic mix of the gardeners and the different farming methods they employ. Some, for example, insist that corn and tomatoes must be planted in separate rows so that the tomatoes can get enough sun. Others argue that the two must be planted together so that the tomato plants can wind their way up the cornstalks. While those from different cultures may disagree on techniques, all agree on the benefits of the program. Ruth Deanda, who farms a large plot with her husband and eight children, saves $50 to $60 a month in grocery bills. . . . "I think [the garden] made a difference, especially after the disturbances. It shows that people of different races can work together."

The success of the Garden Angels can be measured in a variety of ways:

> Today approximately 300 families grow food for themselves on about 15 acres of land. . . . The garden is self-governing. The gardeners elected a gar-

den committee, which oversees cleanups, acts as a liaison between the gardeners and the foodbank, and lets the Foodbank staff know when they have special needs. . . . Perhaps most important of all are the other products of the garden. It is a place where people can just watch their food grow, a place where families can garden together, a job skills training site (if you don't water the plants, they die), and a place that shows Los Angeles is not just a place of guns and hatred, but a place where people can work together to help each other and the community. (Bloch, 1998, p. 1)

The Garden Angels, however, did not become successful overnight or even in a year. According to Feldman, 1993, p. B4):

"Everyone wants things happening in a year because it's a benchmark—one year after the riots. . . . But it took longer than a year for people to end up in the state they were in. And it will take more than a year to get out of it. This is a long-term thing and we're literally planting seeds." Besides, proponents say, most would agree that the goals are worthwhile. "This is about feeding people." . . . Moreover, community gardens promote family togetherness and can serve as a source of pride and industry.

The Garden Angels garden, in true fashion for a community capacity-enhancement project, also beautified the neighborhood

In a neighborhood dominated by auto salvage and recycling businesses, the garden serves as an eye-pleasing and eye-opening respite, providing proof that with adequate soil and water, one can grow a wide variety of fruit and vegetables virtually anywhere in Los Angeles. Aesthetics, however, are the least of it. . . . "Our goal is to give people who lack resources additional resources to help themselves." (Feldman, 1993, B4)

The Victoria Hills project in Kitchener, Canada, discussed in Chapter 8, provides a perspective on how a community can use vacant lots as the basis for a crime-prevention program.

Consisting of a vacant lot surrounded by a school and three high-density, low-rent apartment buildings, the Victoria Hills site had become overgrown, garbage-strewn, and intimidating place to the more than 1,200 residents of the area. Illegal activity in the area closest to Mooregate Crescent resulted in police constantly being called to this locale. Considered "an unsafe and negative presence in the community," many residents simply avoided the place. . . . Recognizing this problem, Constable Rob Davis . . . spearheaded a successful transformation of the area. . . . Specifically, Constable Davis introduced the idea of a community garden, effectively assigning a purpose to the space and compensating for its lack of legitimate activity and overt signs of ownership. (McKay, 1998, p. 1)

The results of transforming this vacant lot were, similar to reports in the literature covered in Chapter 4, indicative of the potential of community capacity-enhancement projects, such as gardens. As McKay (1998, p. 1) reported:

> The results were tremendous. In the first summer of activity, police incidents at the three apartment buildings surrounding the site dropped by 30%. The results continued to improve in 1995 and 1996 with reported police incidents dropping by 48.8% and 55.7% respectively. Plus, local residents now have their own fresh vegetables to eat. Nowhere has the crime rate changed more dramatically than at 80 Mooregate Crescent—a previous trouble spot. Crimes reported at this location decreased 75.4% in 1996, from a pre-garden high of 187 to a post-garden low of 46.

A qualitative perspective on the improvement, however, places these statistics within a community context:

> As impressive as these results are, a qualitative measure of safety showed that participants also experienced a decrease in their concerns about property vandalism and walking in their community at night. Indeed, residents cited many factors contributing to a safer feeling in their community. Most prevalent among these were "the physical presence of people in the garden late into the evening;" the fact that they "knew more people in their neighbourhood;" and the feelings that the neighbors were also watching out for them, their children, and their property." These increased feelings of trust and friendship soon translated into more interaction between ethnic groups and increased cohesion in the community. A boost in community pride was also evident, as qualitative survey responses showed that people now feel "good about the fact that they are involved in their community" and are "more attracted to living in their community." Other positive developments included a feeling of empowerment by the residents and a general physical improvement of the area. Even outside observers saw benefits to the community. (McKay, 1998, pp. 1–2)

The descriptions of the benefits derived from the gardens far exceed beautification of a community and a reduction in crime, although achievement of these two goals should never be minimized. Many lessons were learned by both the community and the practitioner, according to McKay (1998, p. 4):

> The introduction and development of a community garden is a classic example of . . . placing a safe activity in an unsafe area. In Victoria Hills and other communities, such as Selby-Dale in Saint Paul, Minnesota, "the garden has both taken away a negative presence in the community, an unsafe vacant lot, and added a very positive and safe presence, a community garden." It is the challenge of planners, city officials and police officers to recognize the deleterious effect empty spaces have on a community, to guard against their presence, and where empty spaces are unavoidable, to mitigate their impact. By encouraging the sale of undevelopable parcels of land

to adjacent landowners, empty spaces can be eliminated. Where they are unavoidable, creative partnerships and solutions must be sought to make these spaces part of, and not apart from, the communities in which they are found.

Once a community garden is established, it often brings tremendous benefits to the community. Nevertheless, governmental authorities often attempt to eliminate gardens in an effort to create more housing or commercial development (Kirschbaum, 1998a). A recent national survey by the American Community Gardening Association found that only 1.5 percent of all the community gardens surveyed in thirty-eight cities were in permanent ownership by the community or a land trust (Monroe-Santos, 1998. Consequently, it is not unusual for a community garden to be vulnerable to the wishes of a government and land developers.

Land in urban areas is attractive for development because of the scarcity of land. The following case example shows the importance of gardens in organizing a community in ways that were not possible before the garden existed, as evidenced in many New York City communities. As Martin (1998, p. A28) reported:

> In a city woefully short of both open space and affordable housing, Giuliani administration officials are taking steps to create more housing at the expense of some rare patches of greenery. . . . The housing agency [Department of Housing Preservation and Development] announced plans in 1996 to put up for development or sale the approximately 325 gardens over which it already had direct jurisdiction. Now, it will take over about 400 parcels currently controlled by the city's property agency, the Department of Citywide Administrative Services.

The move by the New York City government has not been passively accepted by community gardeners, however.

> But gardeners and environmental groups expressed outrage over the move, saying the gardens lend a touch of beauty and foster community spirit in otherwise gritty neighborhoods. "Mayor issues death certificate to community gardens," read the headline of a statement by the Neighborhood Open Spaces Coalition, an environmental advocacy group. (Martin, 1998, p. A28)

Approximately four hundred community gardens that were built on New York City-owned property are being legally represented by the New York City Coalition for the Preservation of Gardens.

> The coalition has attempted persuasion along with litigation. "We have seen a slow development of awareness even in the city council and various bureaucracies. . . . We have reached out to developers. . . . These neighbor-

hoods have been reborn and are now attractive to developers because of the efforts of these people." (Finkel, 1998, p. 7)

The move by the city to create gardens has, by all accounts, been successful not only in beautifying neighborhoods but in creating a sense of community in the process. However, in attempting to convert these gardens into buildable lots, the city has aroused a sense of outrage in many of these neighborhoods:

> The housing agency began its campaign to redevelop the garden sites in late 1996 by evicting gardeners from 50 of them and beginning development plans. Construction has started on a few sites, and design has been done on others. At about the same time, the department announced that all gardens under its jurisdiction would be open for development or sale. Now, its inventory of garden sites has more than doubled, though they still represent a small fraction of the 11,000 city-owned vacant lots." (Martin, 1998, p. A28)

The campaign by gardeners and their friends has represented an important dimension of community capacity enhancement. Namely, the project, in this case a gardening program, has resulted in groups of community residents coming together to garden and, in the process, organizing themselves as a political and social action force, when none existed before the initial intervention (Baker, 1997; Kinzer, 1994; Lii, 1997; Trust for the Public Land, 1994).

The following Massachusetts case (Jamaica Plain, Boston) is as an excellent example of how the threat to a community garden unified the community against city hall:

> Penny Yunuba walked a visitor through the neighborhood garden. It was a very short walk. It is a very small garden, 3,324 square feet, the size of a house lot. But, as one of Yunuba's neighbors . . . said, "It has been a focal point for our community, a place where we come together and work together, something good that we've created." Now, residents of this densely populated neighborhood of two- and three-family homes . . . fear they will lose that glue that helps bind them together, and they want the city to help make sure they don't. (Lupo, 1997, p. 1)

The garden, once the site of a home destroyed by fire, was taken by the city and sold to a Boston attorney who allowed the community to use it as a garden until the real estate market became stronger. The current owner wishes to sell the parcel of land, and the community wishes to buy it with help from the city. Although negotiations were still ongoing at the time this book was written, the Boston example clearly shows the power of a community garden to bring a community together to take action against external authorities.

There are a number of strategies that communities can use to ensure that gardens are protected; one approach that is finding increased popularity is the development of a land trust. The following example illustrates the appeal and success of this strategy:

> Chicago's new open space land trust, NeighborSpace, incorporated in May 1996, has its origins in a formal open space plan for the city that recommended setting up some kind of entity to purchase, hold and provide insurance for small neighborhood spaces—community gardens and other green areas. In a city with an estimated 70,000 vacant lots and all the usual social ills, community gardening and greening have taken off in the past five years. The city's Greencorps program trains and employs people in landscaping and horticulture who then help neighbors build gardens, to the tune of about 100 a year. . . . At least 300 gardens have been established and 100 people trained since the program began in early 1995. Neighbor Space acquires public land in various ways at the request of neighborhood groups and block clubs. (Kirschbaum, 1998a, p. 8)

NeighborSpace's funding and land-acquisition approach is unique, multifaceted, and collaborative in nature.

> Unlike Boston's trusts, it does not depend primarily on grants, foundations and private money. Although a separate nonprofit 501(c) (3), Neighbor-Space was set up through an intergovernmental agreement and has guaranteed funding for three years from the City of Chicago, the Chicago Parks District, and the Cook County Forest Preserve District. Each of these three government groups appoints a politician and a bureaucrat to the 10-member board, and three members come from the private sector. The board has approved 25 acquisitions so far. NeighborSpace acquires city-owned property by transfer for $1, tax-delinquent property from Cook County, Chicago Parks land by transfer, and private property from individual owners. (Kirschbaum, 1998a, pp. 8–9)

The example of the Greening of Harlem Coalition integrates much of what has been covered in the previous chapters about the role of gardening in community capacity enhancement. The project, which originated in 1989 is sponsored by the New York City Department of Parks, but its success can be attributed to the vision and dedication of one employee, Bernadette Cozart. Ms. Cozart took the challenge of introducing community gardening into Harlem on an unprecedented scale and doing so with minimal support (financial, supplies, and otherwise). The development of collaborative relationships with organizations that normally do not work together proved successful.

> Cozart built alliances with individuals and groups in Harlem neighborhoods who wanted to create community gardens and restore local parks and playgrounds, and then formalized the network, naming it the Greening of

Harlem Coalition. The Coalition members came from key community institutions, such as Harlem Hospital, Mt. Zion, and St. Mary's Churches, and the Upper Room AIDS Ministry, and from local block associations and tenant groups, including the Edgecomb Avenue Block Association and Security Block. She welcomed into the Coalition city agencies, who assisted with services like trash pickup from vacant lots, and the National Resources Defense Council, which offered legal assistance in getting nonprofit status for the Greening of Harlem. (Hynes, 1995, p. 5)

The gardens created through this intervention are extensive in the amount of land they occupy and the social goals they address. As Hynes (1995, p. 6) noted:

The Greening of Harlem rises from and thrives on neighborhood involvement. The seventeen grassroots gardens—designed, built, and tended by neighborhood people and community institutions with Cozart's guidance since 1989—are a small but potent symbol of local love and labor. This community reclamation of abandoned lots, parks, and playgrounds; the modest reversal of neighborhood disintegration; and pride in the greening of Harlem, is largely financed by the labor of Harlem people and by an informal economy based on begging, borrowing, and bartering. The story of the Greening of Harlem is fundamentally the story of an unconventional coalition of women that includes a surgeon, a homemaker turned community activist, the founder of a park conservancy, and a city parks department gardener.

The coalition did not concentrate just on creating gardens out of vacant community lots, it also sought to convert unused or underutilized land belonging to organizations, such as a hospital. An institution like a hospital lends itself to a gardening program and efforts to beautify the neighborhood, particularly if the hospital is centrally located geographically and socially. As Hynes (1995, pp. 7–8) stated:

While a hospital may seem an unlikely place to launch a community greening program, Harlem Hospital—a magnet for the community—was a natural starting point. The Uptown Chamber of Commerce meets here; so does the Pastors Association. The hospital is home to the Harlem Horizon Art Studio, where hundreds of children study art and go to exhibits and sell their work in New York City galleries. The Harlem Dance Clinic is another hospital project, begun for young patients and now open to the community as well, whose members have performed at Lincoln Center, various universities, the United Nations, and in cultural exchange programs in the Caribbean, Europe, and Russia. Although terminally underfunded, the hospital is nonetheless a hub for the community. . . . Harlem Hospital appears side by side with the Apollo Theater and a local radio station as favorite Harlem neighborhood institutions depicted on large, vibrant murals painted by children under the guidance of local artist Bryan Collier, and hung in their playgrounds and school gardens.

Another example of a Harlem community garden created on the grounds of an institution, in this case one devoted to helping emotionally disturbed women and men, is the garden planted at Bishop House. A request was made to the coalition to help create a garden, according to Hynes (1995, p. 11):

> Bishop House had initially paid a contractor thousands of dollars to install a garden; nothing few in the fill laid over a plastic liner sprayed with herbicides. . . . The Coalition was called to rescue the project. When Cozart asked the Bishop House residents about their preferences for the garden, they asserted that they wanted tranquility and beauty in their garden. However, the mental health professionals who ran the facility preferred plants for cottage industries, such as herbs and flowers for making potpourri. "I went with the residents," said Cozart emphatically; together they designed a garden with bold and brilliant color, winding walkways, and benches. With two hundred dollars and leftover plants she collected from city agencies and landscape contractors, Cozart designed and built the Bishop House garden with the residents and staff. This backyard refuge, only a few steps from drug-ridden streets, attracted songbirds, hummingbirds, and butterflies.

The example of the Philadelphia Green Program brings to the foreground the importance of collaborative ventures involving the private and public sectors (Avery, 1997; Ferrick, 1997; Mukherjee, 1995; Peirce, 1995; Yant, 1997). The Philadelphia Green Program was initiated by the Pennsylvania Horticultural Society in 1993. The program sought to use gardening as a community revitalization tool—converting lots and other parcels of land into gardens and, while doing so, increase the organizing skills of the community residents.

A set of structural economic factors made the use of gardens an attractive tool for community capacity enhancement in Philadelphia:

> a realization of stark facts: Philadelphia has lost 450,000 residents in the last 25 years. There are 27,000 abandoned homes, 16,000 vacant lots. Neighborhoods are emptying. And, to use the words of urban consultant Gertrude Spilka: "They look like hell." (Ferrick, 1997, pp. A1, A19)

The Philadelphia Green Program involves three key city agencies (the Planning Commission, the Redevelopment Authority, and the Office of Housing and Community Development), two foundations (Pew and William Penn), and the Horticultural Society. Its approach toward community gardening serves to operationalize the philosophical thrust of this program:

> Kennsington grew up as a factory neighborhood. It is interrelated with narrow streets that are lined with rowhouses, most of them two-story workingmen's homes of the 1800s. Of the 8,600 parcels of land in the neigh-

borhood, 1,100 are empty lots or vacant structures, mostly rowhouses. This is a vacancy rate of 13 percent—double the city average. . . . "We are trying to address every piece of vacant land in this neighborhood. . . . We are trying to create the people system that can handle it and we're trying to come up with creative horticultural ways to stabilize the land." The strategy is to take the neighborhood's greatest physical liability—empty land and abandoned houses—and turn it into an asset. . . . The key is density. By any modern measures, Kennsington is too dense. Despite losing 23 percent of its residents since 1970, it still has two to three times more people per acre than newer city neighborhoods. Housing was clustered in walking distance of factories. Amenities—parks, recreation centers—are few. People yearn for more space." (Ferrick, 1997, p. A19)

Philadelphia Green's Latino-focused project, Norris Square Park in Greene Countrie Towne, served as a central point for the generation of multiple community capacity-enhancement projects (see Figure 11.4). Gardens, weather permitting, provide communities with an opportunity to grow food that has historically been a staple of their cultural heritage.

This project also served as a vehicle for integrating a host of cultural themes:

> The demonstration compost project and environmental park, the eleven tree-lined blocks, and the fifty-nine flower and vegetable gardens which comprise the [community] are a "dream for everybody." . . . Las Parcelas is

Figure 11.4. Norris Square Park, Philadelphia. A project of the Pennsylvania Horticultural Society's Philadelphia Green Project. Photo credit: Ira Beckoff.

its centerpiece, with sixteen family vegetable plots; an orchard planted with peaches, pears, nectarines, and grapes; La Casita (a small traditional Puerto Rican house built by neighbors); perennial and herb gardens; ornamental grasses; and a patio for cookouts. Iris [one of the coordinators] credited a group of ten women ("they are," she added, "humble and speak no English") who have done most of the work. The women call themselves motivos—ones who are motivated and who want to motivate others. During the winter they meet weekly to discuss Puerto Rican history, see films, and enjoy Latino food and music; during the growing season they cultivate many Norris Square neighborhood gardens. (Hynes, 1995, p. 73)

The community, like many other urban-based communities, had a negative reputation in Philadelphia. The experience of working together in a gardening effort led the residents to work together in another capacity: to fight drugs. As Hynes (1995, pp. 73–74) noted:

This neighborhood was one of the worst areas in drugs, known as the Badlands. The community came together—Anglos, Dominicans, Cubans, Puerto Ricans, blacks—and formed United Neighbors Against Drugs. Twenty to forty of us met at Norris Square Park and walked the neighborhood every evening, lingering on corners where the largest drug dealing went on.

Gardening not only serves to generate food, but can play an instrumental role in beautifying a community by dramatically changing an environment, as evidenced in Photograph 11.5.

However, it can also motivate a community to build structures that encourage residents to come together, as evidenced in Norris Square.

Gardening, however, must not be fraught with expectations that it will solve an entire neighborhood's problems, although there is much that can change as a result of it, as a community leader of the project for children (quoted in Hynes, 1995, pp. 77–78) eloquently noted:

"I cannot promise them they're going to get a good education. I cannot promise them they are going to graduate from high school or go to college. I cannot tell them they will have a job. I can tell them they will have fresh produce to eat; I can promise them they will have beauty." She can also promise children that they will grow up in a neighborhood unified by its successful struggle to evict major drug dealers and drug trafficking, a neighborhood where the cultural and botanical legacy of Puerto Ricans fills vacant lots that once had been taken as if by eminent domain by drug dealers. She can promise them what no amount of income and no amount of security systems, guards, guns, and locks in suburbs and new towns can buy—the hard-woven fabric of neighborhood. She can promise that the gardens, with their murals, sculpture, and horticulture, will exhibit the artistry of the informally-trained artists of their community.

Figure 11.5. Norris Square Park, Philadelphia. A project of the Pennsylvania Horticultural Society's Philadelphia Green Project. Photo credit: Ira Beckoff.

The final case illustration does not conform to the examples of community gardens used in this book, but it has been included because of its potential to reach people and create a sense of belonging in a variety of settings. The example of labyrinths (shapes that are designed, many based on ancient sources, to encourage people to follow them and, while walking, to experience the benefits associated with solace and contemplation) have increased in popularity during the 1990s (Davis, 1998; L. Goldstein, 1998). Although labyrinths are not restricted to any particular setting, they have added significance in urban areas because of the paucity of open space that can be used for meditation.

The benefits associated with the use of labyrinths are many, including the creation of a sense of connectedness, and make them attractive for inclusion in community-based gardens with sufficient space to accommodate them. As Goldstein (1998, p. 1) reported:

> When the Rev. Battle Beasley spray-painted 12 large concentric rings on the grass in his front yard three years ago, he handed out fliers to his neighbors explaining that it was a copy of the labyrinths found in medieval Christian cathedrals, and he invited them to walk it. His neighbors stayed away. . . . But word of the labyrinths in Mr. Beasley's yard traveled quickly, and it is now drawing pilgrims from all over the state. On a recent Sunday afternoon, 17 people paced in the labyrinth simultaneously, each lost in private preoccupations, each navigating the turns at a different pace. . . . In an

age when many Americans are looking beyond the church pulpit for spiritual experience and solace, a growing number have rediscovered the labyrinth as a path to prayer, introspection and emotional healing. While walking the labyrinth can be no more magical than a walk in the woods, those who walk them often say it focuses their mind, slows the breathing and can induce a peaceful state or help them confront problems.

The popularity of labyrinths has increased dramatically in recent years, as evidenced by a web site listing over one hundred labyrinths across the United States and the various settings they can be found in. According to Goldstein (1998, p. 16),

> A women carries a cloth labyrinth to jails in San Diego for prisoners to walk. Students at several universities in California walk them before exams. Last year, the California Pacific Medical Center, an acute-care hospital in San Francisco, unveiled a painted labyrinth outside the entrance that is now walked by emergency room nurses as well as surgery patients and their families. At least three more hospitals, including Morristown Memorial Hospital in Morristown, N.J., are planning labyrinths of their own.

The movement to create labyrinths has been fueled by the benefits participants received from their walks. These gardens, if you wish, can easily be transported to any community in the United States. They may be closely tied to established houses of worship or, like some community gardens, to human service organizations. Nevertheless, the reader should be aware of these types of movements because they can be easily integrated into the community gardens discussed in this book.

Playgrounds

Playgrounds provide communities with an opportunity to bring together multiple generations in service to their youngest members. The community capacity-enhancement projects lend themselves to involving hundreds of people in pursuit of a common goal. Nevertheless, as was noted in earlier chapters, these types of projects are labor intensive and usually require extensive planning over one-year period. Although the actual building may take only a few days, much, work has to be accomplished to lay the necessary groundwork for the construction. The cases presented next illustrate several different aspects of community-build playgrounds.

The examples of two community-built playgrounds in Harlem (New York City) have been selected because they were not constructed in the usual way over an extended weekend and involving a large construction crew. These playgrounds were built over a period of several months and did not involve hundreds of residents. As Yarr (1998, p. 20) indicated:

> In New York City, environmental designed Sam Kornhauer makes school playgrounds on a smaller scale, with design input from parents, teachers

and students. In partnership with the Board of Education and the Harlem Hospital Injury Prevention Program, Kornhauser has designed several school playgrounds in Harlem. Because Kornhauer works with the landscape, instead of forcing a generic structure onto it, his custom-built playgrounds usually cost no more than one quarter the cost of a commercial playground. . . . Still they achieve . . . [the] main aim, which is to give residents a sense of pride and ownership in the project, by making the playgrounds relevant to each community.

As noted in Figure 11.6, children in Community School (C.S.) 200 chose to design and construct seats for a stage that represent buildings located in Harlem. As a result, the seats are both decorative and functional.

Children's participation in the design of a playground is essential in operationalizing the principles of community participation (Shell, 1994). What children may consider important structures may not be similar to those that adults consider important. As Figure 11.7 shows, children in C.S. 200 decided to paint a map of Harlem, with the Hudson River and Palisades in the distance, in their playground.

Relevance to a community can be achieved through a variety of participatory means:

by incorporating themes from the students' curriculum and familiar elements from the school and the neighborhood, so that each playground is a literal reflection of the people and place it comes from. One . . . playground is a map

Figure 11.6. "Seats for Outdoor Stage Painted as City Blocks in Harlem by Children of C.S. 200." Sam Kornhauser, Schoolworks, New York. Photo credit: Sam Kornhauser.

Figure 11.7. "Map of Harlem Looking West to Hudson River and New Jersey Palisades." By the Children of C.S. 200. Sam Kornhauser, Schoolworks, New York. Photo credit: Sam Kornhauser.

> of Harlem, including the murals the kids painted of their own house facades; another is an outdoor version of the nearby Museum of Natural History. But . . . [the] playgrounds usually feature some elements in common: a garden area, a clubhouse, and some kind of theater space. (Yarr, 1998, p. 20)

The inclusion of space that can be used for a variety of purposes allows the playground to grow with the community because it can be continually used throughout childhood. This feature, in turn, makes the playgrounds more conducive to involving children of various ages, so they are not restricted to use just by young children. Figure 11.8 illustrates this point; it shows the children's incorporation of an outdoor stage and classroom space in their "Apollo Theatre" section of the playground at (P.S. 197 in Harlem. This playground was also designed and constructed to reflect the neighborhood. As Hiss and Koren (1993, p. 80) reported:

> So there's a large garden, with roses and vegetables, at the P.S. 197 playground, and all the equipment has been built to look like something in central Harlem: one piece is a store; another is an apartment house with a stoop; and there's a fire engine, an ambulance, a stage like the one at the Apollo Theatre, and a crawl-through tube in a structure that represents Harlem Hospital.

The P.S. 197 playground also has a quartet of murals painted by the students that represents an attempt to broaden the horizon of their community to include far-off places:

Figure 11.8. "'Apollo Theatre,' Stage and Outdoor Classroom by the Children of P.S. 197." Sam Kornhauser, Schoolworks, New York. Photo credit: Sam Kornhauser.

Each painting depicts a view of the city and beyond. Yankee Stadium and north to the Arctic; the Harlem Bridge and east to Egypt and the pyramids; a neighborhood YMCA and west to Hawaii and Japan; and the Manhattan skyline giving way to a tropical rain forest in the lush, overripe style of painter Henri Rousseau. (Shell, 1994, p. 80)

In Philadelphia's Nicetown neighborhood, a community-built playground is widely acknowledged to be the key factor that galvanized the community, as Yarr (1998, p. 22) noted:

Juanita Hatton is the volunteer president of the Citizens Congress of Nicetown, she's been working for twenty-five years to improve conditions in this inner-city neighborhood, and she ranks the . . . playground built there in April 1997 as the most important development she's been involved in.

"It was nothing but a dirty, disgusting, drug-infested area that was taken and turned into a lovely site and safe for children to play."

The playground's benefit to Nicetown went far beyond the daily satisfaction it brought to countless children and their families or the beautification of an ugly lot:

And the contacts and organizational talent that developed during the construction of the playground continue to bring benefits. The Citizens Congress has arranged for a local hospital to open a clinic on some evenings and Saturdays so single parents can take their children to see a doctor there instead of at the local emergency room, and it's seeking funding to open a full-time clinic in the neighborhood. . . . Most importantly for Juanita Hatton, the skills to organize these things are being passed on to the neighborhood youth. "They know how to come out to meetings and hold their own meetings," she says. (Yarr, 1998, p. 22)

The success of the Harlem and Nicetown community-built playgrounds was possible only because the communities invested themselves in the projects. According to Yarr (1998, p. 22):

Success stories like these make the community-built playground sound like an easy solution to many social ills. It's not. A solution? Perhaps? Easy? Never. . . . Nothing is accomplished until the community gets behind the project, physically and financially. If the process works, it is because hard work towards a common goal brings people together and prepares them for the hard work.

Finally, the case of Coxsackie, New York, shows an increasingly popular approach toward building a playground—hiring a playground construction firm to assist in all phases of the project:

The Coxsackie playground could not have been possible for the community without having a firm like Leathers & Associates assisting the community. Hiring a firm does not mean that the community abdicates its role and responsibility. However, if the firm subscribes to participatory principles, it facilitates the entire planning and building process. The playground cannot be built by an outside firm. Thus, community residents play leadership roles throughout the entire building process. An experienced firm will have clearly articulated principles that it follows in guiding the entire effort. They know the right questions to ask the community, can provide a variety of designs that incorporate the desires of children and their parents, and can help the community anticipate potential trouble areas. The process of building a community playground is never easy. However, it can be made more manageable through the assistance provided by a firm devoted to doing this kind of work.

The example of a project to reclaim playgrounds and parks in Harlem, New York City, represents a slightly different version of building community playgrounds. However, it illustrates other options for community capacity enhancement that do not require that a playground must be built from scratch.

The development of a reclaiming project followed the work undertaken by the Greening of Harlem Coalition, a group of community gardeners, and shows how one type of capacity-enhancement project can lead to the creation of other types (Hiss & Koren, 1993). The development of a community-built playground by the Greening of Harlem Coalition was primarily the inspiration of one individual—Dr. Barbara Barlow, a surgeon at Harlem Hospital. As Hynes (1995, pp. 14–15) indicated:

> The most ambitious and far-reaching of Barlow's injury prevention projects may be the program to restore and return parks and playgrounds—abandoned by the city, haunted by drug dealers, and the refuge of last resort for the homeless—to kids. Like her Coalition partner, Bernadette Cozart, Barlow believes that giving up on parks means giving up on human life, "Concrete doesn't make anyone human, and it certainly doesn't make children human," observed the surgeon.

Under the leadership of Dr. Barlow, and in collaboration with numerous other individuals and organizations, a campaign was launched to reclaim land for use as playgrounds and gardens. As Hynes (1995, pp. 16–17) explained:

> On October 29, 1989, the official annual fall community cleanup day for parks throughout the city, more than seven hundred resident volunteers showed up at Charles Young Park to clean, plant bulbs, and watch the unveiling of a mural painted by one hundred local children. . . . The restoration of Charles Young Park—a waste site of six acres transformed within a few months into the home of the Harlem Little League, an adult softball league, a women's handball association, a rose garden, and an African tulip garden—dramatizes the accomplishments of this almost fail-safe program. Would Charles Young Park ever have been rescued and returned to its community by the Parks Department? Those who have lived with twenty years of municipal neglect of parks and gardens in Harlem say that without the strategic intervention of Harlem Hospital and community groups, many more years would have passed before Harlem's only park with ballfields would have received the investment of capital and resources from the Parks Department.

The Harlem example clearly shows the potential of community capacity-enhancement projects to organize community residents, develop skills and ownership, and beautify the community in the process. This case example interconnects the various types of capacity-enhancement projects addressed in this book—gardens, murals, and playgrounds. The philosophical basis of the Greening of Harlem Coalition is community capacity enhancement, although no mention of this approach is made directly by any of the participants. Nevertheless, the following statement captures the essence of capacity enhancement:

> "The Greening of Harlem is not a 'give you' program like some other greening and open space programs that put in cookie-cutter gardens or make exorbitant amounts of money as another ghetto-pimp program. . . . It is built on tapping people's talents and empowering people. . . . The Coalition has a different kind of power and wealth . . . based on an alternative economy in which each person gives of their talents and networks with community organizations and agencies to get equipment, seeds, and plants. The more that has been taken away from us, the more we got because we became more self-reliant and resourceful." (Hynes, 1995, p. 30)

Thus, the systematic taking back of gardens, as has been done in New York City, would be not be successful for governmental agencies in the Greening of Harlem's gardens and parks. The success of the gardens planted by the coalition can serve as an example of how these projects can be institutionaled without experiencing the limitations usually associated with gardening based on the use of city land. As Hynes (1995, pp. 37–38) noted:

> Community gardens everywhere in the United States have fragile tenure, often because the land being gardened is not owned or leased long-term by the gardeners, but sometimes because the gardeners do not sustain interest in the garden. The community gardens of the Greening of Harlem are moored to (and thus secured by) institutions and community organizations. . . . The Greening makes one believe that every abandoned lot is waiting for a new Harlem Renaissance that will reunite nature with vibrant human life. The expanded sense of environment there—the human, the architectural, the natural, and ethical—enriches and adds complexity to this more-than-a-greenspace program.

The example of Dickerman Park in Somerville, Massachusetts (see Figure 11.9), brings together many of the key elements addressed in community capacity-enhancement projects in an integrated fashion. As Fishman (1998a, p. 1) reported:

> Elected officials, City Year volunteers, adults and children with plastic shovels assembled last weekend to spread mulch, build benches, and otherwise put the finishing touches on the city's renovated Dickerman playground. Organized to increase neighborhood investment in the public area between Ibbetson and Craige streets, the two-day community building event attracted more than a dozen workers on what began as a cloudy Saturday and drew many more to the sunny cookout sponsored by the adjacent Dante Club the following day. About 500 drawings penned by students from four city schools hung around the playground, completing the celebratory atmosphere. The new playground transforms a previously neglected public area with a lone wooden climbing structure.

Figure 11.9. "Dickerman Community Park," Somerville, Massachusetts. Photo credit: Kate Sheridan.

The play area underwent a remarkable transformation and had an impact that went far beyond the usual play area:

> The new playground now has multicolored equipment with swings, towers, and an oversize "steering wheel." It will soon have all new plantings and a ring of push-button water sprinklers circling the equipment, which will also be surrounded by a hard-to-destroy rubberized surface. Steel cutouts designed by Brown School third graders and created by [a local] artist will also decorate the playground, and two metal archways will be added to the entrances. The basketball court, an important draw for older youths, has not been renovated but will remain in place. "It looks almost like an amusement park." (Fishman, 1998, p. 1)

The goals for Dickerman Park reflect the use of the playground to create a sense of community and belonging for residents, according to Fishman (1998a, p. 6):

> City officials and neighbors hope the effort to remake the playground will help people feel invested in its upkeep and limit common maintenance problems, such as broken beer bottles left at night. A core group of about a dozen neighbors has worked on the project for a year and will continue to keep an eye on the playground. . . . "When you put your blood, sweat, and tears into something . . . people are very protective." . . . Volunteers also hoped the renovation would draw neighborhood residents over the long

term; a bulletin board for community announcements was added to the renovation plan at neighbors' request. "There's a mix of families with kids and older families. . . . Hopefully, this will bring people out."

The wide range of cosponsors of the park opens up endless possibilities for generating support (financial, political and social)—important factors in the creation of a community. The addition of the bulletin board is aimed at "formalizing" a mechanism for communication for residents in search of opportunities to connect with each other. The playground planners also sought ways to maximize contact among multiple generations—in essence, they did not just target young children. The playground, by integrating the basketball court, served to provide a venue for other age groups to interact.

The last case example comes from Holyoke, Massachusetts, and merges both playgrounds and murals, illustrating community-build projects from a youth perspective. In 1995, a community-based organization (Nueva Esperanza) and the city government wanted to develop a playground in a primarily Puerto Rican section of the city. The playground was created behind three occupied apartment buildings managed by another agency (Community Builders). A collaborative partnership was developed by these three entities. The project could be successful only if a collaborative partnership could be formed, since no one entity had the necessary resources.

As expected, this community capacity-enhancement project sought to fulfill multiple goals in addition to creating a play space. As McCarthy and Fletcher (1995, p. 1) indicated:

> Our project addresses four interrelated problems in this community. First, it will transform an area composed of the backyards of four multi-family buildings into a safe, beautiful, well supervised place for children to play. The second problem we are addressing is the drug activity around the abandoned building. . . . The third problem is the physical danger this abandoned building presents to the children playing in or around it. The last issue we will address is the lack of parental involvement and supervision.

One of the components of this project sought active and meaningful involvement of the residents of the apartment buildings:

> The residents will also work together to design and construct a park that will meet the needs of the children and will facilitate adult supervision by providing comfortable places for families to use. The youth of this community will design and paint a mural on the back wall of buildings. . . . We will involve the 36 adults and 80 children living in these three buildings as well as ten YouthRap Kids, residents in the buildings. (McCarthy & Fletcher, 1995, p. 1).

Community participation increases the likelihood of community ownership and results in the enhancement of residents' skills in the process. The project hired ten adolescents to perform the construction. These youths participated in a series of workshops and training sessions throughout the summer. McCarthy and Fletcher (1995, p. 2) noted:

> This project will rid the neighborhood of a known site for drug activity. It will create a safe, fun alternative place for children to play. It will facilitate family activities and parental supervision. Allowing the residents to design and construct this part will insure that residents feel an investment in it. It will fit the needs of this community. The process will also teach residents new skills and how to organize into a group that can work together to solve neighborhood problems.

The design phase involved youths in the actual design of the playground. A series of workshops were developed to encourage children to draw pictures of how they wanted the playground to look. These ideas were put to a vote and incorporated into the overall design. The playground design consisted of setting areas, a basketball and volleyball court, a playground and a "tot lot."

The construction of the playground followed the painting of a mural (see Figure 11.10) that was also designed and painted by the children and adolescents of the area (Bobskill, 1995; McCulloch, 1995). The mural shows a playground and children playing on a variety of types of equipment. McCarthy and Fletcher (1995, p. 5) stated:

> The colors and vibrancy of the recently completed mural are indicative of the positive attitude generated by the active participation of the residents through-

Figure 11.10. "Holyoke Community Playground and Mural Project." Nueva Esperanza/ The Community Builders.

out all the phases of this effort. Imre Kepes summed up the effort when she said, "This dream could never have been realized without the active participation of the residents and capacity of the children and the collective effort of many players in the community. We should all be very proud."

Summary. Community-built playgrounds fulfill many different and important roles within communities. The examples provided in this chapter highlight the variety of playgrounds that can be created in schools and neighborhoods. These playgrounds, however, can achieve multiple goals for enhancing community capacity. The skills learned in constructing them and carrying out other facets related to their creation can be tranfered into other arenas. The process of creating community-built playgrounds enhances individuals' skills and sense of well-being, while creating a sense of community. The beautification of a community can also be an indirect benefit of a playground. Playgrounds also foster interactions between neighbors who, on the surface, may have few similarities, and break down stereotypes while doing so.

Sculptures

This section on sculptures reflects a wide variety of types and settings. Community-built sculptures, as noted earlier in this book, rarely stand on their own. They invariably are part of other community capacity-enhancement projects. The South Minneapolis example, covered in various chapters of this book, integrates community sculptures as part of a community art park and mural. These projects were initiated by Neighborhood Safe Art Spot, an organization devoted to involving youths in the creation of public art. As Noriyuki (1995, p. 14) reported:

> It is a small park on the corner of 12th Avenue and Lake Street in South Minneapolis, and it was build by young people in the Powderhorn and Phillips neighborhoods as a fluorescent symbol of unity and peace. Stately stands beneath a mural of doves on the wall of an adjacent furniture store. The birds have been painted to represent the cultures of the world, and they are flying out of an African drum, above a turtle—the American Indian symbol of creation—toward the Earth and a blazing sun, from which emerges a phoenix, a symbol of rebirth. . . . The park is a gift to a community whose peace has been shaken by recent violence.

The integration of sculptures into other community capacity-enhancement projects is not unusual (see Figure 11.11). The sculptures created for the Neighborhood Safe Art Spot are well integrated into the park and, as a result, may not get noticed to the same extent as the gardens or mural. However, they still play a significant role in the park. Three types of sculptures were created by the youths: arches, a peace pole, and a series of tree stumps:

> The sculpture was conceived as a pair of arches that would be an integral part of the park. Arches were selected because the community did not have

Figure 11.11. "Peace Offerings." By the Youth Team of Neighborhood Safe Art, Minneapolis. Executive Director Marilyn Lindstrom.

any and arches were symbolic for welcoming people, particularly newcomers to the community. Arches would be the first and last thing visitors would see as they entered and left the park, helping to create a lasting positive memory of their experience. Entering a park through aches conveyed to the visitor a sense of acceptance, safety, peace, and friendship. These arches were decorated with various symbols representing the multicultural backgrounds of many of the groups represented in the neighborhood. Symbols, such as the Sacred Circle (Native American), an elephant, a man and a mask (African American), and a photograph of a Pow Wow (Native American), reflect carefully researched subjects that are meant to communicate ethnic and racial ride and community unity.

As was noted, the park serves not only as a garden, home to a mural, but as a place for sculptures. In addition to the arches described above, two other types of sculptures were created for the park:

The Peace Pole is strategically located within the park. The "May Peace prevail on Earth" pole communicates to the audience in many different languages: American Sign Language, Braille, French, Spanish, and Chinese. The pole is of a simple design, requiring a minimal amount of maintenance. A series of tree stumps were used and situated throughout the park. Each tree stump was carved in such a way as to allow a design to be pained on the surface, in addition to providing a sitting area. The designs painted on the stumps, like those in other art projects in the park, reflected African American, Asian, Latino, and Native American symbols. The unity of these four parts of the earth was meant as a symbolic message to the internal and external community.

The community sculpture project created in Craig, Alaska, does not fit into the urban thrust of this book, since Craig is an island and has a population of approximately two thousand. The event that led to its creation does fit in, however. The sculpture (a forty-six foot totem pole) was created to memorialize the death of a youth who died of a drug (cocaine) overdose (Frankenstein, 1998). Although initially the sculpture was the result of one individual acting alone, it quickly became a "community" project.

The carver of the sculpture was the child's father, and the pole was dedicated to the youth and all youths in the community as Frankenstein (1998, p. 76) reported:

> Stan Marsden is Tsimshian and a master carver, but when a friend suggested that he build a totem pole in his son's honor, Marsden wasn't quite ready. A year later, however, he picked out a 500-year-old red cedar tree from the island, and decided to carve it. This pole, he decided, would stand not only for the memory of his son, but would also be dedicated to all youth, to sobriety, and to the people who have died of drug and alcohol in Alaska. As community members heard about the project, which Marsden dubbed the Healing Heart Totem Pole, they asked if they could join him in the work.

The nature and design of the pole were highly unusual, although the pole addressed a theme that was common in the community:

> Haida Elder Clara Natkong says she had seen lots of totem poles raised to tell the story of a clan or event, or as a memorial to a leader, but she had never seen a "healing" pole. The problems of substance and violence, especially among the young people in the region, however, have Natkong and many others worried. Southeast Alaska has one of the highest rates of alcoholism, drug abuse, suicide, and teenage pregnancy in the country. (Frankenstein, 1998, pp. 76–77)

The unusual nature of the pole necessitated that the artist seek permission from his family to create a pole for his son and to allow people, native and nonnative, to become involved. Permission was granted for both requests. The pole served multiple goals in addition to bringing together a community, both old and young. As Frankenstein (1998, p. 77) explained:

> In creating the pole, Stan Marsden took a bold step—using a traditional art form to face personal pain and contemporary problems—and he made everyone around him, native and non-native, feel welcome to take part. To help organize a pole-raising ceremony, he enlisted the help of Cindy Gamble, a health educator and clinic administrator, who became chair of the Healing Heart Totem Committee.

The dedication of the pole gave the residents of Craig the opportunity to reach out to others outside the community and to convey a message to both the internal and external community:

> It took six months and forty to fifty helpers for Marsden to carve the pole. Meanwhile, the community organized drug- and alcohol-prevention workshops, talking circles, and potluck meals around the raising. Expanding on the traditional protocol for potlatches, pole-raising, and other ceremonies, they invited people to come by, publicizing the event throughout the region, and in both the United States and Canada. Community members opened their homes to out-of-towners." (Frankenstein, 1998, p. 77)

Although the pole was specifically created in response to the death of one of Craig's own, it served to generate other pole carvings, as community capacity-enhancement projects are supposed to do.

> "The pole was for helping heal damaged emotions." . . . People are still suffering and dying from illnesses and accidents related to drug and alcohol abuse, but every year on the anniversary of the pole raising, the Healing Heart Committee puts on a rose ceremony and other events to promote sobriety and healing. "The community is not cured. . . . But it took a step forward." Now carving another pole, for the senior citizens of nearby Hydaburg, Marsden says that when the community gathers at the annual ceremony, he is reminded of the purpose of the pole, how it brought people together, and what it felt like when they showed up at the work tent and "carved a little love into the totem pole." Standing tall and proud on the edge of town, the pole seems to shout out that native culture is alive and well, and that, on the island of Craig, Alaska, the healing has begun. (Frankenstein, 1998, p. 78)

The Craig totem pole symbolizes the role a sculpture can play in addressing the goals of healing, communication, bringing people together, and enhancing the environment in the process. The creation of the pole served generated other capacity-enhancement projects related to the same art form.

The case of the "Ark" in Newark, New Jersey, is an example of how one individual's dream could not sustain the onslaught of external authorities. The Ark has been selected because it highlights the importance of involving community residents and other parties in helping residents create change. Without the support, projects like the Ark and others are doomed to failure. Vergara (1995, pp. 157–158) described the Ark this way:

> Sited on high ground, the sky visible between the bare beams of the hull, the Ark pointed toward downtown Newark and beyond, to the towers of the World Trade Center, and farther, past the Statue of Liberty, to the Atlantic Ocean and the freedom of the open sea. The Ark was the creation of Kea Tawana, a carpenter, electrical worker, and scavenger who has a sixth-grade education. Kea, a Newark resident for twenty years, created a

unique folk-art monument at the edge of a church's parking lot in the city's Central Ward. Unfinished, the boat possessed a rawness that sometimes surfaces in its stubbornly determined builder as well, and carpentry skills that went into it, the old-fashioned, sturdy, and reassuring presence of Kea's boat belonged to the realms of dreams and play. . . . The Ark could have become a museum of lost communities, and a place for racial harmony. It made peace between a transformed downtown and the disappearing world of the ethnic neighborhoods. It also became a meeting place for blacks and whites. For me, Kea's Ark symbolized an atonement for the burning of so much of the city.

The Ark played an important role in the community by attracting the residents' attention and serving as a vehicle for discussions about its message. The Ark utilized many objects discarded over the years from abandoned and burn-downed houses. (Veraga, 1995, p. 158):

The power of Kea's dream lives with those who saw the Ark, observed her work, and spoke to her. Faces would turn up to look at the ship, and people smiled with a sense of wonder as if seeing something that could not happen."

Nevertheless, efforts to remove the Ark from the spot it was located were eventually successful. As Vergara (1995, p. 159) noted:

To a city that wants desperately to start over again, the boat was an embarrassing nuisance, preserving as it did discarded pieces of Newark's history. It was a reminder of a race riot, fires, abandonment, and disinvestment, precisely what the city is trying to move away from so that it can become part of "normal America." In addition city officials saw the Ark as an "eye-sore" and, since it was built without a permit, as a prominently displayed challenge to their authority.

Not all sculptures created by residents are successful in achieving all the goals that are hoped for. The Ark's success, although time limited, reinforces the importance of community support for such an endeavor. Although the Ark created conversation, it was not a product of a major sector of the community in which it was situated and thus failed to generate the necessary political support to withstand external pressures for its removal.

Key Practice Skills

There is little question that interventions focused on murals, gardens, playgrounds, and sculptures draw on a set of skills that most social work practitioners do not learn in school. Nevertheless, as has been noted, the author does not expect practitioners to be expert painters, gardeners, builders, or sculptors. However, they must be able to understand the processes each of these types of projects entail and be able to locate the necessary expertise when needed, particularly if the experts are outside the community.

Practitioners must be able to help communities negotiate many of the bureaucratic barriers they will encounter in the process of developing projects. The negotiation and paperwork that are often associated with this step can be facilitated by practitioners. Furthermore, social workers can assist communities in obtaining funding and meeting all the requirements that are usually associated with funding—evaluation, record keeping, obtaining political support from key stakeholders, getting the support of media, and so forth. In essence, practitioners need to be able to use the skills they have learned and apply them to capacity enhancement. There is no question that some of these skills must be modified in the process.

Last, practitioners must be prepared to work in settings other than offices and during times and days that they usually do not work. Much work will take place in people's homes, during the evenings and on weekends—in short, when community residents are available. This flexibility is essential if practitioners are to meet the community on its own terms.

Conclusion

The benefits of intervention are multiple for both communities and practitioners. The joy of designing and implementing a plan that has the support of all those involved cannot be minimized. However, plans, no matter how well conceived and executed, invariably require changes to take into account unforeseen factors. Community capacity-enhancement interventions are no different from their conventional counterparts in this respect.

This chapter has highlighted numerous cases in which the original plans needed to be changed as a result of changes in perspectives. The case of Boyle Heights, Los Angeles, is one example. Nevertheless, intervention based on a community capacity-enhancement perspective offers great opportunities for practitioners to be involved in projects that truly make a difference in a community's life.

12

Application of the Framework to Practice: Evaluation

Numerous measures can be used in determine the extent of success achieved by a project. However, the process of systematizing the methods for measuring the success falls within the realm of evaluation. The evaluation phase of community capacity enhancement is just as important as the initial assessment phase. In fact, the success of a mural, for example, must be evaluated using methods and tools that can help generate lessons for a community.

Nevertheless, although few practitioners will argue publicly that evaluation is never necessary, de facto, it does not take place in a manner that befits its importance. And there are numerous instances in which it does not take place at all. Consequently, this chapter examines the reasons for evaluating community capacity-enhancement projects, identifies the challenges, and make a series of recommendations to help practitioners elevate evaluation to a higher level.

Description of the Phase

Evaluation should never be viewed as the final phase. The results gathered through evaluation will prove of immeasurable aid in helping social workers and communities develop more efficient and sustainable enhancement projects. No initiative is perfect. Thus, evaluation must highlight the successes and failures and provide sufficient data to allow for corrections in future endeavors.

This phase provides practitioners with all the same challenges that they faced in the previous stages. Furthermore, practitioners must be creative in developing evaluation mechanisms for gathering important data in a way that is unintrusive to the community—not an easy task for anyone. In addition, if the goals and spirit of community capacity enhancement are carried out, practitioners must develop ways in which to involve the community actively in developing the approach, gathering and interpreting data, and issuing the final report with the requisite set of recommendations.

Goals

Evaluation must provide practitioners with information on the following three areas: (1) process; (2) output; and (3) if possible, impact. Although a sociodemographic profile of those who participated and benefited from the intervention is useful, it is difficult to compile because the residents may be suspicious about giving information about themselves. However, every effort must be made to develop a greater understanding of the characteristics of the individuals who are involved and are targeted by the capacity-enhancement project.

These goals are no different from those of conventional evaluation. However, as is discussed in the section Key Practices Challenges, community capacity-enhancement projects require the use of highly interactive methods to capture the experiences associated with the intervention and must find a meaningful way of generating high participation by the residents in the process.

In addition, any evaluation of community capacity enhancement must actively involve the community in all facets of the evaluation endeavor and in so doing, enhance the capacity of the participants. Thus, costs of an evaluation of a community capacity-enhancement project are much higher than those of a "conventional" type of evaluation. This "investment" in the project and the participants must be systematically built into the evaluation.

Key Practice Concepts

The concept of an "appropriate" evaluation, like those of "participatory" and "empowerment" evaluations, sets the goals and context for an evaluation focused on community assets (Fetterman, Kaftarian, & Wandersman, 1996; Kretzmann & McKnight, 1997a). An appropriate evaluation must be seen as both a process, which is collaborative and capacity enhancing, and as a product. Consequently, all the key concepts related to capacity enhancement must be reflected in any effort to evaluate the impact of a community capacity-enhancement project.

The goal of "codiscovery" in evaluation, namely the answering of questions by residents and those undertaking the evaluation, best captures the meaning of this important but often overlooked and underappreciated phase. Codiscovery, however, is not restricted in any one facet of evaluation; it must permeate the entire process and incorporate and translate the language for all interested parties.

Evaluation must stress participation by those groups who will ultimately be affected by the answers to questions; thus, the participants are principle players, rather than the subjects of the research. As a result, participation can take place through the creation of an advisory committee composed of key stakeholders, residents and nonresidents alike, that will play a significant role in helping to conceptualize, plan, and implement the evaluation. This committee can play a significant role in helping to interpret the results, particularly those that may have been unexpected or puzzling. The committee can also participate in hiring and training residents to conduct interviews or run focus groups and community forums and other direct forms of obtaining information.

Key Practice Challenges

The importance of quantifying change in a community has never been an easy task for evaluators, regardless of their competence. However, this challenge takes on greater importance because of the ever-increasing need to produce results to obtain funding. Like prevention, community capacity enhancement must not only focus on the present, but just as important, must look toward the future to determine success. Thus, the evaluation process must enhance the abilities of community residents to initiate and undertake evaluations.

Hence, the evaluation phase presents practitioners with at least four key challenges: (1) to develop evaluation methods that do not disrupt community life or serve as an undue burden on the participants; (2) to create ways of meaningfully involving (recruiting, training, and supervising) community residents in all aspects of the evaluation process; (3) to devise data-gathering methods that lend themselves to some form of quantification without losing sight of the importance of ethnography, particularly in process evaluation; and (4) to develop measures of success that have legitimacy to both the community and funding sources.

The creation of evaluation methods that can easily be adapted to local circumstances (language, cultures, and so forth) and do not present an undue onus on the community is clearly one of the greatest, if not the greatest, challenge for a social worker engaged in community capacity enhancement. Methods and instruments must be relevant to a community. With community capacity enhancement, this goal takes on added significance because community members will play an active role in all aspects of the evaluation.

Consequently, methods and instruments that make no sense to the participants will, in all likelihood, not be used in the manner they were intended for and thus will severely undermine the quality of the results. A method or instrument is only as good as the individuals who are entrusted to carry them out. Consequently, the time and energy devoted to developing methods and instruments that are "community-friendly" will be time and energy well spent.

Case Illustrations

Case illustrations of evaluations based on capacity enhancement take on added significance because of the importance that funders place on evaluation. The author had great difficulty finding cases in which the evaluation process was well conceived and implemented. Community capacity-enhancement projects that were initiated by communities themselves did not have "formal" evaluations as part of their interventions. This finding should not come as a surprise because communities usually are not accountable to any "formal" funding source.

However, in the case of projects initiated by practitioners, the author found many situations in which the phases involved in developing community capacity-enhancement projects took on far greater significance than the actual evaluation phase. In many ways, these projects did not differ dramatically from more traditional ones. The need for practitioners to be "creative" in developing measures presented an additional set of barriers.

There were instances in which the only data that were gathered were on the number of participants; no effort was made to follow up with the participants within a predetermined period or to assess whether participation resulted in a change in attitude or behavior. In essence, the projects, although firmly based on many of the community capacity-enhancement principles discussed in this book, focused on creating changes in the environment and maximizing community participation.

Many of the projects that use community capacity-enhancement principles cannot be easily measured on a short-term basis, namely, after one year; these projects invariably require long-term evaluations; for example, in the case of community gardens, it takes several years before concrete benefits can be discerned. The nature of community capacity-enhancement projects makes the process of evaluation challenging, but not impossible.

This chapter uses two cases to illustrate various aspects and approaches to evaluation that are critical for community capacity enhancement. The first case involves a youth-focused organization (Gallery 37) in Chicago that utilizes a low labor-intensive approach to evaluate the experiences of youths involved in painting murals. The second case focuses on the pitfalls that may be inherent in engaging residents community capacity enhancement at this point in time. These two cases highlight the richness of community capacity-enhancement evaluation, its challenges, and rewards for communities and practitioners.

Gallery 37 is a Chicago-based youth-focused, arts organization that provides a wide range of art programs through the city's neighborhood organizations, schools, and park districts. One of the primary art projects involves painting murals. The organization's evaluation is primarily process oriented and seeks answers to the following six key question, including basic demographic information on the participants:

1. Describe your project at Gallery 37 in 199—. Did it deviate in any way from the proposed curriculum? If so, how?
2. Describe in detail the final artwork/products created in your project. Please include both visual and nonvisual artwork (writing pieces, plays, or videos).
3. Describe the impact and affect your program had on apprentice artists. Please include any anecdotes and personal experiences your organization and teaching staff had with any apprentice artists. How were these experiences a result of your project and Gallery 37 in general?
4. Did your program meet your proposed goals for benefiting the community, and in what way? How will you meet or improve upon meeting these goals next year?
5. Please describe any significant growth seen in the apprentice artists in the following areas: artistic, vocational, and social.
6. How many apprentice artists participated in your program? Please provide the gender, age, and ethnic breakdown of your apprentice artists.

The six areas covered by Gallery 37's evaluation provide information from a variety of perspectives, with the participants as the primary target. The focus of the evaluation is clearly on qualitative data with direct programming implications. The generation of products, such as photographs, journals, and videos, allows the organization to do a more in-depth analysis beyond the information provided by the project director. The evaluation process, although not ideal, is sufficiently low labor intensive to generate information that is of value to the organization.

The second case illustration was included in this book because it typified the experiences that the author had in finding detailed evaluation components of capacity-enhancement projects. The information was provided to the author on the condition that the respondent would remain anonymous; as a result, the source and location (city and region of the country) of the project is not provided to protect the respondent's identity.

The mural project was based in a midsized city that was experiencing a steady increase in the migration of various Latino groups. A mural would serve as an excellent project for integrating the backgrounds of the many different groups and their hopes for life in the United States:

> The project sought to develop a series of murals that would be shaped by getting community input. The organization sponsoring this project did not have an extensive history with community capacity enhancement. The idea for this project resulted from the interests of a community social worker

who, had not been actively involved in similar projects in the past, but had witnessed one in a nearby city. These murals, although not complex in design, would be pained on walls that were strategically located in the community. Community youths would be recruited and receive the requisite instruction and supervision in painting the murals.

The funding for this project was minimal, so the youth participants were not paid for their work. A tremendous amount of time and energy was spent in "selling" the idea to the agency and key community stakeholders and in getting local establishments to agree to have a mural. In fact, according to the coordinator of the project, it felt like most of the energy went into this phase and that minimal attention was paid into the other aspects of the project, particularly evaluation.

There was really no evaluation of the process and outcome of the project. At the end of the experience, the youths were asked to share their thoughts, experiences, and recommendations. Community reactions were obtained in a way that did not allow the results to be systematically recorded for analysis and generalizability. The coordinator of the project, although somewhat defensive when asked what changes resulted from this project, noted that the murals beautified the neighborhood, the youths learned "a great deal" about working in this medium, and the community seemed generally happy with the experience. The fact that a "formal" evaluation did not transpire did not take away from the positive experience.

The author, although initially taken aback by the coordinator's reaction, was not totally surprised by the response. Community capacity-enhancement projects, as already noted, require the expenditure of a tremendous amount of time and energy in the planning and implementation phases, and evaluation, unfortunately, can easily become an afterthought. When the hoped-for "successful" outcome occurs, there seems to be minimal interest, energy, and resources to examine systematically why a project succeeded, for whom, and what lessons can be learned and shared with other organizations and communities that want to undertake similar types of projects.

Practitioners and communities must develop an awareness of why evaluation is so important in any form of endeavor but particularly with community capacity-enhancement projects. This form of intervention is relatively new in the field of practice and thus is subject to greater-than-usual scrutiny by funders.

There is sufficient flexibility within evaluation to take into account local circumstances, resources, and interests. Thus, this flexibility allows for compromises without sacrificing the integrity of the evaluation or causing major disruptions in a community's life.

Key Practice Skills

An evaluation will be successful only when the practitioner has the technical and sociopolitical skills to conduct an evaluation that is beneficial to all parties. Thus, the ability to develop methods and instruments that are easily understood and acceptable by all parties, particularly the community and funders, is no small fete. The possession of excellent communication skills, sometimes involving more than one language or having access to high-quality translators, is a practice skill that will serve the social worker well in this type of work.

An ability to ground the evaluation within a culturally competent context naturally follows from having excellent communication skills. Urban communities are not homogeneous and often consist of many ethnic and racial groups that do not share similar world experiences, languages, or cultures. An ability to gain access to all these groups in a manner that is culturally competent will go a long way toward ensuring that the results of the evaluation reflect the community's perspectives on the process and outcome.

Having said that, the author is well aware of the difficulties involved in trying to reach out to all significant groups within a community in a manner that is respectful of their cultural backgrounds. No practitioner will have all the requisite skills and knowledge to be able to accomplish this goal. As a result, it requires a team or access to resources that can be tapped at the appropriate time. The practitioner's network must be extensive and firmly grounded in the population groups that are to be served.

The creation of an evaluation document that has multiple audiences as targets necessitates the creation of multiple reports. The practitioner must be willing to obtain the necessary resources and invest the required time to create multiple reports and sometimes in several languages. This does not mean that all the reports will be identical regarding statistics, tables, description of methodology, details regarding study limitations, and so on. Multiple reports may consist of summary letters (highlighting critical aspects of the intervention) to key community stakeholders in their native languages, informing them that they can see the more fully developed report if they so desire. Funders may be more interested in conventional evaluation reports, which are clearly not of interest to the community. This entire effort requires careful thought, time, and planning. Nevertheless, these decisions should not be overlooked in the interest of keeping communities informed and involved.

Conclusion

The importance of evaluation is often attested to in grant proposals and applications. Practitioners are often quick to point out to funders the importance of understanding how the results of projects have changed people's lives and communities. However, although the reality of practice sometimes makes evaluation important in a grant proposal, evaluation loses its significance for practitioners when they carry out the day-to-day activities associated with projects.

Community capacity-enhancement work is no exception to this phenomenon, as witnessed in the case examples used in this chapter. In fact, this form of intervention presents additional challenges for practitioners, making the process of evaluation that much more important and difficult to achieve. Nevertheless, evaluation is here to stay and must be addressed in a serious and comprehensive manner if community capacity enhancement is to enjoy its time in the sun.

Conclusion to Chapters 8–12

The case examples used throughout Chapters 8–12 provide a rich and detailed perspective on the meaning of murals, gardens, playgrounds, and sculptures to community residents in cities across the country. There are no simple and easy ways to conceptualizing these types of projects, nor are these projects restricted to our national boundaries. Nevertheless, they all bring the strategy of community capacity enhancement to life.

The cases presented in Chapters 8–12 reveal a series of rewards and challenges that practitioners will encounter in assessing and helping to create these community-based projects. Work with community capacity-enhancement projects will never be dull; in all likelihood, no two days will ever be alike for practitioners. A cookie-cutter approach to capacity enhancement will be doomed to failure because of the importance of local issues and circumstances that dictate the nature of the intervention.

The case studies also showed a wide variety of approaches and degree of involvement of communities in all facets of the interventions. Some of the cases focused on collaborative relationships between various governmental entities and the private sector; others showed how one project leads to another; and still others were not as successful as the community and practitioner hoped for but, nevertheless, made important gains or raised critical issues for a community.

These case illustrations, however, do not do justice to the importance of community capacity enhancement projects involving murals, gardens, playgrounds, and sculptures. The richness, complexity, and sense of adventure associated with this form of community practice necessitates specially skilled practitioners and organizations that are willing to undertake projects that do not fit nicely into categories for reporting purposes.

These projects represent an investment in the future of communities in addition to meeting their current pressing social needs. Furthermore, as evidenced in all the cases, communities ultimately determine the success or failure of any intervention. As a result, their part must never be lost in conveying their successes and lessons to the "outside" world.

13

Reflections on Practice
(Lessons and Recommendations)

In this chapter, the author synthesizes the lessons learned in undertaking urban-based community capacity-enhancement practice. The rewards, challenges, hopes, and despair that are often associated with practice, be it either micro or macro, in urban areas must energize social workers in their quest for economic and social justice for undervalued groups that often face multiple jeopardies in their lives.

The chapter was written in an informal manner (no use of references, quotes, and so forth), to facilitate communication with the reader. This is a highly unusual practice in a "scholarly" publication, but it gives the author the opportunity to communicate with the reader in a more personal and engaging way. Recommendations for future work in this area are discussed. These recommendations cover a variety of arenas regarding practice and social work education as a means of bringing these two "worlds" together—each informing the other.

Rediscovery of Community

Although the social work profession has a long history of working in communities, it has not stopped other helping professionals from discovering community as a context for services for the first time; unfortunately, these other rediscovery professionals rarely acknowledge that social work has its roots in communities. The viability of the profession in the next century will be contingent on social workers' willingness and skills to providing services to undervalued urban-based groups within a community context.

This context plays an influential role in the assessment and intervention phases of practice, both micro or macro focused. Thus, the profession must reaffirm that its future rests with communities as both settings for intervention and as vehicles for creating change. The profession's failure to embrace work in this arena will result in social workers' inability to reach out, engage, and serve population groups that have multiple jeopardies. These population groups, which often provide great challenges, can be served effectively and efficiently only within their communities.

Nevertheless, because the definition of *community* is ever changing, it becomes more and more challenging for social workers to have a solid grasp of what the term means. Unfortunately, the shifting of definition of community often has an ever-increasing set of "problems" attached to it. Thus, the profession faces the challenge of how to address urban-based, communitywide concerns, amidst global changes that at times appear overwhelming—the shifting of jobs overseas to developing nations, an economy that is ever more dependent on low-paying service jobs with minimal benefits, and a political will that can best be described as punitive toward low-income individuals and their families.

Importance of Cities

Although the issue was raised in Chapter 1 and interwoven throughout this book, it is important to stress the unique characteristics of cities and why practice must take these unique factors into account. There is little dispute that nations throughout the world, including the United States are experiencing massive upheavals resulting from the migration of people from rural to urban areas. Such a global and national trend has a profound impact on how people live, work, worship, recreate, learn, and solve conflicts. The stressors associated with urban living will no doubt increase in influence as we enter an age of increased uncertainty.

Cities in the United States will continue to increase in importance as they solidify as centers of communication, finances, transportation, and education. Furthermore, as cities increase in size and diversity of composition, the social work profession will be called on to play an active role in helping communities address the tensions associated with rapid changes—changes that are complicated when population groups do not share the same languages, cultures, and history. Probably no other profession is capable of achieving this goal.

The profession's history of community-based work, combined with a history of working with newcomers and doing so from a multifaceted perspective, makes social workers uniquely qualified to face the challenge. Thus, practitioners will be called upon to broker between groups in communities, create opportunities for communities to come together and work on common goals, help identify assets, and create capacity-enhancement opportunities. The author believes that the greater presence of social work in urban areas will increase the marketability of social workers.

Finding One's Niche

Community practice, as conceptualized in this book, is not for every macro-oriented social worker. Unfortunately, macro practitioners, the author included, have tended only to sing the praises of community work and hence to romanticize it. However, community work is far from romantic in the conventional sense of the word. Just like agency-centered work, in which practitioners never leave their offices or buildings cannot be labeled boring and prosaic, some social workers may find community work too unpredictable, the agendas too ambiguous, the time frames unrealistic, and the outcomes too much in doubt.

However, for social workers who love the challenge of no two days ever being the same and of holding meetings in places, such as restaurants, beauty parlors, playgrounds, houses of worship, parks, and people's homes, community practice will more than meet their needs for the "unconventional." Community practice means doing work in the "community." Consequently, social workers must be flexible in how they define the work environment when they work in communities, whether urban, suburban, or rural. The author believes that the excitement of doing community social work far exceeds the downside. However, it would be unfair and unrealistic to ignore the challenges inherent in this type of practice.

Social Work Curriculum

The content of community capacity enhancement must be systematically incorporated into all courses and is worthy of separate courses to allow in-depth examination and discussion. The integration of the subject will reenforce the importance of the subject and ensure that it is supported by all aspects of the curriculum—human behavior and the social environment, social welfare policy, research, ethics, and so forth. However, such integration will not guarantee that the material will be addressed and will rely on the interests, experiences, and capabilities of the instructor. Consequently, offering separate courses on community capacity enhancement will guarantee that the content will be covered and given its due attention.

The demand for community capacity-enhancement courses may be limited. However, in those circumstances, it may be possible to develop and use modules, outside speakers, workshops, and the like to inject the subject into the curriculum without having to create new courses into an overcrowded curriculum.

Innovative Practicum Experiences

A serious commitment to develop community capacity-enhancement strategies in urban areas cannot be easily created or, for that matter, be successful, without significant changes in the field practicum experience. Traditional approaches, such as 9 to 5 hours, several weekdays in the field, and an agency-centered base, must be reconsidered. Furthermore, community capacity enhancement does not lend itself to conventional catchment areas and population groups. Therefore, new strategies and structures must be created to fit the model, rather than fitting the model to existing structures.

New strategies for the practice of community capacity enhancement will necessitate new forms of providing supervision, an examination of who can provide supervision, and the development of new measures for evaluating the field practicum experience. A tremendous amount of time and energy will be required to create these new learning opportunities for social work students. Schools of social work and the Council on Social Work Education must be prepared to invest the resources so the profession can be strategically positioned in the twenty-first century.

Collaborative Research and Theory Development

The increased importance of communities and the development of ways to reach and engage them in change makes it essential for social workers to develop collaborative partnership models with communities not only to bring about change but to facilitate the further development of theory regarding community capacity enhancement. The author has no doubt that these goals can only be achieved through collaborative partnerships.

The authors also believes that these partnerships will present the profession with incredible challenges. These ventures are not only labor intensive but may be fraught with all kinds of hazards for practitioners and the organizations that employ them. Overtures to others to form partnerships may require the expenditure of considerable time and effort without producing the desired results. Nevertheless, the challenges that collaborative partnerships present pale in comparison to the benefits that can be derived from working together. Benefits must be viewed both as present and future results once relationships are established.

The benefits and challenges increase dramatically when collaborative relationships necessitate the involvement of entities that normally do not work together. The importance of developing evaluation strategies for examining the results of capacity-enhancement initiatives, for example provide an excellent context for research.

Needless to say, successful ventures resulting in an increased number of new forms of partnerships are rewarding, as is the case in evaluation. However, these types of partnerships can be labor intensive and painful, especially when they involve entities or sectors that social workers rarely reach out to involve, such as the business community.

Implications for International Practice

Social work education, with some notable exceptions, has concentrated on preparing practitioners for work in the United States. The acceptance of a community capacity-enhancement model, however, prepares students for global practice with both industrialized and developing nations. Since resources that are essential for capacity-enhancement practice are within the capabilities of all communities and nations, this model not only will make American students better able to practice in other countries, but it will attract students from other countries. This exchange will benefit all parties, including the profession.

Some practitioners and policy makers would argue that conditions that are normally associated with "Third World" countries can be easily found within major urban areas of the United States. Some of these conditions represent a far greater injustice than that found in "developing countries" because of the wealth surrounding these communities. Thus, capacity-enhancement practice has relevance in any context.

Conclusion

It was not the author's intent to overwhelm the reader with the amount of further work and reflection that need to be accomplished in community practice. However, community social work practice requires a systematic critique of current practice before any advances can occur. Community social work has a tremendous potential to make an impact on undervalued communities in their search for social and economic justice; it can accomplish this lofty goal through a shift in paradigms and the embrace of an assets perspective.

The skills and knowledge areas addressed in this book lend themselves to application in other areas of community social work practice and are not restricted to the use of murals, gardens, playgrounds, and sculptures. There are numerous other types of community capacity-enhancement projects that can be used to achieve the principles identified in Chapter 5. There are many emotions and thoughts related to urban-based practice. The author hopes that this book has captured some of them and provided the reader with a better understanding of the importance of this type of work and how it is central to the mission of social work. Community practice, however, should never be "romanticized" because of the challenges it provides the profession or because it is "where the people are." This form of practice, whether enhancement or problem focused, is not without its frustrations or "politics."

However, if these experiences are placed within the context that is considered "practice," this form of intervention will never lose its importance and the potential impact it can have on large groups of people who are undervalued in this society. Community assets and needs do not come in neatly labeled packages that can easily be identified, categorized, and utilized. In essence, this is what social work is all about—working with people from an assets perspective and being able and willing to address issues and problems from a multifaceted perspective. In short, social workers should not run away from challenges.

Community capacity-enhancement practice will provide the social work profession with an approach that is not only affirming, but can result in dramatic changes in the environment. The practice of capacity enhancement, in turn, can reenergize practice in urban areas of this country at a time when the profession, at least according to the author, is struggling to find its mission in the twenty-first century.

References

Abrahamson, M. (1996). *Urban enclaves: Identity and place in America*. New York: St. Martin's Press.

Academy for Educational Development, Center for Youth Development and Policy Research. (1998). *Community youthmapping*. Washington, DC: Author.

Albrecht, T. L. (1994). Epilogue: Social support and community: A historical account of the rescue networks in Denmark. In B. R. Burleson, T. L. Albrecht, & I. G. Sarason (Eds.), *Communication of social support: Messages, interactions, relationships, and community* (pp. 267–279). Newbury Park, CA: Sage.

America in the '90s. (1991, September 28). *National Journal*, pp. 2315–2333.

American Community Gardening Association. (1997). *Community gardening bigger than you think*. Philadelphia: Author.

Americans in 2020: Less white, more southern. (1994, April 22). *New York Times*, p. 34.

Andranovich, G. D., and Riposa, G. (1993). *Doing urban research*. Newbury Park, CA: Sage.

Andrews, A. C., & Fonseca, J. W. (1995). *The atlas of American society*. New York: New York University Press.

Annual report: From the roots up. (1996–97). Philadelphia: American Community Gardening Association.

Arie-Donch, T. (1990). *Small neighborhood parks*. Unpublished manuscript.

Arie-Donch, T. (1991). *A guide to community built projects: Organizing techniques for making your community self-help project a success*. Unpublished manuscript.

Arie-Donch, T. (1997). Grow or die. Community Built Association News, 5, 3.

Arie-Donch, T. (1998). *Central organizing principles of community built projects*. University of California, Davis: Office of Graduate Studies Master of Science Thesis.

Asare, E. O., Oppong, S. K., & Twum-Ampofo, K. (1990). Home gardens in the humid tropics of Ghana. In K. Landauer & M. Brazil (Eds.), *Tropical home gardens* (pp. 80–93). New York: United Nations University Press.

Avery, R. (1997, October 24). Taking back the parks. *Philadelphia Daily News,* pp. 1, 32.

Badshah, A. A. (1996). *Our urban future: New paradigms for equity and sustainability.* New York: Oxford University Press.

Baez-Hernandez, S. (1995). The *New York Times:* Discursive practice: On moral transformation of ex-graffiti writers. Paper presented at the annual meeting of the American Sociological Association.

Baker, F. (1977). The interface between professional and natural support systems. *Clinical Social Work Journal, 5,* 139–148.

Baker, R. (1997). Where the sidewalks end. *HOPE, 7,* 16–23.

Balgopal, P. R., & Vassil, T. V. (1983). *Groups in social work: An ecological perspective.* New York: Macmillan.

Barnett, A. W. (1984). *Community murals: The people's art.* Philadelphia: Art Alliance Press.

Barringer, D. (1997). The new urban gamble. *American Prospect, 34,* 28–34.

Barringer, F. (1991, March 11). Census shows profound change in racial makeup of the nation. *New York Times,* pp. A1, B1.

Barringer, F. (1993, June 6). Minorities on the move, often unpredictably. *New York Times,* p. E4.

Barton, W. H., Watkins, M. & Jarjoura, R. (1997). Youths and communities: Towards comprehensive strategies for youth development. *Social Work, 42,* 483–493.

Beckwith, M. E., and Gilster, S. D. (1997). The paradise garden: A model garden design for those with Alzheimer's disease. *Activities, Adaptation and Aging, 22,* 3–16.

Bellisle, M. (1996, July 5). Neighbors transform empty lot. *St. Louis Post-Dispatch,* p. 2B.

Berlin, S. (1997). *Ways we live: Exploring community.* Stoney Creek, CT: New Society Publishers.

Bicho, A. N. (1997). Green visions: Indianapolis and Dayton take center stage. *Community Gardening Review, 7,* 20–27.

Billingsley, A. (1968). *Black families in white America.* Englewood Cliffs, NJ: Prentice Hall.

Birkeland, J. (1994). Ecofeminist playgradens: A guide to growing greenies organically. *International Play Journal, 2,* 49–59.

Black, L. (1996). Families of African origin: An overview. In M. McGoldrick, J. Giordano, & J. K. Pearce (Eds.), *Ethnicity and family therapy.* (2nd ed., pp. 57–65). New York: Guilford Press.

Blakely, E. J., & Snyder, M. G. (1997). *Fortress America: Gated communities in the United States.* Washington, DC: Brookings Institution Press/Lincoln Institute of Land Policy.

Bloch, D. (1998). *Urban garden history.* Los Angeles: Los Angeles Regional Foodbank.

Blue, H. (1997, September 24). Murals: The concrete canvas has transformed many neighborhoods and ideas. *Philadelphia New Observer,* p. 1.

Bluestone, B. (1997). *How does Boston rank?: Comparing the Greater Boston region to top 77 metropolitan regions in the U.S.* Boston: John W. McCormack Institute of Public Affairs, University of Massachusetts, Boston.

Bobskill, L. (1995, August 20). Community produces playground. *Holyoke Sun,* p. 14.

Boyle, P. (1998). Write stuff, wrong place: Graffiti wars. *Youth Today, 7, 56,* 48–49.

Breitbart, M. M. (1998). "Dana's mystical tunnel": Young people's designs for survival and change in the city. In T. Skelton & G. Valentine (Eds.), *Cool places: Geographies of youth cultures* (pp. 305–327). London: Routledge.

Breslav, M. (1995). The Portland difference: Oregon's "City of Roses." *Community Gardening Review, 5,* 14–21.

Brieland, D. (1990). The Hull-House tradition and the contemporary social worker: Was Jane Addams really a social worker? *Social Work, 35,* 134–138.

Bronner, E. (1998, April 28). Jews and Arabs, painting a mural together, find a mosaic of mistrust. *New York Times,* p. A10.

Brower, S. N., & Williamson, P. (1974). Outdoor recreation as a function of the urban housing environment. *Environment and Behavior, 6,* 295–345.

Brown, D. W. (1995). *When strangers cooperate: Using social conventions to govern ourselves.* New York: Free Press.

Browne, C. & Broderick, A. (1994). Asian and Pacific Island elders: Issues for social work practice and education. *Social Work, 39,* 252–259.

Brueggemann, W. G. (1996). *The practice of macro social work.* Chicago: Nelson-Hall.

Budowski, G. (1990). Home gardens in tropical America: A review. In K. Landuer & M. Brazil (Eds.), *Tropical home gardens* (pp. 3–8). New York: United Nations University Press.

Bullard, R. D., & Johnson, G. S. (Eds.). (1997). *Just transportation: Dismantling race and class barriers to mobility.* Stoney Creek, CT: New Society Publishers.

Burawoy, M. (1991a). The extended case method. In M. Burawoy, A. Burton, A. A. Ferguson, K. J. Fox, J. Gamson, N. Gartrell, L. Hurst, C. Kurzman, L. Salzinger, J. Schiffman, & S. Ui (Eds.), *Ethnography unbound: Power and resistance in the modern metropolis* (pp. 271–287). Berkeley: University of California Press.

Burawoy, M. (1991b). Reconstructing social theories. In M. Burawoy et al. (Eds.), *Ethnography unbound: Power and resistance in the modern metropolis* (pp. 8–27). Berkeley: University of California Press.

Bursik, R. J. Jr., & Grasmick, H. G. (1993). *Neighborhoods and crime: The dimensions of effective community control.* Lexington, MA: Lexington Books.

Bush-Brown, L. (1969). *Garden blocks for urban America.* New York: Charles Scribner's Sons.

Buss, S. (1995). Urban Los Angeles from young people's angle of vision. *Children's Environments, 12,* 340–351.

Butterfield, F. (1991, February 24). Asians spread across a land, and help change it. *New York Times,* pp. 1, 22.

Butterfield, F. (1992, July 19). Are American jails becoming shelters from the storm? *New York Times,* p. 4E.

Butterfield, F. (1994, October 14). Teen-age homicide rate has soared. *New York Times,* p. A22.

California town hopes eye-catching murals will put it on map. (1996, November 10). *New York Times,* p. 24.

Callahan, J. (1997). Assisted suicide, community, and the common good. *Health & Social Work, 22,* 243–245.

Campbell, R. (1996, December 26). Urban regains its good name: They're keen, not mean, streets these days. *Boston Globe,* pp. D1, D7.

Carrier, J. (1997, May 11). Gardeners, rich and poor, sink roots across Denver. *Denver Post*, p. B-05.

Cavallo, D. (1981). *Muscles and morals: Organized playgrounds and urban reform, 1880–1920*. Philadelphia: University of Pennsylvania Press.

Chalfant, H., & Prigoff, J. (1997). *Spraycan art*. London, England: Thames & Hudson.

Champagne, D. (1994). *Native North American Almanac*. Detroit: Gale Research.

Chao, C. M. (1992). The inner heart: Therapy with Southeast Asian families. In L. A. Vargas & J. D. Koss-Chioino (Eds.), *Working with culture: Psychotherapeutic interventions with ethnic minority children and adolescents* (pp. 25–42). San Francisco: Jossey-Bass.

Chapin, R. K. (1995). Social policy development: The strengths perspective. *Social Work, 40*, 506–514.

Chase, M. (1990, February 14). Volunteers' distress cripples huge effort to provide AIDS care. *Wall Street Journal*, p. 1.

Chaskin, R. J. & Chipenda-Dansokho, S. (1997). Implementing comprehensive community development: Possibilities and limitations. *Social Work, 42*, 435–444.

Chavis, D. M. & Wandersman, A. (1990). Sense of community in the urban environment: A catalyst for participation and community development. *American Journal of Community Psychology, 18*, 55–80.

Chavis, M. E. (1997). *Altars in the street: A neighborhood fights to survive*. New York: Bell Tower.

Chen, D. W. (1997, November 20). New Chinatown statue shows growing role of the Fujianese. *New York Times*, p. A32.

Christianty, L. (1990). Home gardens in tropical Asia, with special reference to Indonesia. In K. Landauer & M. Brazil (Eds.), *Tropical home gardens* (pp. 9–20). New York: United Nations University Press.

City Editor. (1997, April 21). Hundreds of Kimberly-Clark employees and North Oak Cliff residents to build community playground. *PR Newswire*, p. 1.

Cockcroft, E. S., & Barnet-Sanchez, H. (1990). Introduction. In E. S. Cockcroft & H. Barnet-Sanchez (Eds.), *Signs from the heart: California Chicano murals* (pp. 5–21). Albuquerque: University of New Mexico Press.

Cohen, C. S., & Phillips, M. H. (1997). Building community: Principles for social work practice in housing settings. *Social Work, 42*, 471–481.

Coleman, S. (1994a, December 11). Mission's marvelous murals if you go . . . *Boston Globe*, p. B1.

Coleman, S. (1994b, April 17). Their aim is to create an "Avenue of the Arts." *Boston Globe*, p. 1.

Coleman, S. (1997, January 25). Taking it to the walls: The expressive mural. *Boston Globe*, pp. C1, C7.

Collins, A. H., & Pancoast, D. L. (1976). *Natural helping networks: A strategy for prevention*. Washington, DC: National Association of Social Workers.

Collins, J. B. (1996, May 5). Kids to help plan Warner playground. *Chattanooga Free Press*, p. 1.

Community Built Conference. (1997). What is community build? Ithaca, NY: Annual Meeting, pp. 1–2.

Community mapping: Mapping Boyle Heights. (1996). Los Angeles: J. Paul Getty Trust.

Cook, C. D. (1997). Cultivating locally: Community gardening for food security. *Community Gardening Review, 7*, 2–10.

Cooper, M., & Chalfant, H. (1984). *Subway art.* New York: Holt, Rinehart & Winston.

Cooper, M., & Sciorra, J. (1994). *R.I.P. memorial wall art.* New York: Holt, Rinehart & Winston.

Cotter, H. (1998, March 16). A neighborhood nurtures its vibrant cultural history: Price of place for art and artists in the Barrio. *New York Times,* pp. B1, B3.

Cottrell, L. (1976). The competent community. In B. H. Kaplan, R. N. Wilson, & A. H. Leighton (Eds.), *Further explorations in social psychiatry* (pp. 195–209). New York: Basic Books.

Cox, H. (1995). *Fire from heaven: The rise of Pentecostal spirituality and the reshaping of religion in the twenty-first century.* Reading, MA: Addison-Wesley.

Coxsackie Community Playground. (1998). *Volunteer registration form and construction week details.* Coxsackie, NY: Author.

Cundy, K. (1998). Architecture & kids—The curriculum. *CBA News* (Community Built Association), *6,* 4.

Daley, B. (1996, May 5). If we built it, they'll play: Youths, community unite to create havens for kids. *Boston Globe,* p. 33.

Daley, J. M. & Wong, P. (1994). Community development with emerging ethnic communities. *Journal of Community Practice, 1,* 9–24.

Dao, J. (1998, March 18). New York city grows, even as many leave. *New York Times,* p. A23.

Davis, W. A. (1998, July 11). Journey to the center: A new interest in the ancient labyrinth has people walking in circles toward fulfillment. *Boston Globe,* pp. C1, C6.

Delgado, M. (1995). Community asset assessment and substance abuse prevention: A case study involving the Puerto Rican community. *Journal of Child and Adolescent Substance Abuse, 4,* 57–77.

Delgado, M. (1996a). Aging research and the Puerto Rican community: The use of an elder advisory committee of intended respondents. *The Gerontologist, 36,* 406–408.

Delgado, M. (1996b). Community asset assessments by Latino youths: Lessons from the field. *Social Work in Education, 18,* 169–178.

Delgado, M. (1997a). Interpretation of Puerto Rican elder research findings: A community forum of research respondents. *Journal of Applied Gerontology, 16,* 317–332.

Delgado, M. (1997b). Role of Latina-owned beauty parlors in a Latino community. *Social Work, 42,* 445–453.

Delgado, M. (1997c). Strength-based practice with early adolescent Puerto Ricans: Lessons from an ATOD prevention project. *Social Work in Education, 19,* 101–112.

Delgado, M. (1998a). Involvement of the Latino community in ATOD research. *Drugs & Society, 14,* 93–105.

Delgado, M. (1998b). *Social services in Latino communities: Research and strategies.* New York: Haworth Press.

Delgado, M. (1998c). *Social work practice in nontraditional urban settings.* New York: Oxford University Press.

Delgado, M. (In press). *New arenas for social work practice with urban youth: The arts, humanities, music, and sports.* New York: Columbia University Press.

Delgado, M., & Barton, K. (1998). Murals in Latino communities: Social indicators of community strengths. *Social Work, 43,* 346–356.

Delgado, M., & Humm-Delgado, D. (1982). Natural support systems: Source of strengths in Hispanic communities. *Social Work, 27,* 83–89.

Del Pival, J., & Singer, A. (1997). Generations of diversity: Latinos in the United States. *Population Bulletin, 52,* 1–47.

De Parle, J. (1997, December 28). Welfare to work: A sequel. *New York Times,* pp. 14–17.

De Vita, C. J. (1996). The United States at mid-decade. *Population Bulletin, 50,* 1–48.

Didion, J. (1978). *Miami.* New York: Pocket Books.

Doss, E. (1995). *Spirits poles and flying pigs.* Washington, DC: Smithsonian Institution Press.

Dow, W. N. (1997). An urbanizing world. In U. Kirdar (Ed.), *Cities fit for people* (pp. 27–49). New York: United Nations Publications.

Dowdy, Z. R. (1995, August 7). Art with an urban edge: Teacher helps graffiti masters transform drab city spaces. *Boston Globe,* p. 13.

Downs, A. (1997). The challenge of our declining cities. *Housing Policy Debates, 8,* 359–408.

Drescher, T., & Garcia, R. (1978). Recent Raza murals in the U.S. *Radical America, 12,* 14–31.

Dugger, C. W. (1996, March 10). Immigrant voters reshape politics. *New York Times,* pp. 1, 28.

Dugger, C. W. (1997, November 10). Study shows Dominicans sink deeper into poverty. *New York Times,* p. A31.

Dugger, C. W. (1998, July 20). In India, an arranged marriage of 2 worlds: Here and there. *New York Times,* pp. A1, A14–A15.

Dunitz, R. (1993). *Street gallery: Guide to 1000 L.A. murals.* Los Angeles: RJD Enterprises.

Dunitz, R., & Prigoff, J. (1997). *Painting the towns: Murals of California.* Los Angeles: RJD Enterprises.

Dunlap, D. W. (1998, May 1). Next stop murals: Change here for uptown sculpture. *New York Times,* pp. B37, B52.

Dupper, D. R., & Poertner, J. (1997). Public schools and the revitalization of impoverished communities: School-linked, family resource centers. *Social Work, 42,* 415–422.

Emmerij, L. (1997). In the midst of paradoxes: An urban renaissance? In U. Kirdar (Ed.), *Cities fit for people* (pp. 100–108). New York: United Nations Publications.

Engle, D.R. (1997, October 26). Young artists brighten Reservoir Hill buildings. *Baltimore Sun,* p. 15a.

Erkut, S., Fields, J. P., Sing, R., & Marx, F. (1996). Diversity in girls' experiences: Feeling good about who you are. In B. J. R. Leadbeater & N. Way (Eds.), *Urban girls: Resisting stereotypes, creating identities* (pp. 53–64). New York: New York University Press.

Eriksen, A. (1985). *Playground design: Outdoor environments for learning and development.* New York: Van Nostrand.

Erickson, I. (1994, October). A passion for play. *America West Airlines Magazine,* pp. 40–41.

Escobar, D. (1997). *Major murals of 24th street.* Los Angeles: Social and Political Arts Resource Center.

Ewalt, P. L. (1997). The revitalization of impoverished communities. *Social Work, 42*, 413–414.

Facio, E. (1993). Ethnography as personal experience. In J. H. Stanfield II & R. M. Dennis (Eds.), *Race and ethnicity in research methods* (pp. 75–91). Newbury Park, CA: Sage.

Falck, H. (1988). *Social work: The membership perspective.* New York: Springer.

Falender, A. J. (1998, January 4). Greendreams: Boston's boom should allow for essential and aesthetic open spaces. *Boston Globe,* pp. E1, E4.

Feagin, J. R. (1998a). Arenas of conflict: Zoning and land-use reform in critical political-economic perspective. In J. R. Feagin (Ed.), *The new urban paradigm: Critical perspectives on the city* (pp. 181–215). New York: Rowman & Littlefield.

Feagin, J. R. (Ed.). (1998b). *The new urban paradigm: Critical perspectives on the city.* New York: Rowman & Littlefield.

Feagin, J. R., & Smith, M. P. (1998). Cities and the new international division of labor: An overview. In J. R. Feagin (Ed.), *The new urban paradigm: Critical perspectives on the city* (pp. 25–58). New York: Rowman & Littlefield.

Feldman, P. (1993, August 19). Harvest of hope. *Los Angeles Times,* pp. B1, B4.

Fellin, P. (1995). *The community and the social worker* (2nd ed.). Itasca, IL: F. E. Peacock.

Ferrell, J. (1995). Urban graffiti: Crime, control, and resistance. *Youth & Society, 27,* 73–92.

Ferrick, T. Jr. (1997, March 2). Seeing Phila. as a city of green. *Philadelphia Inquirer,* pp. A1, A19.

Fetterman, D., Kaftarian, S., & Wandersman, A. (1996). *Empowerment evaluation.* Thousand Oaks, CA: Sage.

Fiffer, S., & Fiffer, S. S. (1994). *50 ways to help your community.* New York: Doubleday.

Finch, J. (1983). Can skills be shared? Playgrounds in "disadvantaged" areas. *Community Developmental Journal, 18,* 251–256.

Finkel, E. (1998, March–April). Gardens hang in the balance. *Neighborhood Works,* p. 7.

Finn, J. L., & Checkoway, B. (1998). Young people as competent community builders: A challenge to social work. *Social Work, 43,* 335–345.

Firestone, D. (1995, March 29). Major ethnic changes under way. *New York Times,* pp. B1–B2.

Fisher, J. (1998). *Historical resource evaluation report for the San Diego–Cornado Bay bridge, Chicano Park and the murals.* San Diego: Chicano Park Association.

Fishman, S. (1996, November 24). Eco-artists gather at the river: Environmental science and art meld. *Boston Globe,* 15, 18.

Fishman, S. (1998a, May 10). In Somerville, children have new ground for play. *Boston Globe* (City Weekly), pp. 1, 6.

Fishman, S. (1998b, August 23). Program gives disabled an opportunity to garden. *Boston Globe,* p. 4.

Flanagan, W. G. (1993). *Contemporary urban sociology.* New York: Cambridge University Press.

Floyd, L. (1997, September 4). Farm program plants crops of caring teenagers. *Boston Globe,* p. 14.

Folkman, D. A., & Raijk, K. (1997). Reflections on facilitating a participatory community self-evaluation. *Evaluation and Program Planning, 20,* 455–465.

Foner, N. (1987). Introduction: New immigrants and changing patterns in New York City. In N. Foner (Ed.), *New immigrants in New York* (pp. 1–33). New York: Columbia University Press.

Fong, R., & Mokuau, N. (1994). Not simply "Asian Americans": Periodical literature review on Asians and Pacific Islanders. *Social Work, 39,* 298–305.

The Food Project. (1997, Summer). Planting seeds of change. Food Project Happenings (Lincoln, MA), pp. 1–2.

Forte, J. A. (1997). Calling students to serve the homeless: A project to promote altruism and community service. *Journal of Social Work Education, 33,* 151–166.

Frankenstein, E. (1998). Carved from the heart. *HOPE, 14,* 76–78.

Franquemont, E. (1995, December 28). Community playgrounds. *New York Times,* p. C9.

Fraser, M. W. (Ed.). (1997). *Risk and resilience in childhood.* Washington, DC: NASW Press.

Fraser, M. W., & Galinsky, M. J. (1997). Toward a resilience-based model of practice. In M. W. Fraser (Ed.), *Risk and resilience in childhood* (pp. 265–275). Washington, DC: NASW Press.

Froland, C., Pancoast, D. L., Chapman, N. J., & Kimboko, P. J. (1981). *Helping networks and human services.* Beverly Hills, CA: Sage.

Frost, J. L., & Klein, B. L. (1979). *Children's play and playgrounds.* Boston: Allyn & Bacon.

Gale, G. (1996, November). As the plants grow, we grow . . . *Peacework,* pp. 20–21.

Gallagher, W. (1993). *The power of place: How our surroundings shape our thoughts, emotions, and actions.* New York: HarperCollins.

Gallery 37. (1996). *Friends of the Parks final evaluation report.* Chicago: Author.

Gallery 37. (1997a). *Bethel New Life final evaluation report.* Chicago: Author.

Gallery 37. (1997b). *Fellowship House final evaluation report.* Chicago: Author.

Gallup, G. (1979). The cities: Unsolved problems and unused talents. *Antioch Review, 37,* 148–161.

Gardner, J. (1997). Writing off the walls. *HOPE, 8,* 93.

Garr, R. (1995). *Reinvesting in America.* Reading, MA: Addison-Wesley.

Gaston Institute. (1992a). *Latinos in Boston.* Boston: University of Massachusetts.

Gaston Institute. (1992b). *Latinos in Holyoke.* Boston: University of Massachusetts.

Gaston Institute. (1994). *Latinos in Holyoke: Poverty, income, education, employment and housing.* Boston: University of Massachusetts.

Germain, C. B. (1979). Ecology and social work. In C. B. Germain (Ed.), *Social work practice: People and environment* (pp. 1–22). New York: Columbia University Press.

Germain, C. B. (1991). *Human behavior in the social environment: An ecological view.* New York: Columbia University Press.

Giasone, B. (1994, April 4). Kimberly-Clark launches community playground project. *Orange County Register,* p. 1.

Glentzer, M. (1996). Art with a heart. *HOPE, 4,* 62–69.

Goetz, T. (1997, October 19). Why New York taco stands are Chinese. *New York Times Magazine,* p. 59.

Gold, D. (1996). Utilitarian art. *HOPE, 4,* 12–13.

Goldstein, L. (1998, May 10). Reviving labyrinths, paths to inner peace. *New York Times*, pp. 1, 16.

Goldstein, P. J., Spunt, B. J., Miller, T., & Bellucci, P. (1990). Ethnographic field stations. In E. Y. Lambert (Ed.), *The collection and interpretation of data from hidden populations* (NIDA Research Monograph 98, pp. 80–95). Rockville, MD: National Institute of Drug Abuse.

Googins, B., Capoccia, V., & Kaufman, N. (1983). Interactional dimensions of planning: A framework for practice. *Social Work, 28*, 273–278.

Gomez, G. (1996, October 28). Flag issue's really cultural confusion [Letter to the Editor]. *Union News*, p. A6.

Gonzalez, D. (1992, September 1). Dominican immigration alters Hispanic New York. *New York Times*, p. A1.

Gonzalez, D. (1994). Death along New York's bloodiest blocks, graffiti memorials to the departed are the latest refinement of ghetto art. *V.I.B.E., 2*, 65–71.

Gonzalez, D. (1998, April 22). Memorial to a dog. *New York Times*, p. A26.

Googins, B., Capoccia, V., & Kaufman, N. A. (1983). The interactional dimension of planning: A framework for practice. *Social Work, 28*, 273–277.

Gorham, W., & Kingley, G. T. (1997). The need for effective local governance. In U. Kirdar (Ed.), *Cities fit for people* (pp. 357–367). New York: United Nations University Press.

Gottdiener, M. (1994). *The social production of urban space* (2nd ed.). Austin: University of Texas Press.

Gottlieb, B. H. (Ed.). (1981). *Social networks and social support.* Newbury Park, CA: Sage.

Gottlieb, B. H. (Ed.). (1983). *Social support strategies: Guidelines for mental health practice.* Newbury Park, CA: Sage.

Gottlieb, B. H. (Ed.). (1988). *Marshalling social support: Formats, processes, and effects.* Newbury Park, CA: Sage.

Graham, K., & Bios, C. (1997). The complexity of roles in community action projects: The example of the evaluation of "Alternatives." *Evaluation and Program Planning, 20*, 433–442.

Greene, R. R., & Watkins, M. (Eds.). (1998). *Serving diverse constituencies: Applying the ecological perspective.* Hawthorne, NY: Aldine de Gruyter.

Griswold, M. (1997, September 25). World's fair of gardens grow at the city's doorstep. *New York Times*, p. C11.

Guest, C. Z. (1997, August). Garden talk: Good soil is first rule of great gardening. *The Homesteader*, p. 7.

Gutierrez, L. (1990). Working with women of color: An empowerment perspective. *Social Work, 35*, 149–154.

Gutierrez, L., Parsons, R. J., & Cox, E. O. (Eds.). (1998). *Empowerment in social work practice: A source book.* Pacific Grove, CA: Brooks/Cole.

Hair, M. (1996). Roots revival: Gardening angels. *HOPE, 2*, 14–19.

Halbfinger, D. M. (1997a, October 26). Now, in Lower Manhattan: 215 blocks without graffiti. *New York Times*, pp. 31–32.

Halbfinger, D. M. (1997b, December 1). Political role of immigrants is still lagging. *New York Times*, p. A21.

Halpern, R. (1995). *Rebuilding the inner city.* New York: Columbia University Press.

Ham, J. (1998). Designing playgrounds with children. *CBA News* (Community Built Association), *6*, 2.

Hamamoto, D. Y., & Torres, R. D. (Eds.). (1997). *New American destinies: A reader in contemporary Asian and Latino immigration.* New York: Routledge.

Hamilton, N. (1996, December 23). Building neighborhoods with community gardens. *Des Moines Register,* p. 11.

Hancock, T., & Minkler, M. (1997). Community health assessment or healthy community assessment. In M. Minkler (Ed.), *Community organizing and community building for health* (pp. 139–156). New Brunswick, NJ: Rutgers University Press.

Hardcastle, D.A., Wenocur, S., & Powers, P. R. (1997). *Community practice: Theories and skills for social workers.* New York: Oxford University Press.

Hartman, A. (1979). The extended family as a resource for change: An ecological approach to family centered practice. In C. B. Germain (Ed.), *Social work practice: People and environment* (pp. 239–266). New York: Columbia University Press.

Hayward, D. G., Rothenberg, M., & Beasley, R. R. (1974). Children's play and urban playground environments: A comparison of traditional, contemporary, and adventure playground types. *Environment and Behavior, 6,* 131–168.

Hazen, T. M. (1997). Horticultural therapy in the skilled nursing facility. *Activities, Adaptation & Aging, 22,* 39–60.

Henkin, N. Z., Santiago, N., Sonkowsky, M., & Tunick, S. (1997). Intergenerational programming: A vehicle for promoting intra- and cross-cultural understanding. *Journal of Gerontological Social Work, 28,* 197–209.

Herbert, R. (1998, August 14). Dorchester garden cultivates independence among young mothers. *Boston Herald,* 51–52.

Herdy, A. (1997, May 18). Garden feeds the hungry. *St. Petersburg Times,* p. 7.

Higginbotham, E. B. (1994). Black professional women: Job ceilings and employment sectors. In M. B. Zinn & B. T. Dill (Eds.), *Women of color in U.S. society* (pp. 113–131). Philadelphia: University of Pennsylvania Press.

Hill, M. (1996, July 3). D. M.'s inner city turning green. *Des Moines Register,* p. 1.

Hill, R. (1972). *Strengths of the black family.* New York: Hall.

Hines, P. M., & Boyd-Franklin, N. (1996). African American families. In M. McGoldrick, J. Giordano & J. K. Pearce (Eds.), *Ethnicity and family therapy* (2nd ed., pp. 66–84). New York: Guilford Press.

Hinkemeyer, J. (1996, August 10). Personality takes root with the plants. *Rocky Mountain News,* p. 3D.

Hinkle, D. (1997, April 2). Coalition urges using vacant lots for gardens. *Courier-Journal* (Louisville), p. 01N.

Hiss, T., & Koren, E. (1993, May 24). Child's play. *The New Yorker,* p. 80.

Holloway, L. (1993, May 28). Park, however it smells, blossoms on the river. *New York Times,* p. B3.

Holmes, A. (1997, April 28). North side coalition saves Troy gardens. *State Journal* (Madison, Wisconsin), p. 18.

Holmes, G. E. (1992). Social work research and the empowerment paradigm. In D. S. Saleebey (Ed.), *The strengths perspective in social work practice* (pp. 158–168). New York: Longman.

Holmes, S. A. (1998a, February 14). Hispanic births in U.S. reach record high. *New York Times,* p. B1.

Holmes, S. A. (1998b, January 1). Immigration fuels strong population growth in cities. *New York Times,* p. A10.

Holmstrom, D. (1996a). Asset-building: A Minnesota city mobilizes around kids. *Christian Science Monitor Series Reprint*, pp. 6, 7, 8.

Holmstrom, D. (1996b). Black churches put "spirit" into children's afternoons. *Christian Science Monitor Series Reprint*, pp. 6–7.

Holscher, L. M. (1976). Artists and murals in East Los Angeles and Boyle Heights: A sociological observation. *Humboldt Journal of Social Relations, 3*, 25–29.

Holscher, L. M. (1976–77). Tiene arte valor del barrio [Art has value outside of the community): The murals in East Los Angeles and Boyle Heights. *Journal of Ethnic Studies, 4*, 42–52.

Hurt, B. (1998). Child's play—A thing of the past? *CBA News* (Community Built Association), *6*, 2.

Hynes, H. P. (1995). *A patch of eden: America's inner-city gardeners.* White River Junction, VT: Chelsea Green.

Iglehart, A. P., & Becerra, R. M. (1995). *Social services and the ethnic community.* Needham Heights, MA: Allyn & Bacon.

Iltus, S., & Hart, R. (1994). Participatory planning and design of recreational spaces with children. *Architecture and Comportment, Architecture and Behaviour, 10*, 361–370.

IPR Datanote. (1993). *Puerto Ricans and other Latinos in the United States: March 1992.* New York: Institute for Puerto Rican Policy.

Jack, G. (1997). An ecological approach to social work with children and families. *Child and Family Social Work, 2*, 109–120.

Jackson, D. Z. (1989, June 18). Why blacks, Latin-Americans are at a higher risk for AIDS. *Boston Globe*, p. 86.

Jacobson, C. K. (1995). An analysis of Native American fertility in the public use microdata samples of the 1990 census. In C. K. Jacobson (Ed.). *American families: Issues in race and ethnicity* (pp. 119–130). New York, N.Y.: Garland Publishing.

Jason, L. A. (1997). *Community building: Values for a sustainable future.* Westport, CT: Praeger.

Jeffries, A. (1996). Modelling community work: An analytic framework for practice. *Journal of Community Practice, 3*, 101–125.

Jennings, J. (1994). *Understanding the nature of poverty in urban America.* Westport, CT: Praeger Press.

Johnson, D. (1997, October 18). Ethnic change tests mettle of Minneapolis liberalism. *New York Times*, pp. A1, A11.

Johnson, R. (1998, September 6). Demolition in the city, open space in mind. *New York Times* [Connecticut Section], p. 13.

Kaplan, F. (1998, January 1). United New York City, at 100 is still many separate towns. *Boston Globe*, p. A23.

Kaplan, F. (1997, April 12). In NYC, Dominicans feeling political clout. *Boston Globe*, pp. A1, A8.

Kaplan, R. (1973). Some psychological benefits of gardening. *Environment and Behavior, 5*, 145–152.

Kasarda, J. D., Appold, S. J., Sweeney, S. H., & Stieff, E. (1997). Central-city and suburban migration patterns: Is a turnaround on the horizon? *Housing Policy Debate, 8*, 307–358.

Kasrel, D. (1997, November 7–13). Urban anthropology: Outdoor murals brighten the city's canvas. *Philadelphia Business Journal*, pp. 1, 31.

Katz, C. (1998). Disintegrating developments: Global economic restructuring and the eroding of ecologies of youth. In T. Skelton & G. Valentine (Eds.), *Cool places: Geographies of youth cultures* (pp. 130–144). London: Routledge.

Kaufman, M. (1998, April 10). Painting the town. *Philadelphia Inquirer* [Weekend], 23–25.

Keating, W. D. (1996). Introduction: Neighborhoods in urban America. In W. D. Keating, N. Krumholz, & P. Star (Eds.), *Revitalizing urban neighborhoods* (pp. 1–8). Lawrence: University of Kansas Press.

Keating, W. D., Krumholz, N., & Starr, P. (1996). Preface. In W. D. Keating, N. Krumholz, & P. Starr (Eds.), *Revitalizing urban neighborhoods* (p. ix). Lawrence: University of Kansas Press.

Kemmis, D. (1996). Barn raising. In W. Vitek & W. Jackson (Eds.), *Rooted in the land: Essays on community and place* (pp. 167–175). New Haven, CT: Yale University Press.

Kemp, S., Whittaker, J. K., & Tracy, E. M. (1997). *Person-environment practice: The social ecology of interpersonal helping.* Hawthorne, NY: Aldine de Gruyter.

Kessler, K. (1997). An urban state of mind. *Urban Land, 56,* 4.

Kimmelman, M. (1993, September 26). Of candy bars, parades and public art. *New York Times,* p. 43.

Kingry-Westergaard, C., & Kelly, J. G. (1990). A contextualist epistemology for ecological psychology. In P. Tulan, C. Keys, F. Chertok, & L. Jason (Eds.), *Researching community psychology: Issues of theory and methods* (pp. 23–31). Washington, DC: American Psychological Association.

Kinzer, S. (1994, February 18). Berlin journal: Dread of builders in a city woven with gardens. *New York Times,* p. A1.

Kirdar, O. (Ed.). (1997a). *Cities fit for people.* New York: United Nations Publications.

Kirdar, O. (1997b). Overview. In O. Kindar (Ed.), *Cities fit for people* (pp. 1–8). New York: United Nations Publications.

Kirschbaum, P. R. (1998a). Borrowed land, borrowed time: Preserving community gardens. *Community Greening Review, 8,* 2–11.

Kirschbaum, P. R. (1998b). Emerald city: Living up to its name. *Community Greening Review, 8,* 18–25.

Kostarelos, F. (1995). *Feeling the spirit: Faith and hope in an evangelical black storefront church.* Columbia: University of South Carolina Press.

Kretzmann, J. P., & McKnight J. (1993). *Building communities from the inside out: A path toward finding and mobilizing a community's assets.* Evanston, IL: Center for Urban Affairs and Policy Research, Northwestern University.

Kretzmann, J. P., & McKnight, J. (1996a). *A guide to mapping and mobilizing the economic capacities of local residents.* Chicago: ACTA Publications.

Kretzmann, J. P., & McKnight, J. (1996b). *A guide to mapping local business assets and mobilizing local business capacities.* Chicago: ACTA Publications.

Kunzle, D. (1995). *The murals of revolutionary Nicaragua, 1979–1992.* Berkeley: University of California Press.

Kurlansky, M., Naar, J., & Mailer, N. (1974). *The faith of graffiti.* New York: Praeger.

Laird, R. (1992, March). Local mural walks convey pride and sense of history. *San Francisco Peninsula Parent, 17,* 22.

Lakes, R. D. (1996). *Youth development and critical education: The promise of democratic action.* Albany: State University of New York Press.

Lamb, M. (1997, April 11). SPH Prof finds patches of Eden in nation's inner cities. *Boston University Today,* pp. 1, 7.

Landscape Structures. (1998). *Community-built manual.* Delano, MN: Author.

Landauer, K., & Brazil, M. (Eds.). (1990). *Tropical home gardens.* New York: United Nations University Press.

Landers, S. (1998). Settlement houses survive—and thrive. *NASW News, 43,* 3.

Landis, D. (1994, October 2). The new rules of the game: Today's playgrounds are inventive, involving—and sometimes even indoors. *New York Times Magazine,* pp. 48–49, 51.

Langhenry, M. (1997, April 24). Community spirit builds for playground in Alpharetta. *Atlanta Journal Constitution,* p. 01H.

Lauerman, J. (1998, October 11). Someone there is who loves a wall. *Boston Globe,* pp. 1 City, 13 City.

Lawrinsky, R. (1997). Transforming the soul of a city. *Hope, 10,* 20–23.

Layder, D. (1993). *New strategies in social research.* Cambridge, MA: Polity Press.

Leadbeater, B. J. R., & Way, N. (Eds.). (1996). *Urban girls: Resisting stereotypes, creating identities.* New York: New York University Press.

Leary, K. (1991, May 15). Green gaints at jailhouse garden: "Environmental hero" from African visits rehabilitation program. *San Francisco Chronicle,* p. A15.

Leary, W. E. (1994, October 23). Gun violence leading to better care for injuries. *New York Times,* p. 32.

Leathers & Associates. (1996). *Step by step: Innovative strategies for community-built structures and other one-of-a-kind architectural projects.* Ithaca, NY: Author.

Lee, E. (1996a). Asian American families: An overview. In M. McGoldrick, J. Giordano, & J. K. Pearce (Eds.), *Ethnicity and family therapy* (2nd ed., pp. 227–248). New York: Guilford Press.

Lee, E. (1996b). Chinese families. In M. McGoldrick, J. Giordano, & J. K. Pearce (Eds.), *Ethnicity and family therapy* (2nd ed., pp. 249–267). New York: Guilford Press.

Lee, F. R. (1994a, September 10). A drug dealer's rapid rise and ugly fall. *New York Times,* pp. 1, 22.

Lee, F. R. (1994b, September 9). Harlem family battles weight of the past. *New York Times,* pp. A1, B4.

Lee, F. R. (1994c, September 8). On a Harlem block, hope is swallowed by decay. *New York Times,* pp. A1, B8.

Lee, J. A. B. (1994). *The empowerment approach to social work practice.* New York: Columbia University Press.

Leinberger, C., & Berens, S. (1997). Designing for urban parks. *Urban Land, 56,* 54–58, 67–68.

Lerner, R. M. (1995). *America's youth in crisis: Challenges and options for programs and policies.* Thousand Oaks, CA: Sage.

Levinson, B. (1997, August 28). Food project grows kids, *Concord Journal,* p. 14.

Lewin, K. (1951). *Field theory in social science.* New York: Harper & Row.

Lewis, C. A. (1996). *Green nature/human nature: The meaning of plants in our lives.* Urbana: University of Illinois Press.

Lii, J. H. (1997, December 31). Bulldozers stamp out the islands of green. *New York Times,* p. A17.

Limer, T. M. (1998, May 21). Playground effort showcases Coxackie spirit. *Greene County News,* p. A12.

Linger, E. (1995, October 28). It's a jungle (gym) out there: Community playgrounds growing up. *Palm Beach Post*, p. 2B.

Lofland, L. H. (1998). *The public realm: Exploring the city's quintessential social territory*. Hawthorne, NY: Aldine de Gruyter.

Logan, S. (Ed.). (1996a). *The Black family: Strengths, self-help, and positive change*. Boulder, CO: Westview Press.

Logan, S. (1996b). Strengthening family ties: Working with black female single-parent families. In S. L. Logan (Ed.), *The black family: Strengths, self-help, and positive change* (pp. 164–180). Boulder, CO: Westview Press.

Logan, S. (1996c). A strengths perspective on black families: Then and now. In S. L. Logan (Ed.), *The black family: Strengths, self-help, and positive change* (pp. 8–38). Boulder, CO: Westview Press.

Longo, G. (1997). *A guide to great American public places*. New York: Urban Initiatives.

Longres, J. F. (1995). Human behavior in the social environment. Itasca, IL: F. E. Peacock.

Lotozo, E. (1998, January 28). Mural city, U.S.A. *Philadelphia Weekly* [Pop ed], p. 9.

Lubove, R. (1983). *The professional altruist: The emergence of social work as a career 1880–1930*. New York: Atheneum.

Lubrano, A. (1998, April 9). Two art world leaders to share Phila. award. *Philadelphia Inquirer*, pp. A1, A27.

Lueck, T. J. (1997, July 8). New art on Great White Way: Just paint. *New York Times*, p. A17.

Lupo, A. (1997, May 18). They want to keep garden party going. *Boston Globe*, [City ed.], pp. 1, 8.

Lyon, L. (1989). *The community in urban society*. Lexington, MA: Lexington Books.

Madden, J. (1996, November 14). Offending art: Graffiti on Beverly walls attracts attention, criticism. *Salem Evening News*, pp. A1, A10.

Maguire, L. (1991). *Social support systems in practice*. Washington, DC: NASW Press.

Malakoff, D. (1995). What good is community gardening? *Community Gardening Review*, 5, 4–11.

Marcuse, P. (1997). The enclave, the citadel, and the ghetto: What has changed in the postfortyish U.S. city. *Urban Affairs Review*, 33, 228–264.

Margolin, L. (1997). *Under the cover of kindness: The invention of social work*. Charlottesville: University of Virginia Press.

Marin, G., & Marin, B. V. (1991). *Research with Hispanic populations*. Newbury Park, CA: Sage.

Marti-Costa, S., & Serrano-Garcia, I. (1983). Needs assessment and community development: An ideological perspective. *Prevention in Human Services*, 1, 75–88.

Martin, D. (1997, December 14). Public eyesore vs. private park. *New York Times*, pp. 53, 56.

Martin, D. (1998, May 1). Agency taking over gardens on vacant lots. *New York Times*, p. A28.

Martinez-Brawley, E. E. (1990). *Perspectives on the small community: Humanistic views for practitioners*. Washington, D.C.: NASW Press.

Maser, C. (1997). *Sustainable community development*. Delray Beach, FL: St. Lucie Press.

Mays, J. B. (1997, August 16). The process worked, but the art doesn't. *Globe and Mail*, p. C5.

McArthur, B. (1975). The Chicago playground movement: A neglected feature of social justice. *Social Service Review, 49,* 376–395.

McCarthy, P., & Fletcher, E. (1995). *Holyoke community partnership program development application.* Boston: Community Builders.

McCord, J. (1997). Placing American urban violence in context. In J. McCord (Ed.), *Violence and childhood in the inner city* (pp. 78–115). New York: Cambridge University Press.

McCoy, B. N. (1997, April 24). Artistic service: Former Margate painter to meet with president at summit. *Press of Atlantic City* [Lifestyle], pp. B1, B3.

McCulloch, M. K. (1995, August 25). South Holyoke neighborhood playground a child's dream come true. *Holyoke Sun,* p. 11.

McGuire, D. L. (1997). Implementing horticultural therapy into a geriatric long-term care facility. *Activities, Adaptation & Aging, 22,* 61–80.

McKay, M. M., Stoewe, J., McCadam, K., & Gonzalez, J. (1998). Increasing access to child mental health services for urban children and their caregivers. *Health & Social Work, 23,* 9–15.

McKay, T. (1998). From Canada: Empty spaces, dangerous places. *Multilogue* [American Community Gardening Association newsletter], *15,* 1–2.

McKinley, J. (1997, November 23). Fax attack puts garden defender in legal paper jam. *New York Times,* p. A32.

McKnight, J. L. (1995). *The careless society: Community and its counterfeits.* New York: Basic Books.

McKnight, J. L. (1997). A 21st-century map for healthy communities and families. *Families in Society, 78,* 117–127.

McKnight, J. L., & Kretzmann, J. P. (1990). *Mapping community capacity.* Evanston, IL: Center for Urban Affairs and Policy Research, Northwestern University.

McLaughlin, M. W. (1994). Embedded identities: Enabling balance in urban contexts. In S. B. Health & M. W. McLaughlin (Eds.), *Identity and inner-city youth: Beyond ethnicity and gender* (pp. 36–68). New York: Teachers College Press.

McLeroy, K., Steckler, A., Goodman, R., & Burdine, J. N. (1992). Health education research: Theory and practice—future directions. *Health Education Research: Theory and Practice, 7,* 1–8.

McLeroy, K., Steckler, A., Keger, M., Burdine, J., & Wizotsky, M. (1994). Community coalitions for health promotion: Summary and further reflections. *Health Education Research: Theory and Practice, 9,* 1–11.

McRorie, K. (1997). A placed called . . . Chicano Park. *Community Built Association News, 5,* 4–5.

Medoff, P., & Sklar, H. (1994). *Streets of hope: The fall and rise of an urban neighborhood.* Boston: South End Press.

Mercier, C. (1997). Participants in stakeholder-based evaluation: A case study. *Evaluation and Program Planning, 20,* 467–475.

Miller, A. (1995, July 11). A little patch of Eden blooms in the D.C. sun: Community gardens grow food, friendships. *Washington Times,* p. C8.

Mills, E. S., & Lubuele, L. S. (1997). Inner cities. *Journal of Economic Literature, 35,* 727–756.

Milmore, D. (1997, June 22). Growing knowledge: Brimfield effort earns a spot on garden tour. *Boston Globe,* B12, B14.

Minnesota Green. (1992). *Creating community gardens.* Falcon Heights: Minnesota State Horticultural Society.

Mitlin, D., & Thompson, J. (1995). Participatory approaches in urban areas: Strengthening civil society or reinforcing the status quo. *Environment and Urbanization, 7,* 231–250.

Moe, R., & Wilkie, C. (1997). *Changing places: Rebuilding community in the age of sprawl.* New York: Henry Holt.

Mokuau, N. (1995). Pacific islanders. In J. Philleo & F. L. Brisbane (Eds.), *Cultural competence for social workers: A guide for alcohol and other drug abuse prevention professionals working with ethnic/racial communities* (pp. 158–188). Rockville, MD: Center for Substance Abuse Prevention.

Mondros, J., & Wilson, S. M. (1994). *Organizing for power and empowerment.* New York: Columbia University Press.

Monroe-Santos, S. (1998). Recent national survey shows status of community gardens in U.S. *Community Greening Review, 8,* 12, 17.

Moore, J., & Pinderhughes, R. (1993). Introduction. In J. Moore & R. Pinderhughes (Eds.). *In the barrios: Latinos and the underclass debate* (xi–xxxix). New York: Russell Sage Foundation.

Morales, R., & Bonilla, F. (1993). Restructuring and the new inequality. In R. Morales & F. Bonilla (Eds.), *Latinos in a changing U.S. economy* (pp. 1–27). Newbury Park, CA: Sage.

Moran, J. R., & May, P. A. (1995). American Indians: In J. Philleo & F. L. Brisbane (Eds.), *Cultural competence for social workers: A guide for alcohol and other drug abuse prevention professionals working with ethnic/rcial communities* (pp. 3–39). Rockville, MD: Center for Substance Abuse Prevention.

Morgenroth, L. (1997, October 16). Painting the city: Walls come to life with murals comic and controversial, poignant and pointed. *Boston Globe Calendar,* pp. 8–11.

Morrison, J. D., Howard, J., Johnson, C., Navarro, F. J., Plachetka, B., & Bell, T. (1997). Strengthening neighborhoods by developing community networks. *Social Work, 42,* 527–534.

Mose, L. (1997). Reinventing the central city as a place to live and work. *Housing Policy Debate, 8,* 471–490.

Moskow, A. (1997). Havana's self-provision gardens. *Community Gardening Review, 7,* 17–19.

Mukherjee, A. (1995, July 3). Urban gardening revitalizes neighborhoods. *Citizen's Voice* [Wilkes-Barre, PA], p. 6.

Murdock, S. H. (1995). *An America challenged: Population change and the future of the United States.* Boulder, CO: Westview Press.

Naedele, W. F. (1998, January 11). A picture of harmony in Grays Ferry. *Philadelphia Inquirer* [Metro Section], pp. 1–2.

Naparstek, A. J., & Dooley, D. (1997). Countering urban disinvestment through community-building initiatives. *Social Work, 42,* 506–514.

Nash, J. R., & Fraser, M. W. (1997). Methods in the analysis of risk and protective factors: Lessons from epidemiology. In M. W. Fraser (Ed.), *Risk and resilience in childhood* (pp. 34–50). Washington, DC: NASW Press.

National Hispanic Leadership Agenda. (1996). *1996 policy summary.* Washington, DC: Author.

National Research Council. (1994). *Violence in urban America.* Washington, DC: National Academy Press.

Negri, G. (1992, August 1). Empty lots offer fertile soil: Private group helps seniors, inner-city residents convert blighted spaces into garden spots. *Boston Globe,* p. 17.

Negri, G. (1997, July 20). Garden contest blossoms. *Boston Globe* [City], pp. 1, 7.

Netting, F. E., Kettner, P. M., & McMurtry, S. L. (1993). *Social work macro practice*. New York: Longman.

Nguyen, N. A. (1992). Living between two cultures: Treating first generation Asian Americans. In L. A. Vargas & J. D. Koss-Chioino (Eds.), *Working with culture: Psychotherapeutic interventions with ethnic minority children and adolescents* (pp. 204–222). San Francisco: Jossey-Bass.

Newstetter, W. I. (1980). Regulatory principes. In A. S. Alissi (Ed.), *Perspectives on social group work practice* (pp. 101–110). New York: Free Press.

Nicolaidou, S. (1984). A sociology of children's playgrounds in the urban milieu: The case of Athens. *International Review of Sociology, 20,* 200–211.

1997 year in review. (1998). *Chicago Public Art Group Newsletter, 5,* 3–5.

Ninez, V. (1990). Garden production in tropical America, In K. Landauer & M. Brazil (Eds.), *Tropical home gardens* (pp. 186–192). New York: United Nations University Press.

Noriyuki, D. (1995, September 2). Peace offering. *Saint Paul Pioneer Press,* p. 14.

Nwoye, O. G. (1993). Social issues on walls: Graffiti in university lavatories. *Discourse and Society, 4,* 419–442.

Ochoa, V. (1997a). *Chicano art.* El Cajon, CA: Grossman College.

Ochoa, V. (1997b). San Diego: Chicano park. In R. J. Dunitz & J. Prigoff (Eds.), *Painting the towns: Murals of California* (pp. 266–267). Los Angeles: RJD Enterprises.

Ochoa, V. (1997c). San Diego: El centro cultural de la Raza. In R. J. Dunitz & J. Prigoff (Eds.), *Painting the towns: Murals of California* (pp. 26–27). Los Angeles: RJD Enterprises.

O'Hare, W. P., & Felt, J. C. (1991). Asian Americans: America's fastest growing minority group. *Population Reference Bureau, 19,* 1–16.

Ojito, M. (1997, December 16). Dominicans, scrabbling for hope. *New York Times,* p. A31.

Okigbo, B. N. (1990). Home gardens in tropical Africa. In K. Landauer & M. Brazil (Eds.), *Tropical home gardens* (pp. 21–40). New York: United Nations University Press.

Oldenburg, R. (1991). *The great good place.* New York: Paragon House.

Ortiz, V. (1994). Women of color: A demographic overview. In M. B. Zinn & B. T. Dill (Eds.), *Women of color in U.S. society* (pp. 13–40). Philadelphia: Temple University Press.

Page-Adams, D., & Sherraden, M. (1997). Asset building as a community revitalization strategy. *Social Work, 42,* 423–434.

Pasmanick, P. (1997). *A sketchy history of the mural.* Los Angeles: Social and Political Arts Resource Center.

Patton, M. Q. (1987). *How to use qualitative methods in evaluation.* Newbury Park, CA: Sage.

Pear, R. (1992, December 4). New look at the U.S. in 2050: Bigger, older and less white. *New York Times,* pp. 1, D18.

Peirce, N. (1995, November 10). In search of green for brown fields. *Philadelphia Inquirer,* p. 40.

Perez, S. M., & Martinez, D. (1993). *State of Hispanic America 1993: Toward a Latino anti-poverty agenda.* Washington, DC: National Council of La Raza.

Perez-Stable, M., & Uriate, M. (1993). Cubans and the changing economy of Miami. In R. Morales & F. Bonilla (Eds.), *Latinos in a changing U.S. economy* (pp. 133–159). Newbury Park, CA: Sage.

Pessar, P. R. (1987). The Dominicans: Women in the household and the garment industry. In N. Foner (Ed.), *New immigrants in New York* (pp. 103–129). New York: Columbia University Press.

A place for the kids to play: Shortchanged neighborhood meets its own need [Editorial]. (1994, April 4). *Buffalo News*, p. 2.

Plaisance, M. (1996, October 25). Hispanics to rally against councilor. *Union News*, p. B1.

Poole, D. L. (1997). Building community capacity to promote social and public health: Challenges for universities. *Health & Social Work, 22*, 163–170.

Puckett, P. (1995, March 23). Growing with gardens urban landscape: Garden clubs at several area public housing complexes raise food and community spirits. *Atlanta Constitution*, p. 78.

Purdy, M. (1995, July 25). Bars don't stop flow of drugs into the prisons. *New York Times*, p. 1.

Rappaport, J. (1977). *Community psychology: Values, research and action.* New York: Holt, Rinehart & Winston.

Raver, A. (1994, December 29). When hope falters, balm for the soul. *New York Times*, p. C1.

Raver, A. (1999, January 11). New York City's plan to auction off 100 community gardens stirs up tensions. *New York Times*, p. A17.

Reicher, A., & the Green Guerrillas. (1995). Build a garden pond. *Community Gardening Review, 5*, 22–25.

Renkin, A. C. (1998, March 31). For urban wastelands, tomatoes and other life. *New York Times*, pp. A1, A21.

Reppucci, N. D. (1987). Prevention and ecology: Teen-age pregnancy, child sexual abuse, and organized youth sports. *American Journal of Community Psychology, 15*, 1–22.

Ridout, A. (1998)., (1988, February 14). The Food Project. *Boston Globe*, pp. 75–76.

Rivera, D., & Wolfe, B. D. (1934). *Portrait of America.* New York: Covici-Friede.

Rivera, F. G., & Erlich, J. L. (1998a). *Community organizing in a diverse society* (3rd ed.). Boston: Allyn & Bacon.

Rivera, F. G., & Erlich, J. L. (1998b). Epilogue: The twenty-first century—promise or illusion. In F. G. Rivera & J. L. Erlich (Eds.), *Community organizing in a diverse society* (3rd ed., pp. 243–257). Boston: Allyn & Bacon.

Roberts, S. (1994, October 9). Hispanic population outnumbers blacks in four cities as nation's demographics shift. *New York Times*, p. 22.

Robbins, S. P., Chatterjee, P., & Canda, E. R. (1998). *Contemporary human behavior theory: A critical perspective for social work.* Boston: Allyn & Bacon.

Rodriguez, N. P. (1993). Economic restructuring and Latino growth in Houston. In J. Moore & R. Pinderhughes (Eds.), *In the barrios: Latinos and the underclass debate* (pp. 101–127). New York: Russell Sage Foundation.

Romo, R. (1996). Borderland murals: Chicago artifacts in transition. *Aztlan, 21*, 125–154.

Rosen, M. J. (1997). Reviving urban parks. *Urban Land, 56*, 54–57, 81–82.

Rosenfeld, J. M. (1997). Designing urban public plazas. *Urban Land, 56*, 51–53, 66.

Ross, M. G., & Lappin, B. W. (1967). *Community organization: Theory, principles and practice.* New York: Harper & Row.

Rothman, J. (1996). The interweaving of community intervention approaches. *Journal of Community Practice, 3,* 69–99.

Rumbaut, R. G. (1997). Origins and destinies: Immigration to the United States since World War II. In D. Y. Hamamoto & R. D. Torres (Eds.). *New American destinies: A reader in contemporary Asian and Latino immigration* (pp. 15–45). New York: Routledge.

Rusk, D. (1995). *Cities without suburbs.* Washington, DC: Woodrow Wilson Press.

Ryan, A. S. (Ed.). (1997). *Social work with immigrants and refugees.* New York: Haworth Press.

Saleebey, D. S. (1992a). Introduction: Power to the people. In D. S. Saleebey (Ed.), *The strengths perspective in social work practice* (pp. 3–17). New York: Longman.

Saleebey, D. S. (Ed.). (1992b). *The strengths perspective in social work practice.* New York: Longman.

Saleebey, D. S. (1996). The strengths perspective in social work practice: Extensions and cautions. *Social Work, 41,* 296–305.

Salter, R. (1996, August 19). All work for child's play: Communities take playground safety into own hands. *Morning Call* [Allentown, PA], p. D1.

Sarno, M. T., & Chambers, N. (1997). A horticultural therapy program for individuals with acquired aphasia. *Activities, Adaptation & Aging, 22,* 81–91.

Schneekloth, L. H., & Shibley, R. G. (1993). The practice of placemaking. *Architecture and Comportment, Architecture & Behaviour, 9,* 121–144.

Schriver, J. M. (1997). *Human behavior and the social environment: Setting paradigms in essential knowledge for social work practice.* Boston: Allyn & Bacon.

Schwartz, D. B. (1997). *Who cares?: Rediscovering community.* Boulder, CO: Westview Press.

Seelye, K. Q. (1997, March 27). The new U.S.: Grayer and more Hispanic. *New York Times,* p. A32.

Seidman, E. (1991). Growing up the hard way: Pathways of urban adolescents. *American Journal of Community Psychology, 19,* 173–200.

Sells, S. P., Smith, T. E., & Newfield, N. (1997). Teaching ethnographic research methods in social work: A model course. *Journal of Social Work Education, 33,* 167–184.

Selznick, P. (1996). In search of community. In W. Vitek & W. Jackson (Eds.), *Rooted in the land: Essays on community and place* (pp. 195–203). New Haven, CT: Yale University Press.

Shapiro, S. (1997, December 17). Art therapy brightens a city street corner. *Baltimore Sun,* pp. 1D–2D.

Shell, E. R. (1994, July). Kids don't need equipment, they need opportunity. *Smithsonian,* pp. 79–86.

Silvern, D. (1994, January 4). San Bruno jail: Cultivating hope, faith self-respect blooms in inmates' gardens. *San Diego Union-Tribune,* p. A-1.

Simai, M. (1997). A globalizing world. In U. Kirdar (Ed.), *Cities fit for people* (pp. 50–70). New York: United Nations Publications.

Simon, S. & Haller, R. (1997). Horticultural therapy education for older adults. *Activities, Adaptation & Aging, 22,* 125–140.

Simonds, N. (1993, July 21). Helping the hungry with hoes, not handouts. *New York Times,* pp. C1, C6.

Slessarev, H. (1997). *The betrayal of the urban poor.* Philadelphia: Temple University Press.

Smith, D. J., & McCallion, P. (1997). Alleviating stress for family caregivers of frail elders using horticultural therapy. *Activities, Adaptation & Aging, 22,* 93–105.

Smith, H. Y. (1996). Building on the strengths of black families: Self-help and empowerment. In S. L. Logan (Ed.), *The black family: Strengths, self-help, and positive change* (pp. 21–38). Boulder, CO: Westview Press.

Solomon, B. B. (1976). *Black empowerment: Social work in oppressed communities.* New York: Columbia University Press.

Sommer, R. (1994). The social benefits of resident involvement in tree planting. *Journal of Arboriculture, 18,* 98–101.

Sontag, D. (1998, July 21). A Mexican town that transcends all borders. *New York Times,* pp. A1, A16–A17.

Sontag, D., & Dugger, C. W. (1998, July 19). The new immigrant tide: A shuttle between worlds. *New York Times,* pp. 1, 26–28.

Specht, H., & Courtney, M. E. (1994). *Unfaithful angels: How social work has abandoned its mission.* New York: Free Press.

Spencer, S. (1995, May 20). Glorious garden rises in midst of urban decay. *Stockton Record,* p. D6.

Spergel, I. A., & Grossman, S. F. (1997). The little village project: A community approach to the gang problem. *Social Work, 42,* 456–470.

Spradley, J. P. (1979). *The ethnographic interview.* New York: Holt, Rinehart & Winston.

Sprott, G. (1996, June 15). Harvest of hope: A North Tampa community digs in to fight crime—with squash, okra, cucumbers and a variety of beans. *Tampa Tribune,* p. 1.

Stanfield, J. H. II, & Dennis, R. M. (Eds.). (1993). *Race and ethnicity in research methods.* Newbury Park, CA: Sage.

Stake, R. E. (1995). *The art of case study research.* Thousand Oaks, CA: Sage.

Stein, C. (1997, October 26). Economic divide of races persists in eastern Massachusetts. *Boston Globe,* pp. A1, A26.

Stein, L. K. (1997). Horticultural therapy in residential long-term care: Application from research on health, aging, and institutional life. *Activities, Adaptation & Aging, 22,* 107–124.

Stocker, C. (1989, July 5). Still, cultivating the garden of ideals. *Boston Globe,* p. 27.

Stone, A. (1998). The struggle to preserve gardens in NYC. *Multilogue* [American Community Garden Association], *15,* 4–5.

Stoneham, J., & Jones, R. (1997). Residential landscapes: Their contribution to the quality of older people's lives. *Activities, Adaptation & Aging, 22,* 17–26.

Streeten, P. (1997). The culture of cities and citizens. In O. Kirdar (Ed.), *Cities fit for people* (pp. 198–204). New York: United Nations Publications.

Swift, B. (1996). Tidying up New Orleans. *HOPE, 6,* p. 77.

Taaffe, L., & Fisher, R. (1997). Public life in Gulfton: Multiple publics and models of community organization. *Journal of Community Practice, 4,* 31–56.

Tafoya, N., & Vecchio, A. D. (1996). Back to the future: An examination of the Native American holocaust. In M. McGoldrick, J. Giordano, & J. K. Pearce (Eds.), *Ethnicity and family therapy* (2nd ed., pp. 45–54). New York: Guilford Press.

Terry, D. (1994a, September 18). Gangs: Machiavelli's descendants. *New York Times,* p. 26.

Terry, D. (1994b, September 20). More familiar, life in a cell seems less terrible. *New York Times,* p. 1, 40.

Terry, D. (1997, September 19). Where life is sideshow, street art passes limit. *New York Times*, p. A16.

Thaman, R. R. (1990). Mixed home gardening in the Pacific Islands: Present status and future prospects. In K. Landauer & M. Brazil (Eds.), *Tropical home gardens* (pp. 41–68). New York: United Nations University Press.

Tierney, J. (1997a, December 28). Brooklyn could have been a contender. *New York Times Magazine*, pp. 18–23, 37, 47–48.

Tierney, J. (1997b, October 19). New York's parallel lives. *New York Times Magazine*, pp. 51–53.

Torero, M. (1997). San Diego: Chicano Park. In R. J. Dunitz & J. Prigoff (Eds.), *Painting the towns: Murals of California* (pp. 268–269). Los Angeles: RJD Enterprises.

Toufexis, A. (1996, December 15). Johnny Appleseed of the swing set. *Time*, p. 91.

Trefil, J. (1994). *A scientist in the city*. New York: Doubleday, Anchor Books.

Treguer, A. (1992). The Chicanos—Muralist with a message. *U.N.E.S.C.O. Courier*, 45, 22–24.

Trolander, J. A. (1988). *Professionalism and social change: From the settlement house movement to neighborhood centers: 1886 to the present*. New York: Columbia University Press.

Trust for Public Land. (1994). *Healing America's cities: Why we must invest in urban parks*. San Francisco: Author.

Tumin, M. M. (1971). The arts in a technological environment. *Arts in Society*, 8, 183–193.

U.S. Bureau of the Census. (1991). *Money income of households, families and persons in the 1990s: Current Population Reports: Consumer Income* (Series P.-60, No. 174). Washington, DC: U.S. Government Printing Office.

U.S. Bureau of the Census. (1995). *Population profile of the U.S., 1995*. Washington, DC: U.S. Government Printing Office.

Valdes, A. (1995, August 18). Creating a "black family." *Boston Globe*, p. 54.

Vallongo, S., & Mackey, M. (1998, April 28). Getting down and dirty in garden can be healthy. *Boston Herald*, p. H2.

Vasey, D. E. (1990). On estimating the net social and economic value of urban home gardens. In K. Landauer & M. Brazil (Eds.), *Tropical home gardens* (pp. 203–213). New York: United Nations University Press.

Venkatesh, S. A. (1997). An invisible community: Inside Chicago's public housing. *American Prospect*, 34, 35–40.

Vergara, C. J. (1995). *The new American ghetto*. New Brunswick, NJ: Rutgers University Press.

Vernol, C. (1997, April 17). Comm. playground in the works for McQuade Park. *Greene County News*, pp. 1A, 9A.

Vitek, W. (1996). Community and the virtue of necessity. In W. Vitek & W. Jackson (Eds.), *Rooted in the land: Essays on community and place* (pp. 176–184). New Haven, CT: Yale University Press.

Vogel, C. (1997, December 5). When a wall is not just a wall. *New York Times*, p. B30.

Walberg, H. J., Reyes, O., Weissberg, R. P., & Kuster, C. B. (1997). Afterword: Strengthening the families, education, and health of urban children and families. In H. J. Walberg, O. Reyes, & R. P. Weisberg (Eds.), *Children and youth: Interdisciplinary perspectives* (pp. 363–368). Thousand Oaks, CA: Sage.

Walker, S., Spohn, C., & DeLone, M. (1996). *The color of justice: Race, ethnicity, and crime in America*. Belmont, CA: Wadsworth.

Walsh, M. (1996). *Graffito*. Berkeley, CA: North Atlantic Books.

Walter, C. L. (1997). Community building practice: A conceptual framework. In M. Minkler (Ed.), *Community organizing and community building for health* (pp. 68–83). New Brunswick, NJ: Rutgers University Press.

Warren, R. (1998). *The urban oasis: Guideways and greenways in the human environment*. New York: McGraw-Hill.

Watson, J. G. (1993, September 9). Growing your own. *Los Angeles Times,* pp. 1, 6.

Watts, R. J., & Jagers, R. J. (Eds.). (1998). *Manhood development in urban African-American communities*. New York: Haworth Press.

Weber, B. (1997, November 18). Cities are fostering the arts as a way to save downtown. *New York Times,* pp. A1, A24.

Weber, B. (1998, May 27). Dreams on the streets of El Paso. *New York Times,* pp. B1, B8.

Weil, M. (1996). Model development in community practice: An historical perspective. *Journal of Community Practice, 3,* 5–67.

Weil, M., & Gamble, D. N. (1995). Community practice models. In R. L. Edwards (Ed.), *Encyclopedia of Social Work* (19th ed., Vol. 1, pp. 577–594): Washington, DC: NASW Press.

Weisbrod, B. A., & Worthy, J. C. (Eds.). (1997). *The urban crisis: Linking research to action*. Evanston, IL: Northwestern University Press.

Weitz, J. H. (1996). *Coming up taller: Arts and humanities programs for children at risk*. Washington, DC: President's Committee on the Arts and the Humanities.

Wells, S. E. (1997). Horticultural therapy and the older adult population, Part 1. *Activities, Adaptation & Aging, 22,* 1–2.

Whitter, J. K., & Garbarino, J. (1983). *Social support networks: Informal helping in the human services*. New York: Aldine.

Wilkerson, I. (1994, December 13). Crack's legacy of guns and death lives on. *New York Times,* pp. A1, B12.

Williams, D. (1994). Cultural competence: Building a state level system of change in Pennsylvania. *Focal Point, 8,* 15–17.

Williams, M. D. (1993). Urban ethnography: Another look. In J. H. Stanfield II & R. M. Dennis (Eds.), *Race and ethnicity in research methods* (pp. 135–156). Newbury Park, CA: Sage.

Williamson, M. (1997). *The healing of America*. New York: Simon & Schuster.

Wilson, W. J. (1987). *The truly disadvantaged: The inner-city, the underclass, and public policy*. Chicago: University of Chicago Press.

With, T. M. (1996, April 14). From Mexico to Massachusetts: Northeast migration linked to jobs, Prop. 187 and family. *Boston Globe,* pp. 1, 8–9.

Witkin, B. R., & Altschuld, J. W. (1995). *Planning and conducting needs assessments: A practical guide*. Thousand Oaks, CA: Sage.

Wolkomir, R. (1985). A playful designer who believes that the kids know best. *Smithsonian, 16.*

Wong, B. (1987). The Chinese: New immigrants in New York's Chinatown. In N. Foner (Ed.), *New immigrants in New York* (pp. 243–271). New York: Columbia University Press.

Woods, J. (1996, October 30–November 5). Kos-Lecca, mayor swap charges on "unity" mural. *Holyoke Sun,* pp. 3, 8.

Wright, J. W. (1997). *New York Times 1998 almanac.* New York: New York Times.

Wuthnow, R. (1991). *Acts of compassion: Caring for others and helping ourselves.* Princeton, NJ: Princeton University Press.

Wuthnow, R. (1995). *Learning to care: Elementary kindness in an age of indifference.* New York: Oxford University Press.

Yant, M. (1997, June 16). A garden reaps national honors. *Philadelphia Inquirer,* p. 15.

Yarr, K. (1998). Do it yourself playgrounds. *Hope, 15,* 18–22.

Ybarra-Fausto, T. (1990). Arte Chicano: Images of a community. In E. S. Cockcroft & H. Barbet-Sanchez (Eds.), *Signs from the heart: California Chicano murals* (pp. 54–68). Albuquerque: University of New Mexico Press.

Yemma, J. (1997, September 17). America's changing face. *Boston Globe,* pp. A1, A18–A19.

Yin, R. K. (1994). *Case study research: Design and methods.* Thousand Oaks, CA: Sage.

Appendix

Urban Demographics

There is no question that the concept of community plays a central role in the well-being of all people. However, the struggle to achieve a sense of community in urban areas of the country faces tremendous challenges as the result of internal and external forces (Kasarda, Appold, Sweeney, & Stieff, 1997). Cities have experienced, and are projected to continue to experience, prodigious changes in their racial and ethnic compositions. The new groups who are entering urban areas often come from countries that have historically not had a significant numerical presence in the United States (S. A. Holmes, 1998b; Taaffe & Fisher, 1997).

These groups are entering cities that are ill prepared to welcome them and meet the needs that are often associated with uprootedness for poor and low-income people (Hamamoto & Torres, 1979). As Rumbaut (1997, p. 16) noted, "The stories are being told in the news media of the day—particularly in the 'Immigrant Belt' of global cities like Los Angeles, New York, and Miami—are full of the dramatic contrasts and the 'curiously mingled hope and pain' of contemporary immigrants from all over the world who enter, with or without permission, in search of future promise or to escape a tragic past, and of the variety of ways the natives respond, often with alarm, to their presence." Thus, rapid changes in community composition, if not properly addressed, can result in further isolation of and increased fears among groups and the inability to create a sense of community that encompasses all residents.

Given this situation, it is especially critical for social workers and other helping professionals to develop a keen understanding of how the nation's cities have changed dramatically over the past thirty years; it is also essential for them to look toward the future and attempt to predict, as best as possible, how the cities will continue to change in composition. This "strategic" perspective takes on added significance in community practice and should serve as a basis for planning interventions that are proactive, rather than reactive.

The time when homogeneous communities of color were the norm has long disappeared (Sontag & Dugger, 1998). Today, neighborhoods, especially those that are low income and residentially segregated, often consist of many different racial and ethnic groups. Their significant within- and between-group differences make it difficult to generalize about these groups beyond the fact that they share particular neighborhoods (Black, 1996; Chao, 1992; Lee, 1996a, 1996b; Moran & May, 1995; Seelye, 1997; Tafoya & Vecchio, 1996); indeed, it is difficult to generalize what constitutes a neighborhood. Differences related to legal status in this country, English language abilities, levels of acculturation, household composition, and so forth play important roles in differentiating groups of color (Fong & Mokuau, 1994; Higginbotham, 1994; Hines & Boyd-Franklin, 1996; Nguyen, 1992). For example, the diversity between Asian and Pacific Islander groups is also common within groups. Lee (1996b) noted that there is no one Chinese language and that there are at least eight major dialects and two major writing styles. Consequently, significant differences may exist within and among groups.

Urban Demographic Composition

For the purpose of demonstrating demographic trends, four major groups are discussed in this chapter (African Americans, Asian Americans and Pacific Islanders, Latinos, and Native Americans). In 1995 these four major groups, which consist of numerous subgroups, accounted for approximately 70 million people (African Americans, 31.6 million; Asian Americans, 8.9 million; Latinos, 26.9 million; and Native Americans, 2.5 million), or 26 percent of the total population (De Vita, 1996; Yemma, 1995). When possible, data on subgroups are provided to highlight how oppression has manifested itself within and among groups.

African Americans

According to the 1990 U.S. census, there were 30 million African Americans in the United States, an increase of 13.2 percent from the 1990 census (F. Barringer, 1991, 1993), and in 1995, there were 31.6 million (Yemma, 1995). This group is relatively young when compared to the nation as a whole, with a median age of 28 compared to 34 for the entire country (U.S. Bureau of the Census, 1991). In 1994, the median income of African Americans was $21,000, or 83 percent of that of white, non-Latinos ($34,000). Furthermore, the poverty rate of African Americans was 32.7 percent in 1990, similar to the rate in 1980 (32.5 percent).

African Americans and other blacks have a sizable representation in all fifty states (Barringer, 1991). However, a large proportion (53 percent) live in the South, followed by 20.2 percent in the North Central region and 18.7 percent in the Northeast. As of 1990, African Americans were most heavily represented in New York (2.9 million), California (2.2 million), Texas (2 million), Florida (1.8 million), Georgia (1.7 million), Illinois (1.69 million), North Carolina (1.4 million), Louisiana (1.3 million), Michigan (1.29 million), and Maryland (1.19 million) (U.S. Bureau of the Census, 1991). Nevertheless, significant changes occurred during the ten years between the 1980 and 1990 censuses, the greatest increased recorded in New Hampshire (80.4 percent), Minnesota (78 percent), Vermont (71.9 percent), Alaska (64.6 percent), and Maine (64.3 percent) (F. Barringer, 1991).

African Americans are a highly urbanized group; 85.3 percent reside in cities, compared to 71.4 percent of all white, non-Latinos (Ortiz, 1996). They live mainly in the following cities: New York, Chicago, Los Angeles, Philadelphia, Detroit, Atlanta, Houston, Baltimore, Miami, Dallas–Fort Worth, San Francisco, Oakland, Cleveland, New Orleans, St. Louis, Memphis, Norfolk–Virginia Beach–Newport News, Richmond-Petersburg, Birmingham, Charlotte, Milwaukee, Cincinnati, Kansas City, Tampa–St. Petersburg–Clearwater, and Washington, D.C. (Rusk, 1995). New York City, like many other cities across the United States, has witnessed a continued increase in the number and percentage of African Americans. In New York City, African Americans numbered 1.5 million (19.3 percent) in 1970 and 1.8 million (25.2 percent) in 1980, and they are projected to increase to 1.95 million (26 percent) by 2000 (Firestone, 1995).

Asian Americans and Pacific Islanders

According to the 1990 census, over fifty nationalities are often grouped together into the category of Asians and Pacific Islanders. Chinese Americans are not only the oldest Asian group in this country having settled here in the 1840s, but are the largest Asian and Pacific Islander group with more than 1.6 million people, or 22.6 percent of the Asian and Pacific Islander population in the United States (Lee, 1996b; Ortiz, 1994). Undocumented Asian and Pacific-Islanders present an additional challenge for developing a profile of this community. As a group, Asian and Pacific-Islanders number approximately 7.3 million (Barringer, 1991). According to Browne and Broderick (1994) this group consists of thirty nationalities. Asian Americans consist of Asian Indians, Cambodians, Chinese, Filipinos, Hmong, Indonesians, Japanese, Korean, Laos, Thais, and Vietnamese, and Pacific Islanders consist of Polynesians (Hawaiians, Samoans, and Tongans), Micronesians (Chamorros and other groups), and Melanesians (Fijians).

After Chinese Americans, which are the largest group of Asians and Pacific Islanders, the next three large groups are Filipinos (1.4 million), Japanese (845,000), and Vietnamese (600,000) (Butterfield, 1991; Lee, 1996a).

Among the Pacific Islanders, Hawaiians (211,000), Samoans (63,000), and Tongans (17,600) are the most represented of the Polynesian groups; Chamorros or Guamanians (49,000) are the largest of the Micronesian group; and Fijians (7,000) are the largest of the Melanesian group (Mokuau, 1995).

Asians and Pacific Islanders had a median age of thirty years in 1990 (Andrews & Fonseca, 1995) and a median family income of $40,500, significantly higher than nonwhite Latino families with $25,000 (U.S. Bureau of the Census, 1991). Children born to Asian and Pacific Islander women was 1,080 per thousand, slightly lower than that of non-Asians (1,228). Within the Asian and Pacific Islander community, Japanese and Chinese fertility rates are extremely low: 822 and 875, respectively. The other groups have slightly higher rates (De Vita, 1996): Filipinos (1,079), Indians (1,163) and Koreans (1,007), and Vietnamese (1,304). Asians and Pacific Islanders are found throughout all areas of the United States. However, they are concentrated primarily in the West; California (2.8 million) has the largest concentration of Asian and Pacific Islanders (39 percent of the total in the nation and 9.6 percent of the state's total population (Barringer, 1991). Nevertheless, Asians and Pacific Islanders are rapidly increasing in other sections of the country like New York (694,000), which has a higher population of these groups than Hawaii (685,000) (Barringer, 1991).

Asians and Pacific Islanders as a group are highly urbanized, with 93.1 percent residing in cities; Chinese are the most urbanized, with 97 percent, and Japanese are the least urbanized, with 91.6 percent (Ortiz, 1994). However, subgroups of Asians and Pacific Islanders are concentrated in certain cities. Chinese live mainly in San Francisco, Boston, New York, and Washington, D.C.; the Japanese, in Honolulu, Los Angeles, and Seattle; and the Filipinos, San Diego, San Francisco, and San Jose. The Vietnamese are more dispersed, with concentrations in Orange County (California), San Jose, Houston, and Minneapolis (Lee, 1996a). Almost 20 percent of all Hmong residing in the United States live in Minnesota, primarily Minneapolis, and close to 10 percent of all Asian Indians live in Chicago and its vicinity (De Vita, 1996; Holmes, 1998b).

Latinos

According to the 1990 census, there were approximately 22.3 million Latinos (9 percent of the total population); 13.5 million (60.5 percent) Mexican Americans, 2.7 million (12.1 percent) Puerto Ricans, 1 million (4.5 percent) Cubans (Ortiz, 1995; Roberts, 1994). The Latino birth rate reached a record high in 1995, with 669,768 babies born, compared to 532,249 in 1989, an increase from 14 percent to 18 percent of all births; Latina adolescents had 106.7 births per 1,000 in 1995, compared to 100.8 in 1989, the highest of any of group of color in the United States (Holmes, 1998a, p. B1).

Approximately two-thirds of all Latinos were born in the United States (Perez & Martinez, 1993). However, the Latino community has continued to diversify in composition, with other Caribbean (primarily Dominican), Central American, South American, and other Latino groups increasing in representation and accounting for 4.7 million, or 21 percent, of the Latino population (National Hispanic Leadership Agenda, 1996). Dominicans reside primarily in the Northeast, with New York City having the largest concentration (Gonzalez, 1992). El Salvadorians live mainly in Los Angeles, and Nicaraguans live mainly in Florida, primarily Miami.

The youthfulness of the Latino population must be highlighted. The median age of Latinos in the United States is 26 years, compared to 28 years for African Americans, 33 years for Asian and Pacific Islanders, 24.2 years for Native Americans, and 34 years for the country as a whole (Del Pinal & Singer, 1997). Mexican Americans are the youngest of the major Latino groups, with a median age of 24 years, followed by Puerto Ricans (27 years) and Cubans (39 years) (U.S. Bureau of the Census, 1991). Approximately 11 percent of the Latino population is under age 5, compared to 7 percent of non-Latinos; 60 percent of all Latinos are over age 21, compared to 71 percent of non-Latinos; and 11 percent of Latinos are over age 55, compared to 22 percent of non-Latinos (National Hispanic Leadership Agenda, 1996). However, Latinos are the fastest-growing group of those aged 65 and older (National Hispanic Leadership Agenda, 1996).

The fertility rate among Latinos is expected to remain relatively stable until 2010, when it will drop slightly. The rate of children born to Latinas (per thousand) in 1993 was 2,900, and it is predicted to decrease to 2,777 in 2010. In 1993, most births were to women aged 15 to 39 years, and the highest rate was to women aged 20 to 24 (180.5) (U.S. Bureau of the Census, 1995). However, a closer examination of the births to Latina adolescents revealed that in 1995 this group had the highest rate of births (106.7 per 1,000) compared to African American/black adolescents (74.5 per 1,000), and that the Latina rate had increased from 100.8 in 1989 (Holmes, 1998a).

In 1993 Latino households had an average annual income of $23,884, 61 percent less than the average of $39,239 for all households (IPR Datanote, 1993). However, this statistic masks the differences among Latino groups. Puerto Ricans had the lowest average annual income ($20,654), followed by Mexican Americans ($23,018), and Cubans had the highest ($30,095) (IPR Datanote, 1993). As a result, Puerto Ricans had the highest percentage of families living below the poverty level (39.4 percent)—four times that of white, non-Latino, families and significantly higher than Mexican Americans (29.5 percent), Central and South Americans (24.6 percent), other Latino groups (20.6 percent), and Cubans (18 percent) (IPR Datanote, 1993; Perez & Martinez, 1993).

Latinos can be found throughout all regions of the United States and in all fifty states. The Southwest and West account for 57 percent (or 12.6

million) of all Latinos in the United States (F. Barringer, 1991). Approximately 85 percent of all Latinos reside in ten states: California (7.7 million), Texas (4.4 million), New York (2.1 million), Florida (1.5 million); Illinois (897,000), New Jersey (720,000), Arizona (681,000), New Mexico (577,000), and Colorado (419,000) (National Hispanic Leadership Agenda, 1996).

As a group, Latinos are the most urbanized group in the country, with 92 percent residing in cities compared to 73 percent of non-Latinos (National Hispanic Leadership Agenda, 1996). According to the 1990 census (Morales & Bonilla, 1993), there were nine cities in the United States with Latino populations of at least 500,000: (1) Los Angeles (4.8 million), (2) New York (2.8 million), (3) Miami (1 million), (4) San Francisco (970,000), (5) Chicago (893,000), (6) Houston (772,000), (7) San Antonio (620,000), (8) Dallas (519,000), and (9) San Diego (511,000). Latinos currently outnumber African Americans in Los Angeles, Houston, Phoenix, and San Antonio, four of the nation's major cities (Roberts, 1994).

Native Americans

Native Americans numbered 2 million and represented 542 tribal groups in 1990 (U.S. Bureau of the Census, 1991). In addition, they spoke 150 Native languages, and their median age varied from 18.8 years to 26.3 years on reservations lands, with an overall median age of 24.2 years in 1990. Their median income was $21,750, or 62 percent of the national median of $35,225 (U.S. Bureau of the Census, 1995)—a 5 percent decrease from 1979.

The Native American population is younger, in part, because of a higher fertility rate than the total population. According to Jacobson (1995), Native Americans have historically had a substantially higher-than-average fertility rate. Jacobson (1995, p. 122) summed up Native American fertility patterns as follows: "Two conclusions are evident from the data. . . . First, Native American fertility has declined over the past several decades. Secondly, the decline . . . appears to have stopped. Younger cohorts of Native American women (aged 15–34) are now having as many children as Native American women their age did a decade ago. Nevertheless, this rate is about 50 percent higher than that of white American women in 1990." The fertility rate among Native Americans in 1994 was 2,470 per thousand women. Projections indicate that the rate will decrease slightly by 2010 to approximately 2,759 (U.S. Bureau of the Census, 1995).

Native Americans generally cluster in the West, with 66 percent of them residing in ten states (Moran & May, 1995). In 1990, they were concentrated in Oklahoma (252,000); Alaska (86,000); the Southwest, primarily New Mexico (134,000); and the Rocky Mountain states, with Montana (48,000) having the largest number (Barringer, 1991). States like Alabama (117.7 percent), Tennessee (96.7 percent), Florida (88.7 percent), Hawaii

(84.2 percent), and New Jersey (78.3 percent) experienced a tremendous growth in their Native American populations between 1980 and 1990 (Barringer, 1991).

Native Americans are the least urbanized people of color in the United States, with 54.6 percent residing in cities (Ortiz, 1994). Cities, such as Los Angeles (87,000), Tulsa (48,000), New York (46,000), Oklahoma City (45,700), and San Francisco (40,900) have sizable populations of Native Americans. With increased urbanization, however, there are fears that North Americans with one half of more Indian blood will decrease dramatically in the next ninety years as a result of outgroup marriages.

Demographic Projections

Any form of projection can best be described as "an informed guess" based upon past performance. Immigration probably represents the greatest unpredictable factor in making projections (Holmes, 1998b). Nevertheless, an examination of urban demographic projections, with the understanding that changes are possible, is still a useful exercise in developing a profile of what cities will be like in the next fifty years.

Urban demographic trends are revealing concerning the rapid and dramatic changes that have transpired in the United States in the past twenty years and the projected changes well into the next century. Only a limited number of variables are reported here. These variables were selected to provide readers with an appreciation of a selected profile of communities of color, which will enhances their understanding of the challenges that urban-based practitioners face.

The African American community in the United States is projected to continue to increase numerically in the next fifty years—from 45.4 million (15.7 percent of the population) (up from 9.7 percent in 1993) in 2020 ("Americans in 2020," 1994) to 62 million (16.2 percent) in 2020 (Pear, 1992). A higher-than-average fertility rate will be a contributing factor in the growth of this community. The fertility rate for African Americans was 2,470 in 1993 and is projected to be 2,452 in 2050. The high rate is due mainly to two factors: (1) the African American population, with a median age of 28 years, is younger than the white, non-Latino population and contains a slightly larger proportion of persons in the prime reproductive ages and (2) it is projected that for the next ten to twenty years, African Americans are likely to continue to have higher age-adjusted fertility rates than white, non-Latinos (Champagne, 1994).

Asian and Pacific Islanders are one of the fastest-growing groups in the United States having increased 107.8 percent between 1980 and 1990 (Barringer, 1991, 1993; O'Hare & Felt, 1991). They are expected to number 12 million in 2000 and 41 million in 2050, in effect doubling by 2009, tripling by 2024, and quadrupling by 2038 (Pear, 1992). This rapid growth, however, will be due primarily to immigration, not fertility. It is estimated that the number of Asian and Pacific Islanders who immigrate will exceed the number of births of these groups in each of the next thirty years (Pear, 1992).

Latinos, a rapidly growing population in the United States, increased 53 percent between 1980 and 1990 (F. Barringer, 1991). It is projected that they will account for 37 percent of the nation's population growth from 1995 to 2000, 44 percent from 2000 to 2020, and 62 percent from 2020 to 2050 (National Hispanic Leadership Agenda, 1996). According to Seelye (1979, p. A32), "The long-term rise in the number of Hispanic people, who have the nation's highest fertility and immigration rates, will coincide with a decline in that of non-Hispanic whites . . . [so] that by 2028, the number of white Americans who die will exceed those being born."

It is estimated that Latinos will increase to 42.1 million by 2013, 49 million by 2020, and 81 million by 2050, at which time they will be 21.1 percent of the total population (Pear, 1992). In California, Latinos are projected to account for 43 percent of the total population by 2025, up from slightly less than 30 percent in 1997. If these projections are realized, Latinos will be the nation's largest community of color by 2020, surpassing African Americans ("Americans in 2020," 1994).

This increase will be the result of high immigration and fertility rates and low death rates (Barringer, 1991, 1993; Ortiz, 1996; Pear, 1992). However, increases within specific Latino groups can be attributed to a variety of factors. Immigration among Mexican Americans and Central Americans will play a much more prominent role than among Cubans or Puerto Ricans (Ortiz, 1994).

It is estimated that there were about 7.5 million Native Americans before Europeans settled in America (Champagne, 1994). Their number, however, has decreased significantly over the past four hundred years, and it is estimated that they numbered approximately 1.96 million in 1990 (U.S. Bureau of the Census, 1991), 53 percent increase from 1980 (Barringer, 1991). They are projected to double in number by 2050 (Pear, 1992).

Urban Profiles

Seven cities of various sizes and geographic locations have been selected to illustrate how their composition has changed over the past thirty years: (1) Boston, (2) Denver, (3) Houston, (4) Miami, (5) Minneapolis, (6) New York City, and (7) Seattle, Each of these cities' profiles will be discussed from four perspectives: (1) changes in ethnic and racial composition; (2) percentage of families living below the poverty level; (3) identification of key challenges they face; and (4) projected demographic trends, when available, for the next century. Each profile provides the reader with a brief glimpse of historical developments to place these changes within a present-day context. Some of the profiles consist of greater detail than others depending upon the cities' significance and history, major shifts in population composition, and implications for the twenty-first century.

Boston

Boston is the largest city in New England, with a population of approximately 574,300 in 1990. The population of the city has become increasingly diverse. About 23.8 percent (137,000) of the population is African American; 10.8 percent (61,955) is Latino (of which Puerto Ricans are the largest subgroup, with 25,800), and 5.3 percent is Asian (30,400).

In addition, there is increasing diversity within the groups. Latinos are a good example. Historically, the Latino community in Boston was fairly homogeneous, consisting primarily of Puerto Ricans. According to the U.S. Bureau of the Census, of the 36,000 Latinos in Boston (6.4 percent of the total population), there were 19,300 Puerto Ricans (53.7 percent of all Latinos), 2,500 Cubans (6.9 percent of all Latinos), and 1,300 Cuban (3.6 percent of all Latinos). Other Latino groups combined accounted for 12,880 (35.7 percent of all Latinos).

In 1990 the Latino community accounted for 10.8 percent of the total population of Boston. However, the Puerto Rican share of the Latino community decreased to 41.6 percent (25,770), and the share of other Latino groups, excluding Mexican Americans and Cubans, increased to 50.9 percent (Gaston Institute, 1992a). Boston's Latino community also increased in diversity. Since 1990, the Mexican American community has made significant numerical strides and is the fastest-growing Latino subgroup in the city; in 1996, there were estimated to number 20,000 (With, 1996). This new net gain has been fueled by newcomers from California, Texas, New Mexico, and Arizona.

Denver

With its population of 468,000 in 1990 Denver was twenty-sixth in the nation, making it one of the largest cities in that region. Although Denver's 1990 population was 5.9 percent lower than in 1980 (493,000), the city's total population increased dramatically during the 1990s, averaging 10,000 per year during the first half of the decade (Wright, 1997). Its population is considered to be one of the youngest in the United States.

Denver's population of color represented 39.4 percent of the city's total (Wright, 1997). Latinos (primarily Mexican Americans) were the largest group, with 23 percent, followed by blacks-African Americans (12.8 percent), Asians (2.4 percent), and Native Americans (1.2 percent).

Houston

Houston was one of the fastest-growing cities in the United States during the 1980s and 1990s. Large numbers of Central Americans (primarily Salvadorans, Guatemalans, and Hondurans) settled in Houston during the 1980s, not only increasing the city's population but diversifying the Latino community from what had traditionally been Mexican American (Rodriguez,

1993). Latinos numbered 281,000 in 1980 (17.6 percent) of the total population of 1,595,000 (Rodriguez, 1993).

Houston's 1990 population of 1.63 million ranked it the fourth-largest city in the United States. There were roughly equal proportions of Blacks-African Americans (28.1 percent) and Latinos (27.6 percent), followed by Asians (4.1 percent) and Native Americans (.3 percent). The population of color accounted for 60.1 percent of the city's total population in 1990. Furthermore, although the black-African American and Latino populations are almost equally represented, Latinos have made significant strides in the past two decades, increasing from 12.2 percent of the population in 1970 to 17.6 percent in 1980 and to 27.6 percent in 1990 (Rodriguez, 1993).

Miami

Miami has certainly received its share of attention nationally (Didion, 1987). During the 1980s, Miami reaffirmed its position as the major commercial and banking center for Latin America. This period also witnessed a modest increase in the population, from 347,000 to 359,000, ranking Miami the forty-sixth largest city in the United States; the increase in population is almost identical (12,000) from that of the 1970–80 period.

Miami is a diverse city, with Latinos (62.5 percent) the largest group of color (the majority of whom are Cubans), followed by blacks-African Americans (27.4 percent), Asians (.6 percent), and Native Americans (.2 percent). Miami is known for having distinct neighborhoods, such as Little Havana, Little Managua, and Little Haiti, to list some of the best-known ones. The city, however, is considerably more diverse than the statistics seem to indicate. It has continued a process of diversification started in the 1960s. Between the 1960s and 1970s, Cubans were the largest Latino subgroup (70 percent), with Central and South Americans and Dominicans (20 percent), Puerto Ricans (8 percent), and other groups making up nearly 2 percent (Perez-Stable & Uriate, 1993). However, by 1990, the Cuban proportion of the Latino community had decreased to 59 percent, the Central-South American and Dominican proportion had increased from 20 percent to 31 percent, and the Puerto Rican proportion had remained at 8 percent (Perez-Stable & Uriate, 1993).

Minneapolis

Minneapolis's population of 368,000 in 1990 ranked it forty-second among the top fifty cities in the United States (Wright, 1997). Minneapolis has historically been homogeneous from a racial and ethnic perspective, with a population consisting of 93.6 percent white, non-Latinos in 1970; this percentage, however, has steadily decreased from 87.7 percent in 1980, to 78.5 percent in 1990, and to 77.6 percent in 1997 (D. Johnson, 1997). In 1990, blacks-African Americans were the largest group of color (13.0 percent), followed by Asians (4.3 percent), Native Americans (3.3 percent), and Latinos (2.1 percent).

Asians have made the most significant numerical strides during the 1980s and 1990s and currently represent 5.1 percent of the city's total population. According to recent estimates, the number of students for whom English is not their primary language increased 300 percent since 1990, with students now speaking 70 languages in the school system. Asian American children, primarily Hmong, now represent 10 percent of all students, compared to 1 percent in 1970 (Johnson, 1997).

New York City

New York City, with a population of approximately 7.32 million in 1997, consists of five boroughs—Brooklyn, the Bronx, Manhattan, Queens, and Staten Island (Dao, 1998). Each borough has a rich history of attracting immigrants from throughout the world. This tradition continues today; it is estimated that over 100,000 documented immigrants arrive in New York City every year, a two-thirds increase from a decade ago (Goetz, 1997; Holms, 1998b; Kaplan, 1998). More than half the city's residents were born outside the city (2.5 million in foreign lands and more than 1 million in other sections of the United States (Tierney, 1997b).

The representation of immigrants differs according to the borough. For example, almost half of all Bronx residents and a third of Manhattan's are Latino, whereas nearly 20 percent of the residents of Queens are Asian Americans, the highest concentration in the city (Halbfinger, 1997b). During the 1990s, approximately 677,000 newcomers entered the city, and there were 937,000 births and 516,000 deaths (Dao, 1998).

Tierney's (1997b, p. 53) analysis of the impact of these recent arrivers in New York City can also be recorded in countless other cities across the United States: "New Yorkers need their separate worlds to cope with what is the most unnatural aspect of the city: the loneliness of people far from their families. . . . One-third of the city's adults have never married; Manhattan has the highest concentration of single-person households in America except for an island in Hawaii settled as a leper colony. . . . The melting pot could never turn New York into a happy family or any other kind of family. No sane human would ever wish for seven million relatives."

If New York City's boroughs were to be conceptualized as cities, Brooklyn (2.3 million residents) would be the third largest city in the United States behind Los Angeles and Chicago, Queens (1.9 million residents) would rank fourth, Manhattan (1.5 million) would rank sixth behind Houston (1.6 million) and Philadelphia (1.59 million), and the Bronx would rank seventh (1.2 million residents). Only Staten Island (379,000) would not be ranked in the top ten most populous cities in the United States (Kaplan, 1998; Rusk, 1995).

The racial and ethnic composition of New York City has changed gradually and dramatically over the past thirty years. These changes have been the result of an interplay of three critical factors: (1) birth and death rates, (2) in-migration, and (3) out-migration (Foner, 1987). In 1970 the white, non-Latino population represented 60 percent of the city's population; however, in 1990, it was 43.4 percent and in 1995, it dropped to 38.5 percent of the population (Halbfinger, 1997b). It is estimated that their proportion will decrease to 35 percent or lower by 2005 (Firestone, 1995).

Three major groups of color (African Americans, Asians, and Latinos) have played important, yet different roles in changing the composition of that city. Latinos and African Americans numbered almost 2 million each in 1995, or 55.3 percent of the total population; Asian Americans numbered approximately 630,000, or 8.7 percent, up from 6.7 percent in 1990 (Halbfinger, 1997b). The net gain (births/deaths) highlights a higher death rate to birth rate among white, non-Latinos and a significantly higher birth to death rate among Latinos. African Americans have a moderately high birth to death ratio, but more leave the city than move in. The Asian community, which is predominately Chinese, has a low birth rate but a high immigration rate—higher than among Latinos (Wong, 1987).

Among Latinos, Dominicans have made the most significant gains in representation over the past twenty years. They numbered approximately 125,380 in 1980, 332,700 in 1990, and 495,000 in 1997 and are projected to top 700,000 by 2000 and to continue to increase well into the early twenty-first century, making them the largest Latino group in the city, surpassing Puerto Ricans (Dugger, 1996, 1997; Firestone, 1995; Gonzalez, 1992; Kaplan, 1997; Ojitio, 1997; Pessar, 1987).

Seattle

Seattle had a population of 516,000 in 1990, making it the twenty-first largest city in the United States. Its total population increased 22,400, or 4.5 percent, between 1980 and 1990 (Wright, 1997). Its population of color accounted for 26.9 percent of the total population, with Asians (11.8 percent) being the largest group of color, followed by black-African Americans (10.1 percent), Latinos (3.6 percent), and Native Americans (1.4 percent).

Subject Index

Name Index